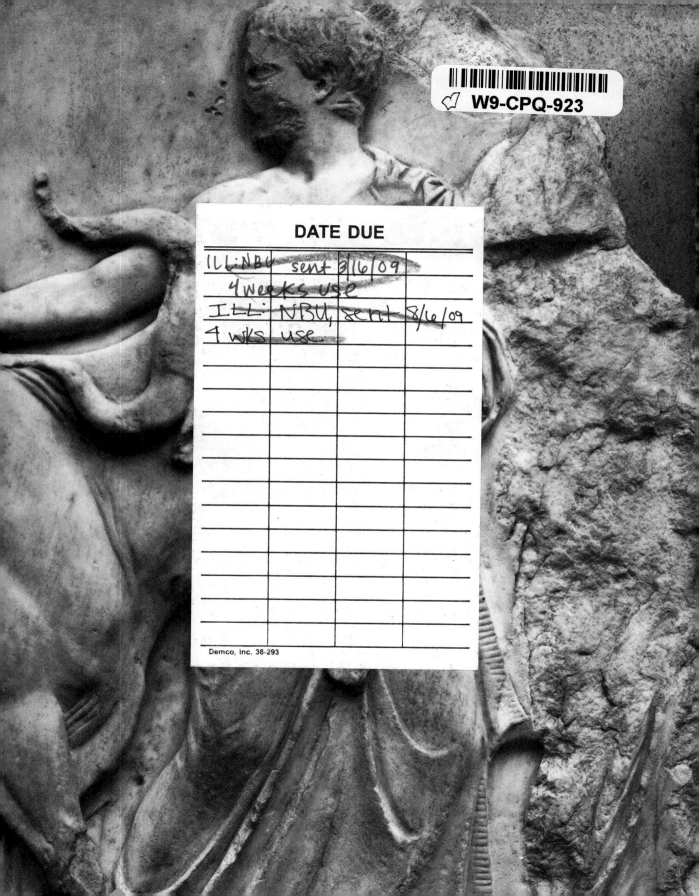

DATE DUE

W9-CPQ-923

CLASSICAL LANDSCAPE
WITH FIGURES

One might say that cities are founded upon the fields and based on the countryside. From the fields come wheat, barley, grapes, wine, oil: food for men and food for other creatures too. If there were no oxen there would be no ploughing, sowing or planting, no herds of grazing cattle. And there would never have been cities. Once founded cities have been linked to the fortune of the countryside, their prosperity and their demise depends on the countryside.
Libanius of Antioch (*fourth century* AD)

Robin Osborne

CLASSICAL LANDSCAPE WITH FIGURES
The Ancient Greek City and its Countryside

Sheridan House

Editorial Adviser: M. H. Crawford,
University College, London

© Robin Osborne 1987

First published by George Philip,
27A Floral Street, London WC2E 9DP.

First published in the United States of America 1987
by Sheridan House Inc., Dobbs Ferry, NY 10522.

ISBN 0 911378 73 1

Filmset and printed by
BAS Printers Limited, Over Wallop, Hampshire

ILLUSTRATION ACKNOWLEDGEMENTS
Antikenmuseum Staatliche Museen Preussischer
Kulturbesitz Berlin p. 19; Bibliothèque
Nationale Paris p. 190, p. 191; John Cherry,
p. 58; Ecole Française d'Athènes p. 65, p. 105,
p. 106; Fitzwilliam Museum Cambridge p. 2,
p. 20, p. 50, p. 122, p. 186; Lothar Haselberger
p. 64; Hirmer Verlag München p. 110, p. 111;
Museum of Classical Archaeology Cambridge
p. 83, pp. 124/5; Museum of Fine Arts Boston
p. 175; National Archaeological Museum Athens
p. 142; Scuola archeologica Italiana di Atene
p. 185; Soprintendenza Archeologica per
l'Etruria Meridionale p. 177; Ronald Stroud
p. 176; Trustees of the British Museum p. 102,
pp. 130/131, p. 143, p. 148, p. 173, p. 189, p. 190;
all other illustrations are by the author.

FRONTISPIECE *This fourth-century figurine of the god
Pan from Attica (14 cm high) reveals clearly his half-
bestial nature: note the horns, hairy legs and goat's
feet.*

Contents

To Anthony Snodgrass

Acknowledgements

It is always the author who learns most from writing a book. What I have learned from writing this one I owe to Paul Cartledge, John Cherry, Michael Crawford, Peter Garnsey, Keith Hopkins, Wim Jongman, Geoffrey Lloyd, John North, Catherine Osborne and Anthony Snodgrass, who read all or part of it in earlier drafts. I owe particular debts to Michael Crawford, who suggested the project to me, and to Lydia Greeves who has patiently taught me how to write. But without the example and encouragement of Anthony Snodgrass I would never have set out on this field of enquiry at all, and this book is for him.

The fieldwork undertaken in writing this book was financed by the generosity of the Faculty of Classics, University of Cambridge, King's College, Cambridge, and the British Academy.

Time-chart

Date BC	Period name	Events	Writers
3000			
2000	Bronze Age		
1000		Fall of Mycenae	
	Dark Age		
900			
800	Geometric		
700			Hesiod
600	Archaic	Solonian crisis at Athens	
		Tyranny at Athens	
500		Democratic reforms at Athens	
		Persian wars	
		Athenian empire	Herodotos
		Peloponnesian War	Aristophanes
			Thucydides
400	Classical	Spartan invasion of Elis	
			Xenophon
			Plato
		Battle of Leuktra	
		Rise of Philip of Macedon	Aristotle
		Death of Alexander the Great	
300			Theophrastos
200	Hellenistic	First Roman intervention in Greece	
			Polybios
100			

INTRODUCTION

'It is necessary to repeat, time and time again, that it is no good being interested simply in the site of an ancient town. An ancient city must always be considered along with its territory, its fields and its forests, which fed it and on which a part of its population lived. The territory cannot be separated from the city. It is always vital to study the territory and to recover its boundaries.'

So wrote the famous French Classical scholar Louis Robert. The point he made was not new, his advice commonplace. But no one, not even Robert, has actually managed to follow that advice. For all scholars' good intentions, the study of the ancient city has remained the study of the town. This book is an attempt to put the countryside back into the picture.

There are good reasons why the countryside has been neglected. The Greeks themselves wrote little about it and Classical scholarship has devoted itself to what the Greeks wrote. Archaeologists too have concentrated until recently on rich sites, and that means on town sites and on sanctuaries and cemeteries. Twenty years ago this book would have been largely inconceivable.

Two things have made this work possible. Ancient historians have been asking new questions, and archaeologists have developed techniques for investigating the countryside. Under the stimulus of modern history and of anthropology, ancient historians have begun to try to answer questions about the ancient world which are not the questions which the Greeks themselves asked. The literary heritage from ancient Greece has been examined for what it implies as much as for what it explicitly states. At the same time archaeologists have begun to explore the surface of the modern Greek countryside systematically for traces of ancient activity. For the first time it is possible to say something about where the ancient population lived at any given time, and about the development of the countryside from one period to another.

This book attempts to put together new questions and new data. It is not simply a summary of the current state of research, and it is not simply a history of settlement in Greece. In the first part of the book I try to present a picture of the nature of the ancient countryside, its settlement and its exploitation. Then, in succeeding chapters, I try to show how this countryside, both in general and in specific cases, had a pervasive influence on the social, military, political and religious life of the Greek city. I try to present the ancient landscape both 'as it was', and as it was seen to be by the Greeks themselves and to explain why they saw it as they did.

The bibliography at the end provides a

9

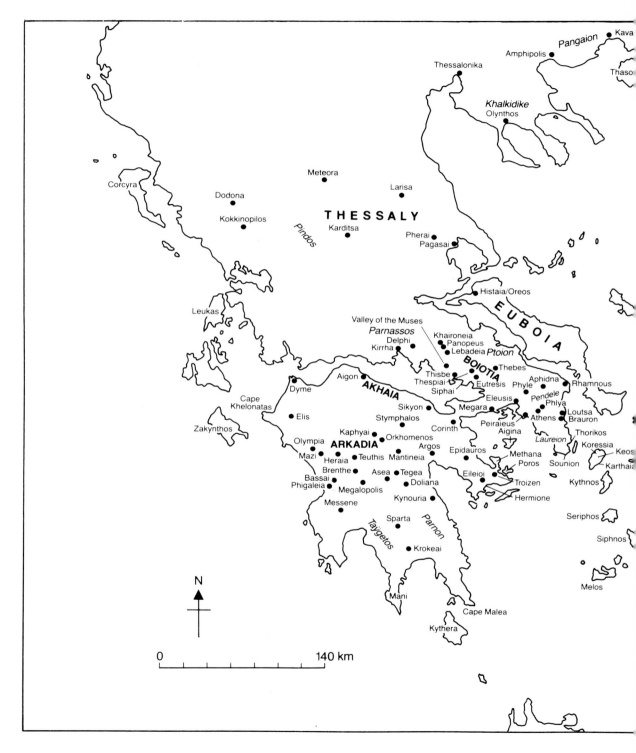

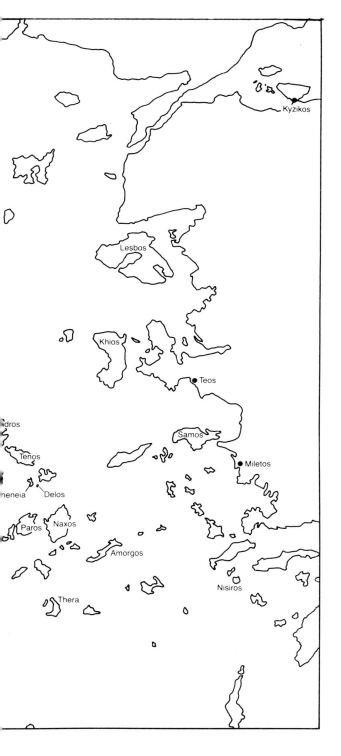

guide to translations and editions of ancient texts quoted in the book. The translations used in the text are my own unless otherwise stated. References for the passages quoted from ancient authors are given in the chapter bibliographies, which also direct the reader to further discussions of the issues and evidence explored in each chapter.

Throughout the book 'city' is used to refer to the independent political unit of town and territory: it does not mean 'urban unit'. 'Town' is used to refer to the largest settlement in a city, even if in absolute terms that settlement would normally be reckoned only a small village. This systematic use of 'city' and 'town' is in fact alien to Greek usage, in which the word used for town and territory, *polis*, was also used to refer to the town alone. If by my usage I have destroyed a significant ambiguity, I hope that this will be justified by an increase in the clarity of the analysis. The territories of various Greek cities were referred to by special terms derived from the name of the town: thus Attica refers to the territory of Athens, Laconia to the territory of Sparta, and the Argolid to the territory of Argos.

The transliteration of Greek is always a problem. Here I transliterate Greek names literally except in those cases where the Latinized form is sanctioned by centuries of usage in the English-speaking world.

All dates before 1500 are BC unless otherwise stated. References to years in the form 329/8 etc. denote the archon year which began in June/July of the current calendar.

1 Greece and the Aegean Sea, showing the regions and cities mentioned in the text.

Note on Greek currency:

1 talent = 6000 drachmas = 60 mnas
1 mna = 100 drachmas
1 drachma = 6 obols

A day labourer in the fourth century BC
could earn $1\frac{1}{2}$ drachmas a day.

THE PARADOX OF
THE GREEK CITY

The dominance of the countryside

To think of Classical Greece is to think of monumental achievements in building, art and literature, of the foundations of European art, architecture and thought. Lavish temples, colossal fortifications, and subtle ruminations on politics, war, and human relations with the divine bulk large in our image of the classical world. But behind this conspicuous expenditure upon sanctuaries and offerings, and this continual involvement in war, lies unseen and unsung the working of the countryside. The vast majority of Greeks were peasants and the characteristic activities of the Greek city, both constructive and destructive, were founded upon the production of the country.

The peasant basis of society determined the nature of warfare. Ancient Greek warfare was a notoriously odd business which depended upon heavily armed infantry (hoplites), who could operate efficiently only on level ground. But Greece is a country with a mountainous terrain which has few open plains. War was endemic in the Greek city; but it took place only over a very limited campaigning season. The peculiarities stem directly from the importance of the countryside. Heavily armed hoplite soldiers may be of no use off the more or less level plains, but when it is these plains which it is most important for the city to defend hoplites

are the best instrument available. Long campaigns may be more cost-effective, but when the soldier is himself the farmer, keeping him from his fields is counter-productive. Even in the great Peloponnesian War between two exceptional cities, Athens and Sparta, at the end of the fifth century, the longest invasion of Athenian territory (Attica) in the first phase of the war was forty days, and all the invasions took place at the very beginning of the grain harvest (late May/June).

Farming is always a seasonal activity, and in Greece the margins of error are often extremely slim, and getting the timing right can be crucially important. Getting the timing right is a primary concern of the poet Hesiod in the poem known as the *Works and Days* composed around 700. Figure 3 shows a calendar of the Greek agricultural year based on Hesiod, other ancient literary evidence, and on modern Greek data. This shows quite clearly that the agricultural year in Greece has two periods of particularly intense activity and two slack periods. The busy times are the grain harvest, which takes place between late May and early July according to the region and to the year's weather, and the combined operation of gathering in the vintage and ploughing and sowing the arable land, which lasts from September to November. The slack times are the periods immediately before and after the grain harvest. Military campaigns tended to concentrate on the slack period of the late spring. One of the major athletics festivals, the Isthmian games, was also held at this time of year, but the Olympic, Nemean, and Pythian games were all held in the period from mid July to September.

This late summer slack period is also the busiest time of year for the building industry. The best illustration that we have of the changing intensity of building activity over the year comes from documents inscribed on

2 The most important cult building at Eleusis was the Telesterion, which was not a temple housing a cult image but a building in which initiates gathered to have the 'Mysteries' of the goddess Demeter revealed to them. Here is part of the portico that was being built in the late fourth century as described in the text.

stone preserved in the Athenian sanctuary of Demeter at Eleusis. Two long sets of accounts which have survived from this sanctuary are invaluable documents of Athenian social and religious history. One set dates from the year 329/8 and records all the expenditure, great and small, made by those in charge of the sanctuary of the goddesses Demeter and Kore during the greater part of the year. These accounts give a good idea of how the overall expenditure of the sanctuary fluctuated during the year (see Figure 3). Expenditure was at its highest at the beginning of the Athenian civil year (mid July to September), low in the early winter and low in June/July, but quite high in February. The other set of accounts, which is roughly contemporary with the first, gives specific dates for work on a particular building project – the building of the portico of the major cult building in the sanctuary,

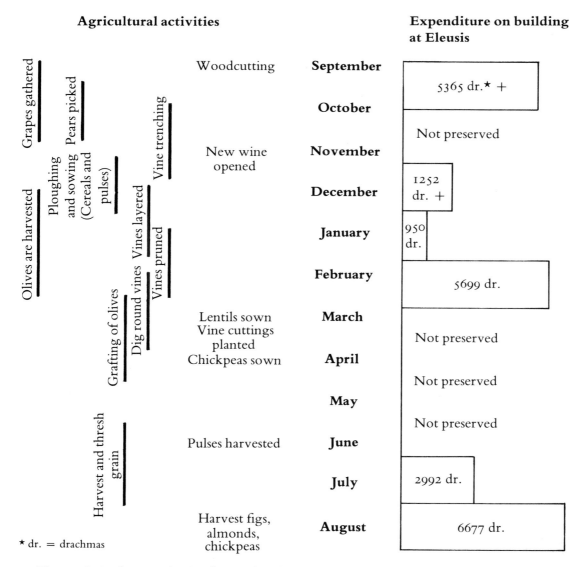

Agricultural activities

Expenditure on building at Eleusis

Grapes gathered

Pears picked

Ploughing and sowing (Cereals and pulses)

Olives are harvested

Vine trenching

Vines layered

Dig round vines

Grafting of olives

Vines pruned

Harvest and thresh grain

Woodcutting

New wine opened

Lentils sown
Vine cuttings planted
Chickpeas sown

Pulses harvested

Harvest figs, almonds, chickpeas

* dr. = drachmas

September	5365 dr.* +
October	
November	Not preserved
December	1252 dr. +
January	950 dr.
February	5699 dr.
March	Not preserved
April	Not preserved
May	Not preserved
June	
July	2992 dr.
August	6677 dr.

3 The correlation between the Greek agricultural year and the Greek construction year.

the Telesterion. Column drums of Pentelic marble were hauled from their quarry to Eleusis for this work. Transport begins during July and continues in the following month, the Athenian month Boedromion, which is when the sanctuary celebrated its major festival, the Greater Mysteries. There seems to have been no further transportation after

the middle of September. Other accounts from the oracular sanctuary of Apollo at Delphi in central Greece suggest that this pattern of late summer building was general.

Building was an occasional activity which relied heavily on casual labour (see Chapter 4). It could only make headway when there was no prior call on that labour. Moving stone required great teams of oxen: up to thirty-three *yoke* of oxen were employed to pull a single column drum from Pendele to Eleusis. Animal power in such quantities would simply be unavailable when harvesting, threshing, or ploughing were taking place. Attica, in fact, was so short of large cattle that on occasion teams of oxen from Boiotia had to be called in to provide the motive power for building activities.

The concealment of agriculture

The nature and needs of the countryside do not dominate only war and building. This book explores at length the way in which the whole political, social and religious structure of the Greek city was shaped by its countryside. But there is a paradox here. On the one hand the productive countryside was of fundamental importance. On the other the arts and literature of Classical Greece largely ignore it. No ancient Greek writer ever describes for us the nature of the countryside, the tasks of the farmer or the lot of the agricultural labourer. We are given no picture of life on a peasant holding, no notion of the strains and stresses of eking out a living in conditions where the rainfall vital for an adequate crop frequently failed to materialize. So great is the repression of the country that even in the case of Athens itself it remains a major scholarly puzzle whether the labour force on the land consisted predominantly of slaves, hired freemen, or family labour.

It might be argued that the paradox is not significant, that writers, and especially historians, took the countryside for granted because it was so universally important. But in a country with a topography and physical geography as varied as that of Greece, the countryside simply cannot be assumed as a constant known factor (see Chapter 2). Dif-

ferent landscapes demand different farming practices, and different farming practices have different timetables and different social and political implications. Greek writers were indeed well aware of this. The fifth-century historian Herodotos' account of his travels in the eastern Mediterranean reveals how acute one Greek's observation of local differences was. The far reaching implications of these local differences are the subject of the little treatise on *Airs, Waters, Places* preserved among the so-called Hippocratic medical writings. The treatise argues that climate and geography are basic determinants of human physical and temperamental constitutions, as its ending summarizes.

'The chief controlling factors are the variability of the weather, the type of country and the sort of water which is drunk. You will find, as a general rule, that the constitutions and habits of a people follow the nature of the land where they live. Where the soil is rich, soft and well-watered and where the surface water is drunk, which is warm in summer and cold in winter, and where the seasons are favourable, you will find the people fleshy, their joints obscured, and they have watery constitutions. Such people are incapable of great effort. . . . But if the land is bare, waterless and rough, swept by winter gales and burnt by the summer sun, you will find there a people hard and spare, their joints showing, sinewy and hairy. They are by nature keen and fond of work, they are wakeful, headstrong and self-willed, and inclined to fierceness rather than tame. They are keener at their crafts, more intelligent and better warriors. . . . If you draw your deductions according to these principles, you will not go wrong.'[1]

The individual observations made in this text have little more than curiosity value; what is important is the structure of the argument. The prejudice of Greeks, who regarded barbarians as unmanly, colours the perceptions of the writer but it cannot obscure the acute awareness of the importance of natural environment for human habits and character. The writer connects human character to rich soil and mild climate in a rather hasty way, but climatic variability and physical geography will bulk large in this book as vital determinants of the agricultural practices and settlement patterns of the Greeks. On the other hand the countryside of *Airs, Waters, Places* is a natural landscape without labour; the countryside I shall present here is a countryside of farmers and toil.

Some literary texts do discuss the countryside, but they do so in a very limited fashion. Two major ancient Greek authors devote a large amount of space to the rural world: the poet and farmer Hesiod, and the soldier and gentleman Xenophon. Hesiod was a second generation immigrant from the coast of Asia Minor. Born in the late eighth century, he lived in what he himself describes as 'the miserable village of Askra, bad in winter, terrible in summer and good at no time of the year.'[2] His low opinion of the Boiotian village of Askra, coupled with his complete failure to describe the surrounding countryside, has made identification of the site of the village difficult, although it is now clear that it lay in a far from unpleasant position in the Valley of the Muses.

The poem *Works and Days* does not give any description of agrarian conditions. It goes through the farmer's year, but it would be an exaggeration to call it a practical manual for arable farming. The poem opens with a brief mythological genealogy for Strife, which turns into a series of moral observations about the occurrence of Strife among men. These observations are aimed at the ear of the poet's brother Perses, by whom Hesiod considers that he has been unfairly treated.

The injunction to perform the necessary tasks on the land at the right time of the year is part of a general advocation of work, and must be seen in the context of the moral exhortation. The poem ends with a list of lucky and unlucky ways to act and lucky and unlucky days for particular activities, such as, 'Don't put the wine jug into the mixing bowl at a party, for a terrible fate is associated with that.'[3] To the modern mind such advice is very different from advice about the best time to plough and to sow, but the motivation for Hesiod is the same in both cases. Far from being innovative or concerned to help those who work the land become more efficient farmers, Hesiod is exploiting the traditional rhythms of the agricultural year for their moral and rhetorical value.

Three centuries later a similar use of the countryside is found in the writings of Xenophon. Xenophon was a prolific writer of an anecdotal kind. He concerned himself with history (military history, of course), popular philosophy, and the pursuits of the gentleman both in the army, for example as cavalry commander, and at leisure in the hunt. One of his shorter works, the *Oikonomikos* or *Domestic Manager*, is devoted to the running of the wealthy household. Agriculture is only part, if an important part, of this, and the way in which it is introduced is significant: 'I think that farming is something which not even those who are blissfully content can do without. The practice of farming is both in itself a great pleasure, and it increases the household, and keeps the body in trim for all that a free man ought to be able to do.'[4] This panegyric on farming emphasizes three things: that it is enjoyable, that it increases the fortunes of the household, and that it keeps the body fit for other things. Xenophon too lays stress on the importance of timely action: farming has the moral value of ensuring that the farmer acts in due season.

The praise of farming is followed by a second panegyric – on hunting. The juxtaposition of these two panegyrics shows just how remote Xenophon is from the real production of the countryside. Historians may have underestimated the degree to which Mediterranean farmers continued to supplement the household food supply by hunting and gathering, but it is certain that in the Attica of the early fourth century hunting can only have been of trivial economic importance. To juxtapose hunting with farming as Xenophon does is to suggest that farming is but a sport, and to undercut its basic importance. Once more we are being treated to the countryside as a moral example.

Later in the *Oikonomikos* Xenophon records a conversation between the philosopher Sokrates and a very rich Athenian estate owner named Iskhomakhos. They discuss the various agricultural tasks, and Iskhomakhos argues that agriculture is a simple matter which can be carried on from a knowledge of first principles. The practical value of this discussion is almost nil. Iskhomakhos suggests, for example, that the amount of seed required per unit area depends upon the richness of the soil, just as the proportion of water mixed with wine depends upon the strength of the wine. All well and good, but no help at all to the poor farmer in his specific situation, for whom it does not even supply a rule of thumb. Because Xenophon wants to play down the technical aspects of farming, he fails totally to describe the very real problems of all farmers in Attica, problems faced even by the exceptionally well-off landowner (see Chapter 2). What he provides instead is a rhetorical exposition of the moral value of working in the fields.

The countryside of the *Works and Days* and the *Oikonomikos* is the creation of their authors; it is not a description of the Greek countryside as it was. Hesiod and Xenophon have selected aspects of country life and have presented them as if they were all that country life was about. Their countryside is a partial countryside, deprived of all signs of work except for the farmer himself, whose daily task becomes a moral exercise and a physical recreation, rather than the very stuff of his subsistence.

The people of the countryside appear only at the margins of dramatic literature. When they come on stage it is as the messengers and supporting cast in tragedies, and as the butt of jokes and jibes in comedies which distance the real life of the agricultural community. Menander's *Disagreeable Man* has as its title figure a farmer who is portrayed living on his own up in the heavily contoured landscape near the cave of Pan at Phyle (see below p. 192) in northern Attica. This farmer is of interest because he has a beautiful daughter. By making his disagreeable man live out on his own in a wild landscape, Menander stresses that he is an unsociable type. In actual fact even this remote part of Attica was peopled: there was a small farming community residing in the village of Phyle, and troops were garrisoned at the nearby fort controlling the pass towards Boiotia. The glimpse which comedy gives of the countryside is extremely partial.

The visual arts are no less selective in their imagery. The little we know of major wall-painting suggests that farming scenes were no more to be found there than they are in free-standing or relief sculpture. Men at work in general rarely find a place in these media, but representations of workshops are not infrequent on painted vases. Vases too, however, show very few agricultural scenes. Figure 4 shows one exception to this exclusion of the rural from vases. The inside of this

4 This unique scene on the interior of an Attic cup found at Vulci in Italy has a hunter with a club in the middle, and ploughing and sowing, together with hunting and stray lizards, round the outside. Compare the ancient plough shown here with that in Figure 36. The cup was made by the potter Nikosthenes in the late sixth century.

ABOVE

5 This early sixth-century bronze statuette from Asia Minor, 13 cm long, shows a plough team turning at the end of a furrow. This moment may have been chosen for its symbolic rather than its agricultural importance: early Greek inscriptions are written 'as the ox ploughs,' from left to right in one line and from right to left in the next.

BELOW

6 This late eighth-century bronze statuette of an ox, 8 cm long, comes from the West Peloponnese, where it was dedicated at a sanctuary.

late sixth-century cup by the Athenian potter Nikosthenes, decorated in the black-figure technique, shows three plough teams and a sower in the main field. Round the outside it has youths hunting fawns, and there is another hunter in the central medallion. The whole scene gives a very general impression of life in the country, an impression in which farming and hunting are mixed together, as they are in Xenophon. This is a passive observer's view of the countryside rather than the view of the active peasant. The vase is a unique piece, and it is notable that the potter Nikosthenes specialized in making pots for the Italian market. Athenians who purchased painted vases seem to have had no interest even in this idealized countryside.

Agriculture featured to some extent in small statuettes of bronze or terracotta. Although they are not common, plough teams are found in both bronze and terracotta, and there was a strong Arkadian tradition of small bronze figures of shepherds. Such figures are, however, virtually confined to the Archaic and early Classical periods, and even then they are far outnumbered by single animal figures – the country without people. These representations of animals are extremely numerous in the eighth and seventh centuries, but they are by no means directly or unequivocally connected with farming (see Chapter 8).

In their literature and their art we see the Greeks as they chose to represent themselves. That self-representation consistently plays down the basic reliance upon the countryside. The views of the country that are offered are selected so that they almost always omit the people and invariably omit the labour. Ironically the only time that agricultural production becomes prominent in the literary record is when home production fails and food has to be imported from outside. Improper dealings among the shippers of grain figure quite prominently in the various surviving law-court speeches from fourth-century Athens. This irony demonstrates both the depth of the paradoxical relation to the countryside, and the importance of unmasking the reality.

The country in the city

The image projected in Classical literature and art is of a countryside which is a separate world. This world runs itself in a healthy but unproblematic way. The people of the countryside ought to be doing the right thing at the right time and ought to be prosperous and morally upright, but they are, at the same time, quite different from those of the political centre, are ignorant of politics and are unsociable. The country is good to draw on for the sake of argument, from time to time, but it does not deserve the close attention of the urbane. Aristotle on more than one occasion extols the importance of city self-sufficiency, but for all the inquiries into animals and plants made by him and by his pupil Theophrastos, no philosopher was will-

ing to look into the working source of this self-sufficiency.

The reality is very different. Far from the country being a separate world, the political centre proves to be permeated by the country at every level. The countryside absorbs the time and energies of the majority of its inhabitants, directs its politics, and drives its calendar of activities. Two examples which concern the very highest levels of Athenian society will clarify this reality.

In 415, in the middle of their long conflict with Sparta, the Athenians were preparing to send a major expedition to Sicily. As the expedition was about to sail a major scandal broke out: pillars of Hermes throughout the city were mutilated and it was reported that the sacred Mysteries of Eleusis had been grossly parodied. In the virtual witch-hunt which followed, a large number of prominent Athenians were condemned and either fled or were executed. Their property was confiscated and lists of the property and the prices fetched in the auctions were inscribed on large stone pillars, which became known in antiquity as the 'Attic stelai.' A number of fragments of these stones have been recovered from the Athenian agora (the centre of Athenian political life). These fragments give a unique, if imperfect, impression of the holdings of real estate and the personal possessions of a small set of relatively rich and relatively young Athenians at a time when Athens was at the height of her power.

The religious scandal of 415 was interpreted in a political light, and attempts were made to manipulate it both against Alkibiades, the most eloquent and forceful of the supporters of the Sicilian expedition, and against Alkibiades' enemies. In both cases personal as well as political friends and enemies were probably involved. It is relatively clear that most of those who lost their property were men whose propertied interests were not so very different from those of Alkibiades himself, who was the son of a distinguished family and capable of prodigious expenditure on items of conspicuous consumption (in particular race horses and clothing).

The authorities responsible for the confiscation worked from Athens out. First they sold off goods in the properties in Athens followed by the properties themselves, and then they worked out to those elsewhere. As a result we cannot, from the partially preserved stones, reconstruct the complete property of any individual, and we do not have a representative cross-section of types of property holding. But for giving a general impression of the holdings of rich young men the stelai are uniquely valuable.

The goods in the properties in Athens are notable for their lack of variety: we find simply kitchen equipment, food supplies, clothing and furniture. Sometimes the amount of clothing does seem excessive, as in the long list of cloaks (perhaps of Alkibiades himself). But the only real luxury items seem to be the pictures collected by one Axiokhos, which may well have been kept in a property outside the town. Most important for what they tell us about connections with the countryside are the stores: these are no mean kitchen supplies, but include unground grain in large quantities. It is almost certain that these stores are stores of the householder's own produce, brought in from fields owned and farmed by the householder.

Until the rural properties of the condemned men were sold, rent and crops continued to come in from them. These give a further indication of the strong rural interests which are revealed to the full when these properties are sold off. Landed interests are universal and agricultural properties are scattered not only through Attica, but also over parts of the Athenian empire. Many of the condemned seem to have been young men who may frequently not yet have inherited the main family properties. But although their holdings may for this reason be untypically dispersed, they do represent one strong, if minority, pattern. Details of a sample of holdings will best convey the situation.

Axiokhos, the man with the pictures, came from Alkibiades' own deme (ward/village) of Skambonidai within the town walls. He has a piece of land at Tho . . . (in or near the town), a tenement house (probably also nearby) and three houses in the country. Two of these are in Attica and are associated with areas of vineyard, and one may be outside Attica altogether. Crops are also received from a piece of land outside Attica.

Euphiletos from the town district of Kydathenaion was the leader of the alleged band of mutilators. He has a house in or near the town, perhaps in Kydathenaion itself, another house in the village of Semakhidai (perhaps in northeast Attica), and plots of land at Aphidna, in northeast Attica, and at Gargettos and Myrrhinoutta, in the Mesogeia plain east of Athens. His land at Myrrhinoutta seems to include another house and a garden.

Aphidna is the home village of another of the condemned, Panaitios, who has even stronger agricultural interests. Stele 2 records the sale of his slave donkey-driver, while later wine is sold from one piece of his land, two oxen from a second, and six oxen, eighty-four sheep with their offspring, and sixty-seven goats with their offspring, from a third. Unfortunately none of the location names is completely preserved, and we do not know whether Panaitios pursued this extensive pasturing activity within Attica or outside.

These examples illustrate the very strong involvement with the countryside which was common to the vast majority of Athenians.

They also show how widely spread the interests of the rich were, spread not only around Attica but also over the Aegean empire. Agriculture was the basis of life and wealth for these people, and although they might reside for much of the time in the town, it is clear that farming was no game for them. They acquired land wherever they could and farmed it as vineyard, arable land, or pasture as suited it, and them, best. The products of the land piled up in their town houses and formed the basis of their subsistence.

The second example comes from a very different, far more anecdotal and far less historically reliable source, the *Life of Perikles* by the Greek writer Plutarch, composed in the early second century AD. In Chapter 16 of the *Life* Plutarch has occasion to mention that Perikles was incorruptible by money, and he makes this his excuse for discussing Perikles' domestic economy: 'Perikles was not, however, altogether lazy with regard to making money. To avoid either losing his own proper inherited wealth through neglect or having it take up a lot of his precious time and trouble, Perikles arranged his household economy in the way which he considered to be the easiest and most efficient. He sold all the annual harvests in one go, and then provided for life and livelihood by buying what was necessary from the market. He was none too popular with his grown sons for this, and he was no lavish supplier of the women. They criticized the day-to-day nature of the expenditure and the limitations upon it, contrasting it with the ever-flowing abundance of great houses, for here every expense and receipt was carefully noted down. The man who kept charge of all this detailed accounting was one of the slaves, Evangellos, suited as none other to domestic accountancy through natural aptitude and the training Perikles had given him.'[5]

This anecdote is only told because Perikles' practice is novel. Generally, as is indeed clear from the Attic stelai, the rich kept their produce for their own use throughout the year, selling what was necessary to meet purchasing needs. Perikles, by contrast, sells everything and only purchases when purchase is necessary. Perikles' innovation is resented by his family. This is partly, no doubt, because it meant that they ended up being less extravagantly supplied. But it may well be also because the dependence which it established upon goods in the market was a dependence normally associated with the poor (see Chapter 5). But even Perikles' innovation is limited. He does not rid himself of the worry of farming; he continues to keep his landed property and to run it himself rather than leasing it out. He converts crops to money in one go, but he still starts with the crops. Perikles had inherited his landed property, but that property was not simply an ornament, it was the root source of the wealth and subsistence of the family. Perikles supplies himself from the income from his land rather than directly from the crops which that land produces, but he still expects the land to be the ultimate source of his livelihood.

Both these examples have been Athenian, but the same interdependence of town and country can be seen in very different circumstances in the history of the Peloponnesian city of Mantineia. In the late fifth century the people of Mantineia lived mainly in one major settlement and enjoyed a political regime that was broadly democratic. Later tradition held that this creation of a single political centre was a product of the deliberate decision of a number of earlier settlements to combine. In the early fourth century the city came into conflict with Sparta, and it is the results of this conflict which are of interest here.

In 384 Sparta responded to what she took to be disloyalty on the part of Mantineia by demanding that the Mantineians pull down their walls. The Mantineians refused, and the Spartan king, Agesipolis, led an army against the city and beseiged it. Mantineia enjoyed a poor defensive position and the Spartans were able to undermine her walls by diverting a stream and to force the city to accept their terms. These terms were that the Mantineians should abandon the town and go back to living in villages. Xenophon, who provides the fullest narrative of these events, remarks of the Mantineian reaction to these terms that: 'They did not like it at first, since they had to demolish their existing houses and build others. But since those who had property were both living nearer to the pieces of land that they had around the villages and were enjoying aristocratic government, being freed from the burdensome demagogues, they were rather pleased at what had happened. The Spartans now sent not a single mobilization officer but one for each village, and the Mantineians joined campaigns much more keenly from their villages than they had when democratic.'[6]

Thirteen years later the Theban victory at the battle of Leuktra freed southern Greece from Spartan domination. Xenophon, again, describes the Mantineian reaction: 'The Mantineians, as people who were already free from outside interference, all gathered together and voted to make Mantineia one city and to fortify that city.'[7] When the Spartans send King Agesilaos to Mantineia to try to stop this he is told 'that all the city had already decided to build fortifications.' The Spartans are extremely annoyed but in the end hostility stops short of a pitched battle. A decade later, however, Mantineia is the scene of a major battle involving forces from a large number of Greek cities. The course

and indecisive result of that battle are not of concern here, but in his narrative of the campaign Xenophon makes a number of significant remarks. As the troops gather, the Boiotian general Epameinondas, coming to help, hurries his cavalry on to Mantineia 'learning that all the cattle of the Mantineians were probably outside, and all the men, particularly as the gathering in of the harvest was taking place'. The Mantineians begged help from the Athenian cavalry as well 'because all the animals were outside, and so were the labourers, along with many free-born children and old men'.[8]

A clear and consistent picture emerges from all these episodes. The basic livelihood of the people of Mantineia rests on farming the countryside, and it does so whether they live in one central settlement or scattered in villages. Living in villages makes cultivating the fields easier, but that cultivation continues even when they reside further away. The threat of war is not enough to interrupt the agricultural activities, but it does lead to a shortage of adult males in the fields and an unusually prominent role for boys and old men, who take charge of the labourers, who were apparently slaves. The town is not simply the base for agricultural activity, it is also the place where the grain is stored and it has enough open space to take all the cattle inside. The countryside and its production are the primary concern of the men of Mantineia, whether they live in one community or in several, and whether they have democratic or aristocratic leanings. If ever there was a clear example of the fact that centralization does not involve any weakening of ties with the land or decline in the numbers employed in agriculture, this is it. Town and country interpenetrate, and the decision to recreate the town is in no sense a rejection of the country.

At the same time it is clear that the question

of centralized or dispersed residence is an important one, about which the Mantineians feel strongly. The ability of the Mantineians to be independent and to act in co-ordination is seen, both by the Mantineians themselves and by their Spartan adversaries, to depend upon their residing in a single centre. In the face of threats from outside, residence in a central settlement is seen to offer a possibility for the Mantineians to defend themselves, which they would not be able to do in their small villages. The question is also tied up with conflicting political views among the citizen body, since residential pre-ference is closely linked with the question

of democratic or oligarchic constitution. Gathered together the poor have a political clout which they lack when divided up. The rich whose land-holdings are concentrated around the old villages become much more conspicuous and dominant when all must reside in the midst of their fields. When all have to travel out from the central settlement to farm their land, at least some of the striking contrast between rich and poor is concealed. To live in a single settlement was to have a community life and community facilities, which no individual village could hope to provide. In all these ways there was, for the large proportion of the free population of Mantineia at least, a world of difference between living together and living scattered, but in both situations the country remained at the heart of the city.

This chapter has attempted to set out and

7 Towns could afford facilities not available in smaller settlements. This surviving theatre at Mantineia, in the centre of the walled area, is of Roman date.

to illustrate the paradox of the Greek city. In literature and art the countryside of the Greek city is never described and rarely discussed. In reality the whole population was intimately involved in the life and production of the countryside and the town never began to be independent of the land around it. The Greek city was not a town and its territory, as it has sometimes been described; it was a variously peopled landscape. The following chapters will explore the nature of that landscape and will attempt to show something of the way in which it was exploited. The consequences of the rural basis of life in the Greek city were manifold – political, religious, military. As these are investigated in the succeeding pages a new framework for comprehending the history of the Greek city will be forged.

FARMING THE COUNTRY

All Greek cities were fundamentally dependent upon their countryside, but there was enormous variation in the particular landforms available to individual cities. This chapter examines the nature of the Greek landscape and its agricultural exploitation, exploring the constraints within which the Greek farmer operated and the effects which these had. The variety of the countryside and the rigours of the climate imposed different conditions in different places and demanded different agricultural strategies. These strategies enabled the country to be highly productive, but not reliably so. Both the form and the success of the strategies directly affected the nature and structure of society and hence the course of much of military and political history.

The formation of the Greek peninsula

The geological history of Greece is complex, and as a result many distinct landforms are found there on a small scale which are found on a much larger scale in other parts of the world. This was already recognized in antiquity. Aristotle writes: 'Rivers which are swallowed up prove the existence of many chasms and cavities in the earth. This happens in many places, for example in the Peloponnese one finds it most often in Arkadia [see Figure 8]. The reason for this is that the country is mountainous and yet there are no outlets from the basins to the sea. Thus these parts get filled up, and since there is no outlet the water flowing in from above forces its way out and finds a way through to the depth of the earth. In Greece such things only ever happen on a small scale, but there is such a lake beneath the Caucasus which the locals call a sea [the Caspian].'[1]

On a geological time-scale Greece is a young country, formed at the same time as the Alps, between 100 million and 25 million years ago. Subsequent geological events have had a further considerable effect on the landscape: the rich agricultural basins of Thessaly and Boiotia, and the volcanic islands in the southwest Aegean, came into being only about 2 million years ago, and the Corinthian Gulf, large parts of the western Peloponnese, and the plain of Thessalonika in northern Greece have been shaped even more recently. Greece is still today the most geologically active part of Europe, suffering frequent earthquakes.

The variety of the landscape resulting from this complex history is not simply a matter of interest to the geologist. The nature of the rocky skeleton, so often itself protruding through the thin covering of soil, materially affected the possibilities for human exploitation. Different rocks weather in different ways and provide soils that are more or less

8 Inland lakes drained by swallow-holes are a not infrequent product of the limestone geology of the Greek mainland. One such is the Stymphalian lake, seen here. This lake was the scene of one of Herakles' legendary labours, when he shot down the bronze man-eating birds which had taken up residence on the lake. The level of the lake fluctuated in antiquity, and today the waters cover part of the ancient town of Stymphalos, traces of the walls of which can be seen disappearing below the lake surface.

9 The remarkable rocky fingers of the Meteora in Thessaly are a product of the erosion of sediments deposited some 20 million years ago, and are unparalleled elsewhere in Greece.

fertile and more or less subject to erosion. Also only some rocks were valuable in themselves: not everywhere in Greece had access to good marble for building (see Chapter 4), and the peninsula of Methana had a virtual monopoly within southern Greece of the fine-grained igneous rock used for millstones.

The territories of the Greek cities were often tiny, and as a result there was frequently nothing in common between the terrain of one city and that of another. The cities of Thessaly enjoyed broad expanses of gently rolling or even completely flat plains, but although they had no shortage of arable land they often had problems with drainage. Just to the south, however, the cities of Phokis and Lokris nestled in a mountainous landscape: terraces often had to be built before cereals or tree crops could be grown here and pastoral activities necessarily played a large

part in the agricultural strategy. In other cases sheer differences in altitude resulted in similar landforms of very different potential for the farmer. Argos in the northeast Peloponnese has an extensive coastal plain ringed by hills, a territory suited both to arable agriculture and to tree crops, but less suited to pastoral farming because of shortage of water. Nearby Mantineia and Tegea (see pp. 23-25 and 49), in an upland basin some 700 m above the sea, had abundant flocks and herds, but were too susceptible to frosts to be able to grow olives. The Greek landscape has both rugged and smiling faces, and provides both fertile and barren landscapes at all altitudes. It frequently invites settlements, but equally frequently forbids communications between them. And just as there is no one Greek landscape, so there could never be any one single way of agricultural life. At any one time different

Greek farmers faced very different problems in their fight to force a living from the earth. But one factor in particular meant that the success of the farming enterprise was always in doubt for every farmer—the climate.

The climatic constraints

For most Greeks it was the nature and distribution of the soil which most directly determined their settlement and social interactions. How much soil there was and what crops it would produce were in part determined by the climate. Extravagant claims have sometimes been made that the climate at various particular periods of antiquity was dramatically different from that of the present day, so different that it was difficult for men to survive at all. Recent work, however, has made it clear that the broad pattern of the Greek climate has remained the

same for the past three or four millennia at least. There have certainly been some minor short-lived changes and local peculiarities and some of these have indeed affected agriculture, but broadly speaking the climate posed the same problems for the ancient farmer as it does for his modern Greek counterpart.

Climate has been responsible in some cases for soil erosion and soil deposition, but more frequently man's activities have played some part in such geomorphological changes. Ever since the earliest settled agriculture of the Neolithic, men have changed the land they live in by what they have done – and not all those changes have been designed or desired. In Greece the traces of such changes can be seen from the Bronze Age onwards, as hillsides have been grazed, terraces built and abandoned, forests felled or allowed to grow up in areas no longer in agricultural use. There is no simple pattern to these changes in the landscape, however. There has been no general trend towards the increasing denudation of the natural vegetation on soil of the countryside. The changes that have occurred have usually been local ones, often determined by peculiarly local circumstances. Sometimes it has been the exploitation of the land that has led directly to loss of soil or of ground cover, but equally often the building of terraces and field walls has maintained the landscape and it has been the removal of the human presence that has led to its degradation.

10 Much of the Greek countryside can be cultivated only once it has been terraced. The building and maintenance of terraces demands much time and effort, and thus terrace construction and abandonment (as here in the eastern Argolid) is a good indicator of changing pressures on the land.

Much of the Greek countryside is marginal for arable agriculture and even for the growing of tree crops such as olives and figs. The decision to cultivate a particular area will therefore often have depended upon a very delicate calculation of likely productivity and likely demand. Minor local changes in geomorphology therefore would have had a dramatic effect upon farming practices. Those minor changes are sometimes easy, and sometimes impossible to trace today; as a result our ability to assess the exploitation and productivity of any particular area of ancient countryside varies from area to area. The very variety of the landscape forbids overhasty generalization or rapid global estimates.

The fundamental importance of the climate in determining not just the soil but what that soil produced was recognized in antiquity. Aristotle's pupil, Theophrastos, writes: 'The mix of the air and the general nature of the seasons is of prime importance for the growth and nourishment of plants. When rain and fine weather and storms are timely all bear well and have much fruit, even if they grow in salty or light soil. Well does the proverb say: "The year bears the crop, not the soil." The land does make a big difference, but not just by being heavy or light, sodden or dry: the surrounding air also makes a difference. Some light and poor lands yield perfectly well because they are favourably disposed for breezes off the sea.'[2]

Greece as a whole enjoys a generally Mediterranean climate, the bulk of rain falling between October and May and very little during the summer. Northern, and particularly northwestern, Greece, however, falls between an area of Mediterranean and an area of continental climate, where most rain falls in the summer. Thus the wettest month in southern Greece is December, in northwest Greece October; the driest months in the

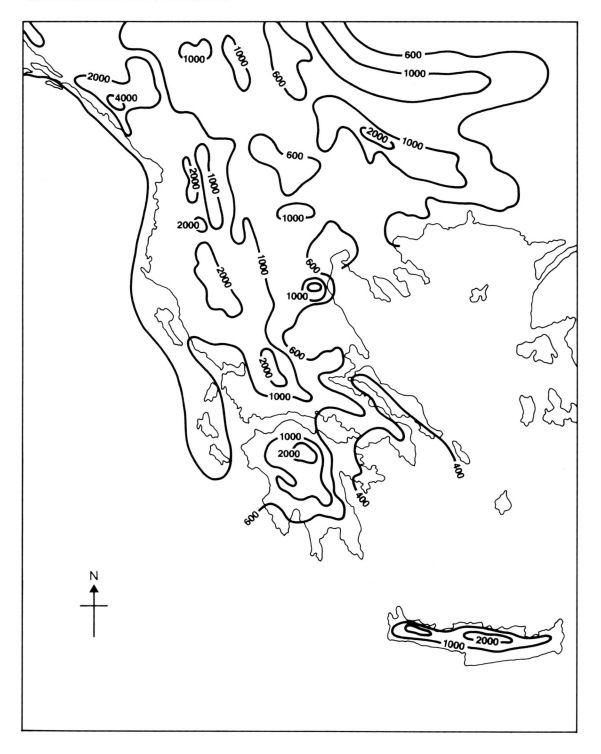

south are July and August, but in the north-west March is driest. Amounts of precipitation vary as widely as its distribution: Attica, the Cyclades and the southern tip of the Peloponnese receive less than 400 mm of rain a year; the mountains of the Peloponnese and of northwest Greece receive upwards of 2000 mm, and in the Ionian islands 150 mm and more may fall in a single day. Some Aegean islands have less than fifty days a year with any rain, but in southern Thessaly twice as many can be expected.

Within this overall pattern there may be very considerable local variations, as was recognized in antiquity. Aristotle writes in the *Meteorologica*: 'Sometimes it happens that drought or rain affects a great area of country at the same time, but sometimes the effect is only local. For often the country in general receives due rainfall for the season or even more, but in one part of the country there is drought. And occasionally the opposite is true: when all the country around has but moderate rainfall or even a drought, one particular part receives boundless supply of rain.'[3]

Some of these local variations are closely linked to the physical geography of the country and are more or less constant. A striking example of the effect of topography on rainfall occurs in Boiotia in central Greece, where Thebes, the most important city in antiquity, has on average some 477 mm of rain each year, but Lebadeia, the modern regional capital some 30 km west-northwest and also an ancient city site, receives some 732 mm. What makes the difference here is the fact that Lebadeia is under the shadow of

11 The 'contours' of this map (in mm) link places of equal average annual rainfall. Note the enormous difference between what can be expected annually in eastern and in northwestern Greece.

Mt Parnassos. A similar phenomenon is found in Thessaly, where Karditsa in the upper plain receives 907 mm of rain a year, Larisa in the lower plain 490 mm. In this case the contrast between the two areas is further magnified: not only does Karditsa itself directly receive some of the very high rainfall of the Pindos mountains, it also receives enormous quantities of water draining in winter and spring from the Pindos themselves.

Other local variations in rainfall are the product of the particular year's weather. Examples from the opposite ends of the Greek mainland will illustrate how common and how problematic these fluctuations in the rainfall at a particular place are (see Table 1). Kavala, ancient Neapolis, on the north coast of the Aegean, had an average annual rainfall of 549 mm in the 1960s. This average hides the fact that in the driest year of the decade (1964) it had only 252 mm, and in the wettest (1969) 897 mm. At Athens in the 1950s annual rainfall varied from a low of 216 mm (1959) to a high of 560 mm (1953). Nearby Eleusis shared the same general pattern of rainfall as Athens, but in 1959 it had 280 mm and in 1953 only 427 mm (its wettest year was 1955 when it recorded 740 mm, when Athens had just 548 mm). Overall there are few areas of Greece where the rainfall in any particular month does not vary by more than 60 per cent from year to year.

This interannual variability might simply lend spice to life were it not that even the *average* annual rainfall in many areas of Greece is barely sufficient to support the basic staple crops. Barley will produce a decent crop on 200 mm of rain a year (provided the seasonal distribution of the rain is not too maverick), but wheat is seriously affected if the rainfall falls below 300 mm in the year, legumes if it falls below 400 mm. Thus even at Kavala, which on average has abundant water supply

33

Table 1 Variations in annual rainfall at Kavala, Athens and Eleusis (in mm)

Kavala		Athens (Helleniko)		Eleusis	
Year	Annual Total	Year	Annual Total	Year	Annual Total
1961	589	1951	346	1951	361
1962	541	1952	433	1952	358
1963	418	1953	560	1953	427
1964	252	1954	414	1954	497
1965	376	1955	548	1955	740
1966	744	1956	281	1956	374
1967	488	1957	305	1957	433
1968	599	1958	349	1958	401
1969	897	1959	216	1959	280
1970	585	1960	356	1960	444
Average	549	Average	381	Average	432

for all these crops, the driest year of the 1960s will have knocked out all but the barley crop. At Athens sufficient rain for legumes was received in only four years during the 1950s, sufficient for wheat in only seven (1957 was marginal), and in the driest year even the barley crop will have been threatened (19 mm, almost 10 per cent, of the rain in that year came in a July storm). The rain that matters is that which falls during the months when the crop is growing. This varies from crop to crop, but the most important months are from October to May. Because summer rain is so frequently received in the form of torrential storms which may bring up to 50 mm in an hour, it frequently does more harm than good to crops (although it may usefully top up supplies for human consumption).

There is abundant evidence for crop failures and food shortages in antiquity. Because people could vary the amount of grain they consumed only within rather narrow limits (between starvation on the one hand and satiety on the other), the fluctuations in the grain supply are very closely

reflected in fluctuations in the grain price. Good and bad years for grain in Attica and in the areas from which Athens imported grain are traceable through the records of the grain price, which fluctuates dramatically over short periods of time. An inscription dated to about 330 records the gift of a very large quantity (probably 4830 metric tonnes) of grain (wheat?) from Cyrene in north Africa to cities throughout Greece (see Figure 12). The recipients include cities in Thessaly and Elis as well as cities of the dry southeast, and this suggests that in this year there was a very widespread corn shortage through the whole peninsula. (The grain trade is further discussed in Chapter 5.)

How did ancient farmers cope?

Strategies Gifts of grain from friendly cities elsewhere might conveniently stave off the worst effects of food shortage, but they could

12 *The corn given by the north African city of Cyrene to the cities of Greece in c. 330 was distributed widely through the southern part of the mainland and the islands.*

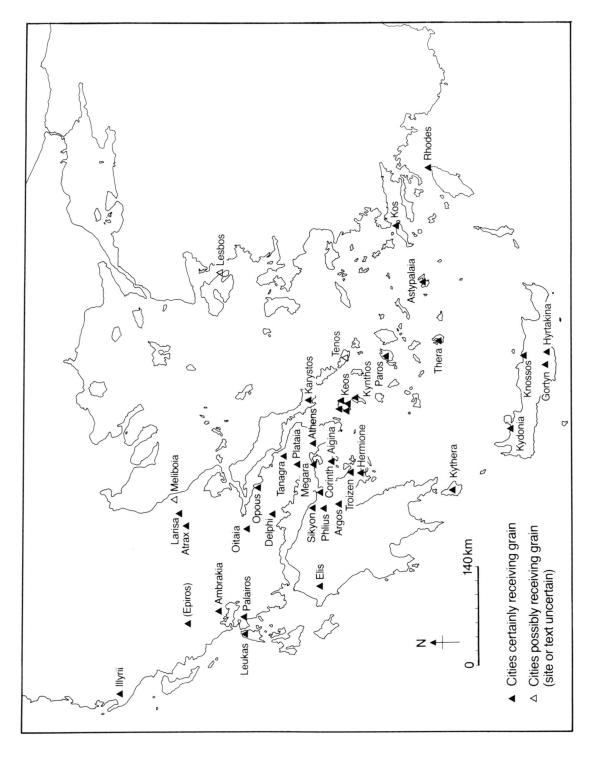

Lesbos

Kos

Rhodes

Astypalaia

Hyrtakina

Tenos

Thera

Knossos

Paros

Karystos

Kynthos

Gortyn

Athens

Keos

Kydonia

Tanagra

Plataia

Aigina

Meliboia

Opous

Megara

Corinth

Hermione

Delphi

Sikyon

Troizen

Larisa

Atrax

Oitaia

Phlius

Argos

Kythera

(Epiros)

Ambrakia

Elis

Palairos

Leukas

N

Illyrii

140km

0

▲ Cities certainly receiving grain

△ Cities possibly receiving grain
    (site or text uncertain)

hardly be built into the farmer's regular calculations, or form part of his strategy for coping with the rigours of the ever unpredictable climate. The direct evidence for how the farmer coped is very limited: none of the surviving writings from antiquity openly discuss the problem. But, on the basis of indirect literary and epigraphic evidence and with the help of comparative data, it is possible to suggest the strategies pursued by the ancient farmer.

Modern Greek farmers face the same problems as the ancients did, for, as we have seen, the climate is no kinder and no more predictable now than ever it was. The means at the disposal of the farmer have, however, changed enormously. On the one hand the internal combustion engine has enabled irrigation to be carried out in places where previously it was unthinkable, and chemical fertilizers have done much to improve the status of marginal soils. On the other hand the introduction of new crops has made it more possible to specialize in the crop to which the ground is most suited. Certain areas of Greece now grow large quantities of cotton for cash, others tobacco, others currants, and so on. While it makes sense today for territory which is marginal for the cultivation of the basic staple cereals to be used for whatever crop it is ecologically most suited for, the scope for doing this in antiquity was severely restricted. Ancient Athenian specialization in olives has been thought to be indicated by the fact that the law-giver Solon prohibited the export of all agricultural produce except olives. Similarly, the survival of two laws on the wine trade from the island of Thasos, together with the massive evidence for the production of amphorae in which wine was transported, suggests that in antiquity Thasos was dominated by the vine – although today there are very few vines and

agriculture is oriented towards the olive. Macedonia was relatively well covered with forest in antiquity, and there is little doubt that it came to realize the value of these timber resources and to exploit them: in the late fifth century Perdikkas, King of Macedon, agreed with the Athenians that they alone were to receive oars from his dominion, and at the end of the century the Athenians made another agreement with his successor Arkhelaos which involved the sending of Athenian shipwrights to Macedon in order to construct a fleet in the shortest possible time.

But although a single crop might dominate exchange relations between one city and another, the idea that any city seriously limited the variety of its agricultural production is supported by little good evidence. Even in the rather special case of timber, Macedonia has no sort of monopoly of supplies: we hear of timber coming from various parts of Arkadia, from Sikyon, Elis, Corinth, Kos and Rhodes, as well as from the further reaches of the Greek world – south Italy, Sicily, the Black Sea and Cyprus.

There is much evidence that most cities of Greece aimed at a general self-sufficiency in staples. The practice of growing a little of everything is true of cities as a whole and of individual farmers and plots of land. This is most clearly and nicely illustrated by some fourth-century documents relating to the leasing of public land. A small group of land leases from Attica and from the Aegean island of Amorgos, at a time when it was dominated by Athens, include detailed instructions on farming practice. These instructions lay down the crops to be grown and the methods of cultivation. Such detail is of the very greatest interest, although it is not clear whether the specifications reflect normal practice or impose special conditions.

The long and well-preserved lease from

Arkesine on Amorgos reads as follows: 'The lessee ... will pay the rent in the month Thargelion [May] every year, free of all taxes. If he fails to pay there shall be exacted from the lessee and his sureties a fine equivalent to half the rent. He is to plough half the land each year, and not all the land in a single year. He is to dig round the vines twice, first in Anthesterion [February] and again before the twentieth of Taureon [April], and round the figs once. If he fails to do this he must pay a fine of an obol for each vine or fig tree round which he fails to dig, and 3 drachmas for each zugon [a measure of land of uncertain area] he fails to plough. ... He is to build up again all walls that collapse, on pain of a fine of a drachma for each fathom of collapsed wall. He must repair all the walls along the road and leave them in good condition at the end of the lease. He is to apply 150 loads of dung a year with a basket holding 1 medimnos and 4 hemiekta [about 70 litres], or pay a fine of a $\frac{1}{2}$ drachma for each basket shortfall. He must swear to the temple magistrates that he has indeed applied this manure in accordance with the agreement. He must keep the roofs watertight, and hand them over in this condition. The vines that are cut down the temple magistrates will sell. The lessee will dig trenches in the month Eiraphion [December] where the magistrates mark them out, 4-foot ones and 3-foot ones, and will put in the plants in the presence of the temple magistrates, planting each year twenty vines, at the spacing ordered by the magistrates, and ten fig trees, and he must build a wall on the land. The storage jars shall be considered security for the building of this wall, and the lessee will make a pledge to the magistrates. For failure to do this the fine shall be 1 drachma per plant. ... '[4]

This lease relates to a piece of land sacred to Zeus upon which are some buildings, probably field stores to judge by the reference to storage jars, a vineyard, a number of fig trees and some arable land. There are no olives. The lease is particularly concerned with the trees and vines, and this is no doubt because of their capital value as a long-term investment. The instructions for the arable land are much more cursory, limited to ensuring that its fertility is not undermined by over-exploitation. How much land is involved is impossible to tell. A precise amount of manure is specified, but we do not know enough of ancient manuring rates to calculate the area on this basis. What is clear is that it is not expected that the arable land will all be given over to a single crop. This is equally true of all other pieces of leased land where we know anything in detail of the farming regime. The lessees of these tracts of public land were generally rich men, farming this land in addition to land of their own and not residing on the land they leased. Nevertheless it is clear that they grow a little of everything on the land, just as if they were dependent on it for their very subsistence.

The evidence for the way in which Classical farmers exploited the land which they themselves owned is less detailed and explicit. Two important facts can, however, be established: most holdings consisted of a number of small plots scattered about; and most farmers grew a wide variety of crops. The most famous description of an Athenian estate comes in a law-court speech designed to convince a jury of the excessive wealth of a man named Phainippos. In some ways this estate is far from typical: it is almost certainly on marginal land at the very edge of the fertile Mesogeia, and it is all one continuous tract. The description is nevertheless very revealing. The most important product of the land is grain. There are two threshing floors on the estate, and various buildings which are used as corn stores. The grain crop, which is possibly wholly barley, is sufficient for some to be sold off shortly after harvest. Wood is also a significant source of revenue: the speaker claims that six donkeys are employed throughout the year carting wood, and that this brings in 12 drachmas a day. The speaker visited the land in August, a slack period in the farming year and just the sort of time when the labour force would be turned to such tasks as wood-cutting: Hesiod recommends that September be given over to wood-cutting. Twelve drachmas a day would hardly be enough to keep six donkeys and those in charge of them, and so those donkeys are more likely to comprise the total animal labour on the land than a special team devoted to timber. Nevertheless the description makes clear the mixed exploitation of the estate, which is also said to produce a large amount of wine.

The fragmentation of holdings is well brought out by the Attic stelai discussed in Chapter 1. The properties of the upper crust of Athenian society, with whom the Attic stelai are concerned, might be widely scattered and some of the more distant were no doubt run by agents. Even men whose holdings were concentrated in a single area and who oversaw the farming themselves seem rarely to have had all their land in one continuous tract. This is nicely shown by a document recording the sale of the property of the fourth-century politician Philokrates after he had been condemned in the courts. The stone is unfortunately badly preserved, but it still shows that Philokrates possessed at least six separate pieces of land at his native village of Hagnous (again in the Mesogeia). Two of the pieces of land have buildings on them, and at least five of the six are very close together in the same area.

The rich had the resources to purchase plots of land outright or to lease them, and there is evidence that they showed an interest in acquiring even plots of extremely small size. The poor had much more circumscribed opportunities to acquire land, and we know much less about the nature of their holdings. Some scattered land-holdings certainly came about through the processes of inheritance. In the vast majority of Greek cities inherited land was normally split equally between surviving sons, and in certain circumstances the marriage of people from different locations could lead to the accumulation of disparate lands in a single household. But amongst poor families there may have been little or no property to inherit. The privilege of possessing a fragmented holding was yet one more way in which the rich could not only maintain but increase their advantage over the less well-off.

To describe fragmentation of farmland as a privilege goes against a basic tenet of modern agricultural economics. This holds that scattered lands are inefficient because of the travelling time which their exploitation involves. For the subsistence farmer it may be much more important to avoid years with no crop at all than to save time, a commodity which the family supplies in plentiful quantities. For such a farmer a fragmented holding is a positive asset. The variety of landscape and the fluctuation in rainfall which Greece enjoys mean that it is extraordinarily unwise to concentrate on growing a single crop or on exploiting only one tract of land. Such concentration may produce a massive crop in the year that offers ideal growing conditions, but it will run the risk of producing no crop at all in another year. Growing a variety of crops begins to spread the risk: conditions which will decimate the wheat crop may but slightly reduce the barley yield; even if the entire cereal crop is lost for one year the problems

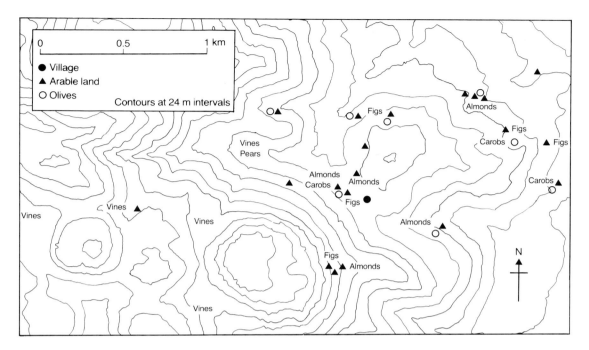

13 *This map shows the lands belonging to a single family in a Methana village in the 1970s. Note the number of plots of land and how scattered they are. By growing a variety of crops in a variety of locations the family effectively halved the risks of crop failure. (After Forbes)*

of securing seed-corn for the next year may be partially offset by the fact that the tree crops will already be provided for. Growing crops in a variety of places spreads the risk still further. It will enable a variety of different ecological conditions to be exploited – lands that drain more or less well, lands with and without access to springs and hence the possibility of irrigation, exposed hillsides and sheltered valleys, thin hill-slope soils and deeper alluvial fans, terraces and plains, varieties of aspect, and so on. The combined strategy of growing a variety of crops and of growing each crop in a variety of locations will mean that really bumper years will be forfeited, but it will also mean that it is extremely unlikely that there will be a year in which all crops in all places are completely wiped out.

Unfortunately we cannot trace on the ground what effect these agricultural strategies had on the landscape of antiquity. Field boundaries rarely leave archaeological traces

and still more rarely can be linked to a particular owner. The situation in modern Greece is, however, to a large extent comparable. The land is still characteristically farmed in very small fields, the boundaries of which are not always clear on the ground. The *average* size of field in Greece in the 1960s was just under half a hectare. Work done in the southern Argolid and on the Methana peninsula, where the rugged nature of the land exaggerates ecological variation over a small ground area, has shown how Greek farmers exploit their fragmented holdings and the advantages they gain from them. One farmer had 3 hectares of land spread over 20 plots. The most distant plots were 8 km apart and separated by 700 m in altitude. The yield from individual plots varied by some 27 per cent, but the total yield from all together varied by only 16 per cent: the farmer had effectively halved his problems.

This pattern of extreme fragmentation is the one that is, and almost certainly has been for a long time, prevalent in southern Greece and on the islands. It is not prevalent through the whole of Greece, however. Climate and landscape impose different constraints in different places. At the margins of agricultural viability a farmer may need both to grow a variety of crops and to grow them in a variety of places. Other farmers in less severe conditions may employ either strategy on its own. Thus Phainippos seems to own only a single piece of land, but he grows a variety of produce. A fourth-century will from the sanctuary of Dodona in Epiros shows an anonymous figure pursuing a different strategy: '[Name, lost] bequeaths to the association all his landed possessions: arable land at Kossos, a meadow at Atherios, a vineyard near Kotas, and a building plot.'[5] Dodona lies in the northwest of Greece where, although there is still a large amount of variation from year to year, the total precipitation is dependably large, and cereal crops are less likely to be threatened by drought. (Corfu, off the northwest coast, is in fact one of the wetter places in Europe, with some 1100 mm or more annually.)

Farming methods The variations in climate and soil and the range of strategies employed by farmers to cope with them mean that it is very difficult to reconstruct Classical agricultural practices in detail or to estimate their productivity. Nevertheless certain basic features can be reconstructed.

Agricultural technology was primitive: the plough was a simple ard which broke the soil but did not turn it. The fullest ancient des-

cription of a plough is provided by Hesiod. Hesiod assumes that the farmer will construct his own wooden plough, and this is not entirely a literary artifice. The plough did not change significantly over the subsequent centuries; only in the Roman era was metallurgical skill applied to it. But the ard should not be considered as an inefficient and underdeveloped modern plough: it is a totally different instrument. As well as its role in preparing the seed-bed, it was equally important in the conservation of moisture. Fallow land, in particular, was ploughed repeatedly during the year in order to keep it clean and also to maintain some sort of tilth so as to reduce moisture loss through capillary action. Ploughing between vines and olives had the same aim.

Ploughing with the ard in this way had to be supplemented by turning the soil and breaking up the clods with a mattock. The precise way in which plough, spade and mattock were combined was dependent on the crop and the soil involved. Theophrastos, who is sensitive to the different needs of different soils and who has a considerable understanding of soil mechanics, is emphatic that some digging is good for all crops because it mixes in air and makes the soil at the same time both damper and lighter. Different types of soils were worked at different seasons: Theophrastos suggests that as a general rule damp and heavy soils should be both ploughed and turned in the summer, light and dry soils in the winter. He goes on to note that it may actually be harmful to do the wrong thing to a soil: deep ploughing is said to render Syrian soil hard as rock, while the Thessalians have developed a special mattock so that they can turn over a greater depth of soil. It would be interesting to know whether this relates specifically to the upper plain of Thessaly with its drainage problems and anaerobic (glei) soil, but Theophrastos does not go into detail.

As all this will have made clear, ancient farming is extremely labour intensive. Animal power is of rather limited use: oxen, mules and donkeys can pull the plough and carry the crops, but they cannot help with the digging, pruning or harvesting. Much of the farm labour is heavy manual work, demanding only restricted skills. The farmer's knowledge and experience comes into play chiefly in the timing of what he does and in tree and animal husbandry. Getting the timing right is dependent upon intimate knowledge of local landscape and climate; a rigid application of Hesiod's rules would be likely to lead to inappropriate action as often as not. Significantly the leases specify particular months rather than particular days, leaving the farmer to play it by ear from year to year.

We can show that there was an awareness of some relatively sophisticated agricultural practices in ancient Greece, but we cannot hope to trace how these practices were put into operation in any particular place. Theophrastos is the most important witness that we have, but he is far removed from the daily toil of the fields and is interested in the plants and not the farmer. In many ways it is not what he says that is significant, but rather the very fact that the concepts and vocabulary existed with which he could express himself. Theophrastos is, for instance, well aware of the importance of both soil structure and soil nutrients. He recommends that light and heavy soils be mixed to improve both structure and nutrient status. He knows about the problem of the leaching of nutrients from the topsoil, and says that deep digging will improve fertility, the soil that is underneath acting as a sort of manure for the soil on the top. Theophrastos nowhere describes systematic crop rotation, but he is aware that chick-

peas and beans effectively fertilize the soil. Interestingly he considers the practice of turning in the pulse crop once it has flowered a peculiarity of the Thessalians and Macedonians. Xenophon knows the practice of turning under grass as green manure and one of the fourth-century Athenian leases allows the lessee to fallow half the land in pulses as he chooses, but we cannot tell whether either of these practices was common.

There is more general evidence for biennial fallow. Leases of farmland commonly insist on it and expressly forbid annual cropping. This is hardly surprising since anything which reduces the fertility of the land in the long term is against the interests of those leasing out the land, while for the lessee there is considerable attraction in getting as much as possible out of the land during the relatively short time for which he holds it. 'Sowing barley in the straw' was a proverbial ancient Greek phrase for annual cropping, and the very existence of such a phrase suggests that some did take this calculated risk. The very poor may have had no choice. Those under less pressure could afford longer periods of fallow. Theophrastos suggests that farmers particularly concerned with weed control might leave land fallow for two years, working it frequently and sending in animals to eat off any growth that appears. Different farmers no doubt did different things in different places at different times, but it looks as if decisions could at least be taken in the light of considerable understanding of the various possibilities and their consequences.

It is common in Greece today to see cereals being grown under olives. The practice of getting a double crop off the same land in this way was certainly known in antiquity, and it may have been followed quite extensively, but Theophrastos regards double-cropping as strictly for special circumstances, particularly

Table 2 The provisions of Classical and Hellenistic agricultural leases

	Aitolia, polis of Thestia. Pleket 1.47	Gambreion. SIG³ 302	Keos, polis of Poiessa. SIG³ 964	Khios, phratry of Klytidai. Pleket 1.40	Attica, cult of hero Iatros. Pleket 1.43	Attica, cult of Egretes. ii² 2499	Attica, deme of Teithras. Pleket 1.41	Attica, deme of Peiraieus. ii² 2498	Attica, deme of Prasiai. Hesperia 31	Attica, deme of Prasiai. ii² 2497	Attica, deme of Peiraieus. ii² 2496
Date	C2	326	C5/4	c. 350	333	306	c. 350	321	C4	C4	C4
Leasing body	polis	?	polis	phratry	cult	cult	deme	deme	deme	deme	deme
Length of lease	—	?	—	—	30	10	all time	10	—	all time	all time
Rent	?1	?	30	420	20	200	—	—	—	—	54
No. of annual payments	—	?1	1	1	1	2	1	2	?2	2	2
Tax liability	—	—	—	Yes	—	None	Yes	None	—	None	None
War damage clause	—	—	—	Excluded	—	—	Yes	—	Yes	—	—
Includes building	Yes	Yes	Yes	Yes	Yes	Yes	—	Yes	Yes	—	Yes
Cultivation regime prescribed	—	Yes	—	—	—	—	—	In part	—	—	—
Cereals	—	Yes	—	—	—	—	—	Yes	—	—	—
Biennial fallow	—	—	—	—	—	—	—	Yes	—	—	—
Pulse crop for fallow	—	—	—	—	—	—	—	No	—	—	—
Vines	—	?	—	—	—	—	—	—	—	—	—
Olives	—	?	—	—	—	?	—	—	—	—	—
Figs	—	—	—	—	—	—	—	—	—	—	—
Wood-cutting and felling forbidden	—	—	Yes	No	—	Yes	—	—	—	—	—
No manure removal	—	—	—	—	—	—	—	—	—	—	—
No topsoil removal	—	—	—	—	—	—	—	Yes	—	—	—
Irrigation	—	—	—	—	—	—	—	—	—	—	—
Water course	Yes	—	—	—	—	—	—	—	—	—	—
Garden	—	Yes	—	—	Yes	—	—	—	—	—	—
Pasture	—	—	—	—	—	—	—	Yes	—	—	—
Tree-planting enjoined	—	Yes	—	Yes	Yes	—	—	—	—	—	—
Burials prohibited	—	—	—	—	—	—	—	—	—	—	—
Area of land (one plethron=0.1 ha)	—	—	—	—	—	—	—	—	—	—	—

Lease location and reference	Attica, deme of Rhamnous. ii²2494	Attica, deme of Rhamnous. ii²2493	Attica, deme of Aixone. ii²2492	Attica, phratry. ii²1241	Olympia, *Insch. von Olymp.* 18	Amorgos, Arkesine. *SIG³*963	Thespiai. *BCH* 61.217ff.	Thespiai. *IG* vii 1739–42	Thasos, Garden of Heracles. *IG* xii suppl. 353	Delos, temple estates. *Insc. Dél.* 503 etc.	Rhodian Peraea, Amos, Frazer and Bean 8–10
Date	C4	339	345	300	C5	C4	220s	240s	C3	C4–2	C2
Leasing body	cult	deme	deme	phratry	?private	polis	polis	polis	cult	temple	community
Length of lease	—	10	40	10	all time	—	25	20	—	10	50
Rent	—	—	152	600	kind	—	—	—	—	—	240 (eg)
No. of annual payments	—	1	1	2	1	1	1	1	—	—	2
Tax liability	—	—	None	None	—	—	—	—	—	—	—
War damage clause	—	—	Yes	Yes	—	—	—	—	—	—	—
Includes building	—	Yes	No	Yes	—	Yes	—	—	Yes	Yes	Yes
Cultivation regime prescribed	Yes	Yes	Yes	Yes	—	Yes	—	—	?Yes	—	Yes
Cereals	Yes	Yes	Yes	Yes	Yes	Yes	—	—	—	Yes	—
Biennial fallow	Yes	Yes	Yes	Yes	—	Yes	—	—	—	—	—
Pulse crop for fallow	—	Yes	—	Yes	—	—	—	—	—	—	—
Vines	—	Yes	Yes	Yes	—	Yes	—	—	—	Yes	Yes
Olives	Yes	?	Yes	?	—	—	—	—	—	—	—
Figs	Yes	Yes	—	Yes	—	Yes	—	—	—	Yes	Yes
Wood-cutting and felling forbidden	Yes	Yes	Limit	Yes	—	—	—	—	—	—	Limit
No manure removal	—	Yes	(soil)	—	—	—	—	—	?Yes	—	Yes
No topsoil removal	—	—	Yes	—	—	—	—	—	—	—	—
Irrigation	Yes	—	—	—	—	—	—	—	—	—	—
Water course	—	—	—	—	—	—	—	—	Yes	—	—
Garden	Yes	—	—	—	—	—	—	—	Yes	—	—
Pasture	—	—	—	—	—	—	—	—	—	Yes	—
Tree-planting enjoined	—	—	—	—	—	Yes	—	—	Yes	—	Yes
Burials prohibited	—	—	—	—	—	—	—	—	—	—	Yes
Area of land (one plethron = 0.1 ha)	—	—	—	—	18 pl.	—	—	7 pl.	—	—	—

those in which an excess of moisture needs to be taken up by vegetation. Theophrastos is frequently concerned with damp and waterlogged conditions. He advises against digging deeply round plants in the wet since standing water will induce rot and he notes the varieties of vine and cereals which best stand up to damp conditions. Although he claims that all trees, even olives and pines, like damp and shade he knows that wood from too wet conditions is not good. Drought is not the only problem in a Mediterranean climate.

Ancient agricultural productivity It is clear then that, however primitive his technology, the Classical Greek farmer did not simply plough on in ignorance or at random. The evidence does not, however, give us any means of gauging how efficient or productive his husbandry was. In the following section the various ways of assessing ancient agricultural productivity are reviewed and some calculations are made. Although any estimates we make can only be tentative, they have a considerable bearing on the number of people the territory of an ancient city could support.

It has often been assumed that the best guide to the productivity of ancient agriculture is given by the productivity of modern Greek agriculture at the turn of this century, before the major introduction of chemical fertilizers and mechanization. This assumption has led to a very pessimistic view of the degree to which Greek cities could grow enough food for themselves, and to tremendous problems reconciling estimated food supply with ancient population figures. The problem with the assumption is that it ignores the fact that agricultural productivity is not determined simply by technology, but also by the amount of labour put in. In early twentieth-century Greece wheat yields were

as low as 500 kg per hectare, with a seed to yield ratio of 1:3; but recent work has suggested that in the Neolithic era Greek agriculture may have achieved 1000 kg per hectare from just 100 kg of seed. This simply reflects the fact that gardening is more productive than extensive farming: constantly working the soil prevents weeds and conserves moisture. Constant effort is abundantly repaid by higher yields.

Global figures of whatever sort are likely to be more misleading than helpful when applied to a particular holding or small region. A particular farm will enjoy its own peculiar soils and its own peculiar situation; there will be a history to its exploitation and this will have left its mark in terms of olive groves, established vineyards, terraces, wells, and so on. In recent years archaeologists have sometimes attempted to assess the agricultural resources available to ancient sites by examining the territory close to the site, usually everything within an hour's walk. The potential ancient land use is deduced from the present day soils and terrain which are classed as suitable for arable crops, trees or pasture. An adjustment is made for the less efficient use of distant land, and a hypothetical figure for total production is calculated. This technique is of some use for small sites in geographically well-defined areas, where it can indicate whether a town, a village or only a single farmstead could be supported from local resources, and hence the extent to which the actual settlement depended on outside or non-agricultural resources. The method is, however, fraught with problems. The distribution of land exploited by a settlement was determined by social factors as well as by ease of access. Pastoral land in particular was very frequently exploited at a considerable distance from a settlement, especially where the shepherds were slaves, but as modern

Greek practice shows, even arable land may have been cultivated at a great distance from the farmer's residence. Today's landscape rarely gives any hint of the intensity of the ancient exploitation, and the ubiquity of mixed farming in antiquity means that it is virtually impossible to make a division between arable and tree crops on the basis of soil alone. This sort of analysis is of little help in assessing the agricultural strength of a Classical city.

It is also important to bear in mind that when calculating the agricultural production of people who are largely practising subsistence farming what is important is not the maximum production, nor the average, but the production in bad years. If a city grows beyond what can be supported by its territory at the worst of times, it will need to develop links with the outside world in order to make up the shortfall. Figures from early twentieth-century Greece are of interest here, for they reveal very clearly the startling difference in production from year to year. In the first decade of this century wheat yields in Thessaly ranged from 1,118,111 quintals in 1902/3 (a quintal is 100 kg) to a low of 407,607 quintals in 1905/6. In human terms this is the difference between enough grain to feed 550,000 people for a year and enough to feed just 200,000.

These modern figures illustrate the nature and scale of the problems in assessing ancient agricultural performance and its demographic implications. To gain an impression of the absolute level of ancient production, however, it is necessary to take a more abstracted approach. The bulk of Classical agricultural production consisted of wheat, barley and olives. These were grown in different proportions in different places, and it is not possible to do more than speculate about the proportions of each grown in any particular region or place.

Experimental archaeology elsewhere and reasonably well-attested parallels from parts of Greece under Turkish rule in the early modern period suggest that it will have been possible to obtain wheat yields of 1000 to 1500 kg per hectare in at least some areas of Classical Greece, with a seed to yield ratio of 1:10. Even at the lower end of this production scale one hectare will yield 900 kg net of seed, and this is enough to feed four to five people for a year. Barley yields substantially more heavily than wheat but has a slightly lower calorific value: a hectare of barley will therefore support about the same number of people as a hectare of wheat, or slightly more. If biennial fallow was generally practised then two hectares of land were required to produce one hectare of cereal crop.

Olive production is more difficult to assess. The olive is notoriously biennial in its cropping pattern, good and bad years regularly alternating. Olives over a wide area tend to share the same good and bad years. Production figures from different parts of Greece today range very widely, depending upon the extent to which oil production has been commercialized. In antiquity a hectare of olives (about a hundred trees) will have yielded 150 kg of oil in the off year, 400 kg in the good year. Again in some areas these figures may have been comfortably exceeded. Assuming a production of 550 kg per hectare over the biennium, a hectare of olives will have yielded about 70 per cent of the calorific value of a hectare of wheat or barley. But if the cereals were grown with biennial fallow, the olives would actually yield almost half as much again as a hectare of cereal land over the two year period. If cereals and olives are grown on the same land the yields of both fall, but their combined yield is still likely to be greater than the yield of either grown on its own, although only by some 10 to 20 per cent.

If these calculations are of the right order, then even in bad years 3 hectares of land will have produced enough food to feed a family of five, no matter how the land was cropped. It follows from this that Classical Attica, which covered an area of some 2400 km², about 40 per cent of which was probably exploited for agriculture of some sort, will have had the capacity to support a population of around 150,000 from its own resources. The actual population of Attica is rather difficult to calculate. The ancient literary texts give enough information to enable an estimate of citizen numbers in the fifth and fourth centuries to be made with some confidence: citizen families probably accounted for some 60,000 to 80,000 people. The population of resident foreigners fluctuated considerably, but probably never exceeded about 20,000. The difficult calculation is that of the number of slaves. Scholars have disagreed radically about slave numbers in Athens, estimating anything from 20,000 upwards. What is interesting in the context of the question of food supply is that on a conservative, but not unreasonable, estimate of 50,000 slaves, Attica will have had a total population of around 150,000. This would mean that the whole Athenian population *could* have been supported from the territory of Attica itself alone. This does not, of course, mean that it was. Social and political factors as well as more directly agricultural ones will have determined the relative attractions of very intensive as opposed to rather more extensive farming. The importance of the calculation lies in the limit which it establishes. (The extent of Athenian need for imported grain is discussed further in Chapter 5.)

There are some production figures from antiquity, but they are of little use to us.

Records from Eleusis detailing the small shares of wheat and barley which Athenian farmers were obliged to contribute to the sanctuary of Demeter and Kore enable a deduction to be made about the absolute amount of wheat and barley produced in a single year. Each Athenian tribe had to give $\frac{1}{600}$ of its barley crop, $\frac{1}{1200}$ of its wheat, and the preserved figures point to a cereal production of some 120,000 quintals of barley and 16,500 quintals of wheat in about 330. Unfortunately there are good independent reasons for thinking that this particular year was a rather bad one for cereals. More seriously still we have no way of calculating the proportion of Athenian agricultural land that was devoted to cereals as opposed to olives. Because of this we cannot even begin to guess what the total agricultural production of the territory in this year might have been.

The intensity of agricultural exploitation will inevitably have varied from farmer to farmer, from time to time, and from place to place. Farmers with only limited land at their disposal will have had no alternative but to work that land intensively; in times of great population pressure the demand for food will have intensified the exploitation of the fields; some territories will have offered more scope for intensification than others. Some indication of this variation in practice can be gleaned from some land leases of the Hellenistic period which relate to the Boiotian city of Thespiai and to the Cycladic island of Rheneia.

It has been argued that almost the whole of the island of Rheneia was occupied by estates owned and leased out by those who managed the famous sanctuary of Apollo on the tiny neighbouring island of Delos. The southern half of the island covers an area of some 625 hectares, and it seems that in the 280s the estates here paid some 4606 drachmas of rent. This works out at 7 drachmas per hectare. Detailed records of wheat prices for the year 282 from Delos show that the price fluctuated between $4\frac{1}{2}$ and 10 drachmas per medimnos (one medimnos = about 52 litres). Thus the lessee could pay off the rent if his estate produced at the rate of just one medimnos of wheat per hectare – 41 kg per hectare. Of course wheat itself was not the sole product of these estates; we know that most also had vineyards and cattle pasture. Nevertheless the remarkably low figure does suggest that this island landscape was not subject to, and perhaps not capable of, intensive arable farming.

At the end of the third century the Thespians bought up and leased out some land at a rent of 20 drachmas a hectare. The grain price at this time was not appreciably higher than it had been in 282. Thus the Boiotian lessee had to be at least three times as productive as his Delian counterpart in order simply to pay off his lease. This would hardly have been difficult, but it does suggest that those leasing out land at Thespiai had rather different expectations about agricultural productivity compared with those of the managers of the Delian temple estates.

The contribution of pasture The Delian estates include steadings for sheep and cattle, and the will from Dodona, quoted previously (p. 40), includes a meadow. Pastoral production played a part in the overall agricultural strategy of many Greek farmers, but it is difficult to assess how important that part was, either generally or in a particular region.

Pastoral farming is itself very diverse. It is possible to pasture sheep and goats entirely on land that is otherwise unexploited, and this practice is particularly common with goats. But it is also possible to pasture intensively, using irrigated meadow lands and grazing

stubble and fallow land. The latter practice actually assists the arable farmer by on-the-spot manuring and because cereals will produce more ear-bearing stalks if the earliest shoots of the young plants are eaten off. In this way the necessary exchange between pastoralist and arable farmer takes a more active form than the simple interchange of meat and milk products for grain and oil.

Ancient literature tends to treat pastoralism and arable farming as exclusive options. Pasture is seen as the characteristic mark of the landscape with no human presence. A common Athenian piece of rhetoric in the political oratory of the fourth century is that the policy of an opponent will lead to the desolation of Attica so that it becomes one enormous sheep pasture. Yet there were flocks of sheep even in Attica and they were not all grazed on bare hillsides. One fourth-century land lease includes a tract of coastal pasture near the Peiraieus to which the lessee gains exclusive rights.

Pasturing rights were closely guarded and pasturing on common land was not open to all. Even in territories where pasture was relatively abundant cities guarded it jealously: at Tegea in Arkadia the right to pasture animals is limited to citizens or those to whom a specific grant is made, and in some circumstances a fee was charged. Land ownership in general in Classical Greece was restricted to citizens (that is, native-born free adult males), but the specific controls on pasturing are particularly important because of their implications for the movement of animals between summer and winter pastures. This practice of long-distance transhumance has long been familiar in Greece, although today it is again unpopular with bureaucrats. In ancient Greece there was certainly some movement of animals according to season, but this movement must have been largely confined to the territory of a single city.

Explicit literary reference to transhumance is extremely rare. Sophokles' version of the legend of Oidipous has a famous meeting between a Theban and a Corinthian shepherd on Mt Kithairon, but there is not much else. Aristotle remarks in connection with the large cattle of Epiros that Epiros possesses a large amount of good pasture and meadows suitable for *every* season, and this implies that some movement of animals was routine and recognized to be climatically enforced. But Epiros in fact lies outside the area of the Greek city, and the same political controls upon movement may not have applied there.

The most interesting case of all involves two cities in western Lokris in central Greece. In the early second century the cities of Myania (modern Hagia Efthymia) and Hypnia (perhaps near modern Tritaia south of Hagia Efthymia) (see map p. 139) made an agreement, one of the clauses of which runs as follows: 'If one of the shepherds who has pastured his sheep in the area in the past brings his sheep before they are dipped, let him take them away once he has dipped them. But all the shepherds who have not previously used the land as pasture, but have dipped their sheep [elsewhere], when they come to pasture sheep in this place, may remain and fold their sheep here for ten days.'[6] Since the object of the agreement is to have *closer* co-operation between the two cities, this inscription shows very clearly the problems which the movement of shepherds and their flocks were felt

14 Part of the fourth-century town wall of ancient Myania in Lokris (on the site of the modern village of Hagia Efthymia), just south of Amphissa.

to create. The presence of flocks from another city is seen as a threat to the sovereignty of the city.

Lowland grazing grounds seem to have been in short supply. One indication of this comes from the frequency with which sanctuaries feel that they have to control grazing on sacred ground. Thus the lease of sacred ground on Amorgos (see p. 37) forbids anyone to pasture sheep on the land. These prohibitions are partly a product of the fear that the presence of animals may lead to pollution. This aspect comes over particularly strongly in a fourth-century document from the Aegean island of Khios: 'Decision of the council when Tellis was magistrate in the chair. No pasturing or dumping of manure in the grove. If anyone does pasture sheep, or bring in pigs, or graze cattle, then whoever sees this is to inform the magistrates known as the kings. The shepherd, swineherd or cowman is to pay a fine of $\frac{1}{12}$ stater per head of cattle grazed. If anyone is caught dumping dung he shall pay 5 staters before he is right with the god. If the man who sees does not inform let him owe 5 staters to the god.'[7]

Some of the regulations are not so blankly negative. One document which is particularly interesting for the positive assumptions which it makes comes from fourth-century Tegea: 'The priest may pasture twenty-five sheep, a yoke of cattle, and a goat. If he breaks the law there is a pasturing fine. The sanctuary registrar is to exact the fine. If he fails to exact the fine he shall owe 100 drachmas to the people and be accursed. The official in charge of sacrificing may pasture any animal that is without blemish in Alea and pay a pasturing fine for any not physically perfect. ... For the last three days of the three major festivals all restrictions on pasturing are to be suspended, as long as there is no pasturing in the concourse. A pasturing fine is to be exacted

from anyone pasturing there. No foreigner or citizen is to pasture in Alea unless he has come for the feast. Strangers who have come down for the feast may pasture one yoke beast for a day and a night. If he pastures any more than this he is to pay a fine of 1 drachma per large animal and the pasturing fine for a smaller. The sacred animals are not to be pastured in Alea more than a day and a night if they happen to be driven through. If they are pastured for more, then the fine is to be a drachma for each larger animal, an obol for each smaller and a drachma per pig, unless the herdsman has managed to get special permission from the fifty or the three hundred. ...'[8]

This document assumes that the various officials connected with the temple will have animals in need of pasture. But a priest who has a yoke of cattle as well as a small flock of sheep will be a man who practises both arable and pastoral farming. Visitors to major festivals are assumed to come by animal (probably ass), whether local or strangers, and it is thought important to make provision for these beasts. Animals grazing sacred land must be without blemish, and the fine for pigs that overstay the time period is particularly high. The temple has its own herd of sacred animals which can be expected to have to move through the sanctuary when travelling between pastures. These animals are presumably destined for sacrifice, and the contrast between this Tegean practice and the Athenian practice of buying sacrificial beasts in the market no doubt reflects the much greater part played by pasture in Tegean society.

In Arkadia animals seem to form part of every farmer's strategy. In Athens animals are rare – the Athenians never give pasturing rights to anyone, because no one would think of using land for pasture in normal circumstances. In the Aegean islands the situation

49

appears to have been different again: only rough pasture was available, but in some places there were considerable amounts of this and considerable competition for its use. A regulation from the small island of Herakleia even seems to envisage men using force to bring in goats to graze there!

Because pastoralism means movement it causes friction. The shepherd needs to be able to move and be independent of settlements, but he also needs to make contact with those settlements in order to exchange his products for theirs. The countryside of the shepherd is a different countryside from that of the arable farmer, but the two countries must meet. The countryside of the Greek city, fragmented into independent political units whose

15 Pigs were a problem for some sanctuaries, but they played a central part in the cult of Demeter (see p. 174 and Figure 57) and finds of votive pigs often mark sanctuaries of that goddess. This pig rattle (12 cm long) comes from the sanctuary of Demeter at Eleusis and dates to about 400.

16 When the border between Delphi and Ambryssos (modern Distomo), described in a second-century document, is traced on the ground, it is found to cut right across an important modern route for the movement of animals from winter pasture in the Pleistos valley and around Arakhova to summer pasture high on Parnassos in the area of Kalyvia Arakhovas.

borders do not respect the need for pasture at all seasons, is not made for the shepherd. The stronger the political identity and exclusiveness of the city, the more difficult life for the shepherd.

This is nicely illustrated by the political boundary between Delphi and the territory of the Ambryssians and Phlygonians which is described in detail in a second-century inscription. This boundary can be traced with some confidence on the ground, and it runs between modern Arakhova and its summer village (Kalyvia Arakhovas) in the large plain above. Thus the political boundary actually interrupts a passage which in more recent times has been not simply the casual path of sheep, but the route of the seasonal migration of human residence.

The shepherd's need constantly to be on the move and to breach political boundaries was a source of tension both within cities and between cities (see Chapter 7). But for all his

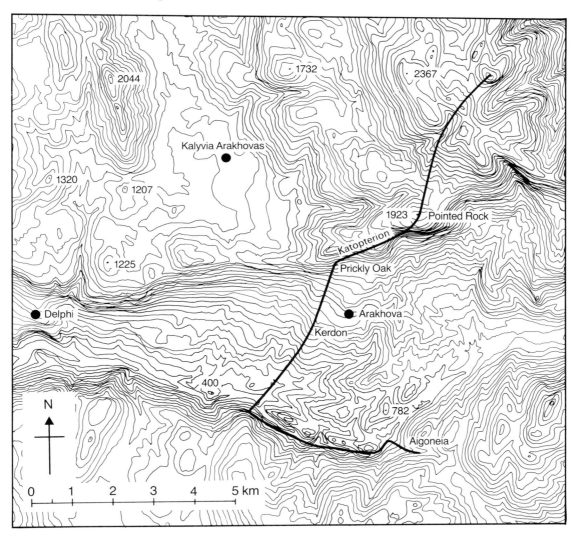

pursuit of self-sufficiency and for all his cultivation of a subsistence strategy, the arable farmer was equally in need of contact and exchange. The nature of climate and landscape and the potentials and demands of crops and animals all conspire to prevent farming becoming a safe or parochial enterprise. The threat of shortage to come in time of plenty, the dearth in lean years, the impossibility of growing thirsty crops in dry areas, or growing olives at high altitude (olives are not normally found above about 360 m) of pasturing large cattle without abundant mountain pastures, of practising intensive arable agriculture if bound to move with the flock, all of these made exchanges between neighbours, between communities within a city, and between cities both essential and fundamental. It is only exchange which made agricultural settlements in Greece possible, and contact across political boundaries must always have preceded the establishment of those boundaries. The constraints under which agriculture operated governed settlement and society also; agricultural choices are also social choices, and as farming strategies varied from area to area and from century to century, so too the patterns of settlement and the structure of local society varied. The next chapter will look at the evidence for the settlement history of Greece in the Classical period and explore some of the variations.

3

A SETTLED COUNTRY?

'But Theophemos, instead of following on to the money-changer's and collecting the fine, went and took fifty fine soft-woolled sheep of mine and their shepherd and all the hardware involved in shepherding; then he grabbed a young servant boy carrying a bronze water-vessel which I had begged from another and which was worth a lot. And they weren't satisfied with getting these, they invaded my land – I have a farm near the race-course and have lived there since I was a young lad – and first they made a surprise assault on the slaves, and when these got away from them and ran off in various directions they went to the house, knocked down the gate that leads to the garden . . . attacked my wife and children and made off with all the goods and chattels that were left to me in the house.'[1]

This passage from a fourth-century law-court speech gives a vivid picture of the more violent side of Athenian life. It also displays, with unusual clarity, the social geography of Athenian agriculture. The speaker has a variety of agricultural interests at various distances from his dwelling: he has a flock of fine sheep, apparently kept for wool rather than for meat or milk; arable land where a number of slaves are involved in agricultural tasks; a garden, walled and close to the house, perhaps devoted to vegetables; and a house which he later reveals to possess a courtyard

where meals are eaten, and a strongroom or tower where servant girls live and work. As one moves away from the dwelling farming becomes less intensive – changing from gardening to pasturing – and the nature of the workforce employed also varies. The flocks are entrusted to a specialist shepherd, non-specialist house-slaves are employed on the arable land, and the women, both slave and free, are kept inside the dwelling itself. Settlement, agriculture and social structure are bound up one with another.

This interrelation of settlement and agriculture is equally a feature of the life of the city as a whole. In the case of the city of Mantineia, presented in Chapter 1, there is explicit ancient acknowledgement of this: Xenophon records that the propertied Mantineians were pleased with the splitting up of the city into villages which the Spartans insisted upon, because it meant that they came to live nearer to their land. The same strong ties with the land were shown up when Megalopolis ('Great City') was artificially created as a strong centre for Arkadia against Sparta by the grouping together of some twenty or more earlier settlements; not only was there discontent in the years immediately following the foundation in c.370, but the geographer Strabo, writing some 350 years later, explicitly notes that there had been a decline in the number of farmers in Arkadia,

17 Megalopolis was founded in c. 370 by bringing together the people of a number of small Arkadian settlements to form a single large city as a bulwark against Sparta. The town had no natural defences and this view from the theatre looks out over the administrative and religious centre, cut by the river Helison.

and that land use had changed from arable to pasture 'especially for horses and asses.'[2]

The fact that Megalopolis survived and that a single city centre was soon recreated for Mantineia indicates that even in Arkadia agriculture was by no means the only determinant of settlement. Social structure, economic factors, and political institutions all react to and interact with the pattern and organization of settlement. Subsequent chapters will try to unravel some of those inter-relations. This chapter presents the evidence for the nature and pattern of settlement in the Greek cities in antiquity. It discusses the problems involved in interpreting both the literary and the archaeological evidence, and explores the connections between settlement and land use. Settlement patterns varied greatly from period to period and from area to area, and this variation was intimately connected with the physical geography and the agricultural exploitation of the local landscape. Although agricultural factors are examined first, these were not necessarily of prime importance in determining settlement.

The traditional settlement history

There is a story of the development of settlement in Greece which is recurrent in the ancient literary sources. It tells how early Greece was settled in scattered villages and how these were then gradually or suddenly brought together to form the concentrated residential and political centres of the Classical cities. Here is Strabo's version: 'The present city of Elis had not yet been founded in Homer's time; rather the countryside was inhabited in villages . . . in fact it is pretty well the case that the other places in the Peloponnese mentioned by Homer are not called cities but territories, each having collections of several villages. The cities that are famous later were founded from the grouping together of these – so Mantineia was formed from five villages by the Argives, Tegea from nine, Heraia from nine by Kleombrotos or Kleonymos. Similarly Aigion was made into a city from seven or eight communities, Dyme from eight.'[3]

There is no doubt that Strabo is thinking in terms of a movement of population from a number of villages into a single centre. The aim of his remarks, however, is not to describe changes in the nature of settlement of the countryside but to explain the formation of political units, the origins of the Classical city. This motive comes out particularly clearly in the account of the formation of Athens given by the historian Thucydides: 'Under Kekrops and the first kings up until Theseus, Attica was always settled in separate towns which had civic institutions and magistrates of their own. In times of security they did not come together to consult with the king, but they ran their own affairs and made their own policy. Some of them even made war – for instance the Eleusinians with Eumolpos made war against Erekhtheus. But when Theseus became king, being a capable and intelligent man, he both organized the territory in other respects and put down the councils and magistrates of the other towns, making all into a single community, the present city, with a single council and set of civic institutions. They continued to enjoy their own lands as before, but they had to use the one city.'[4]

The political aspect of this tradition makes it misguided to consider this tale of the formation of cities from scattered settlements to be a folk memory of an actual historical event. The stories, although related to particular cities, provide an explanation of how the Classical Greek city came to be which is very close to that offered in more abstract form by the opening sections of Aristotle's *Politics*. There Aristotle argues that cities are formed through necessary and natural forces which compel men to live in groups. Since neither male nor female can continue alone they must unite and form a household. While the household is sufficient for everyday needs the more occasional demands which the household itself cannot meet demand the union of several households into a village. The village is a sort of extended household and so tends to be ruled by its senior member as a petty king. But the village cannot meet every need, and it is to create a unit that is perfectly self-sufficient that the city is formed, 'created for the sake of life itself, but existing for the sake of the good life.' It is because the city must be formed to enable life at all that Aristotle says that 'man is by nature a political animal,' that man naturally lives in a city.[5]

It is highly significant that ancient writers present what is really an analytical explanation for the city in the form of a story of a movement from scattered to nucleated residence patterns. These writers see living in villages as a mark of the barbarian, and the development of all that the Greeks valued most is seen to hang on the intense communal life of the city. The story thus tells us a good deal about attitudes to the countryside, but it tells nothing about the history of settlement patterns. To uncover this we must turn to non-literary sources.

The archaeological evidence

Men who use pottery unavoidably break it and the fragments remain to reveal where they have lived and worked. The potsherds may be covered up by later deposits, whether from continuing habitation on the same site or of soil, but they are rarely totally removed or obliterated.

Archaeological investigation of the remains of the past, particularly in Greece, has traditionally concentrated on the intensive examination of particular remains through excavation. The sites to be excavated have been determined by the presence of monumental standing structures, such as temples, fortifications, and tombs, or by the chance discovery of individual outstanding objects during the routine processes of agriculture and building. Such investigation frequently yields abundant detailed information about a single structure or group of structures, but it can rarely be sufficiently extensive to give information about a settlement as a whole. The excavation of residential buildings rarely yields outstanding individual objects and as a result few domestic complexes have been investigated in this way. Moreover, even in the best conditions the excavation of part of a single site can reveal little or nothing about the relationship between that site and other local settlements. The discovery of the pattern of human presence in a landscape must proceed in a totally different way, for it demands extensive knowledge of the whole country and not detailed knowledge of small portions of it.

Extensive survey of the Greek countryside has a long and not undistinguished history. Generations of Classical scholars have attempted to trace on the ground the cities and other sites mentioned by ancient writers, and in particular in the catalogue of ships in Book Two of Homer's *Iliad* and in Pausanias' *Guide to Greece*. This latter, topographical work has been invaluable, but it naturally concentrates on major settlements and monuments. This reinforces the predominance of such sites as are mentioned in the literature and does nothing to fill in the picture where the literary sources are silent. On the contrary, it perpetuates the picture of the landscape created by ancient writers, the very town-based and town-biased picture which I am attemping to supplement. If we are to recreate the ancient countryside as a whole we must know about *all* the traces of ancient presence in an area of country. Such knowledge can only be achieved by intensive and systematic surveys. Changes in the natural landscape through erosion and deposition, coupled with continuing human occupation and use of the land, mean that even the most thorough of surveys can recover no more than a partial picture. But at least the partiality is not one imposed by the archaeologist. Since intensive survey is least good at recovering town sites that have been continuously occupied, its only systematic bias is directly counter to that of the ancient writers.

Such detailed searches can only be carried out by closely organized and recorded field-walking. This has only been undertaken to any extent in Greece during the last fifteen to twenty years, and as a result the spatial information which the historian of settlement requires is only available for a very small proportion of the Greek landscape. Nevertheless, the data which such surveys have given not only enable a number of individual landscapes to be reconstructed in detail, but also aid the interpretation of the less complete record from other areas, where knowledge is often plentiful but unsystematic.

Intensive surveys produce information about the location of cultural material from the past in the landscape in a quantity unknown before. But the quality of the data is often very poor. Whether surface finds have lain for 2000 years uncovered and exposed to the elements, or whether they have been brought to the surface by natural or artificial means, earthworms or earth-movers, they rarely fail to reveal the hardships which they have suffered. Surface finds tend to be much more worn and abraded than those recovered from excavation, and as a result they carry much less explicit information about their original appearance. They also tend to be far less numerous, for what is on the surface represents but a small and highly variable proportion of what is still buried. All of this makes the interpretation of the material extremely difficult. It is not easy to reconstruct a detailed settlement history when the reticent potsherds fail to give clear evidence either of their date or of the precise nature of the human presence which deposited them. To take a specific example, it may be difficult to distinguish between the scatter of glazed tile and black-glazed pottery that is produced by a small and ephemeral building and that produced by a tomb. Scatters of pottery consisting largely of coarse ware with a small quantity of finer pottery can only be dated by that finer pottery, and even then, if the quantity of fine pottery is small or the quality indifferent, the dating may be only to within 250 years. In these circumstances it is often impossible to come to any confident assessment of the duration of occupation marked by a scatter.

Despite all this, it *is* now possible, as it was

not even twenty years ago, to make some assessment of the nature and history of Classical settlement in Greece. The limits within which any history is written remain broad, however, and the room for speculation in the explanation of that history is large.

The variety of the Greek landscape and the dependence of the Classical city upon home agriculture create necessary links between settlement and landscape. Thus different regions have different settlement histories, and a single region may be settled in contrasting ways at different times. There are, however, also some strong correlations between the settlement patterns of different regions in a single period, and this implies that settlement was also influenced by factors that were neither local nor purely agricultural.

Survey has confirmed that the Greece of the later Bronze Age was unevenly but often densely occupied, but it has done nothing to relieve the blankness of the so-called Dark Age (tenth and ninth centuries). Depopulation and disruption were such that continuity of occupation from the end of the Bronze Age to Archaic times can be demonstrated at hardly a handful of sites in the whole of Greece. It is clear that the human landscape of Archaic and Classical Greece was a creation in a space uncontrolled by earlier occupation. The rate at which this wild landscape was developed, and the nature of its exploitation, were, however, far from uniform.

On the island of Melos the period from 950 to 500 saw the appearance of a very large number of small sites, perhaps totalling more than a hundred for the island as a whole (which has an area of 151 km^2). The site of the Classical town of Melos seems to have been the earliest to be (re-)occupied, and the other sites spread out gradually from this nucleus. They show little clear variation in size or type, and those responsible for the fieldwork suggested that on average they covered about 1 hectare each. These sites were presumably small villages or groups of households whose life revolved round farming the land in the vicinity and which were largely independent of one another.

It is difficult to judge how completely this spread of settlement exploited the agricultural resources of the island. If the number of sites was governed by the agricultural capacity of the land, then it might be expected that the number of settlements would cease to grow once the country was fully exploited. But in fact the number of settlements does not simply cease to grow, it goes into a relatively

steep decline in the sixth century. This decline in the number of sites occupied is accompanied by an increase in the size of some of the sites that remain, notably of the political centre at ancient Melos. In the Classical period the number of sites occupied is only some 80 per cent of the seventh-century peak; the number of sites occupied in the third century is only half the Classical total. It cannot be proved that all the sites from which there is seventh-century pottery were occupied at the same time, but the greater number of sites occupied during that century does suggest that settlement choice was influenced by different factors than from those operative in the Classical period. This change in settlement priority must involve a change in the way the relations between land and residence were perceived, a change induced by new social priorities.

18 The acropolis of the town of Ancient Melos on the bay of Melos. Ancient Melos was the dominant settlement on the island throughout the Classical period.

Living in small settlements is anti-social, conducive neither to the communal activities and celebrations which demand aggregation, nor to the acquisition of specialized social, economic or political roles. In a small community, as Aristotle saw, there is little room for a wide variety of statuses or for the development of extensive chains of dependence. Living apart binds man and land together in both a positive and a negative way: positively, the man who lives in a small settlement together with little more than his, perhaps extended, family is unlikely to have to go far even to his most distant fields, and the location of his land may have little more than a marginal effect on the intensity with which he cultivates it; negatively, that man is also more tied to the fluctuations in the output of that land, for in his solitary state he will find it much more difficult to form and use the sorts of social contact which can be vital for the efficient disposal of a surplus or for making up a short-fall. Those who choose to live apart do so in order to maximize their contact with the land, but this does not necessarily mean that they take the course which offers least risk.

This raises the question of why the less sociable option had any attractions at all for the Melians of the Archaic period. The answer lies partly with the nature of Melos, partly with the state of development of Melian and Aegean society in the eighth and seventh centuries. Melos was formed by volcanic activity, and its soils are exceptionally rich in minerals and by the standards of the Cyclades very fertile. Intensive agricultural exploitation brings rich rewards, and the dangers of soil exhaustion are comparatively small. The rich soil does not cushion the farmer against the unpredictable climate, however. The Melian soil has a rather low capacity for retaining water and ground-water supplies

are short. Even at the best of times water is not plentiful. Cushioning the effects of the years of dearth which the climate brings demands building up contacts with other communities. As long as such contacts are rudimentary and cannot be relied upon, the farmer has little option but to get the most he can out of the Melian earth. It may be no accident that, as soon as exchange networks become developed in the later part of the Archaic period, the Melian farmer begins to move into larger settlements.

There is a clear resemblance between the development of the settlement pattern on Melos and the ideal pattern of city formation envisaged by Aristotle. The land was quickly colonized as small groups hived off from an initial settlement, formed family groups and small villages, and gradually coalesced into larger villages. These larger villages became ever more closely related to the central settlement which itself increased in size. This pattern bears far less resemblance, however, to the historical development of settlement as it is becoming known on the Greek mainland and even on other Cycladic islands.

There is a striking contrast between the Melian story and that which is coming to light on the island of Keos, some hundred kilometres to the north. Here settlement restarts much later after the Dark Ages: there is a little geometric pottery from the acropolis at Koressia, but otherwise little proof of human presence in the eighth century anywhere in the northern part of the island. Settlements begin to spread over the landscape during the seventh and sixth centuries, but even at its densest Archaic occupation was only half as thick as it would become in the late Classical period. Thus the people of northern Keos continue to move into the countryside at the very time when the Melians are retreating from it.

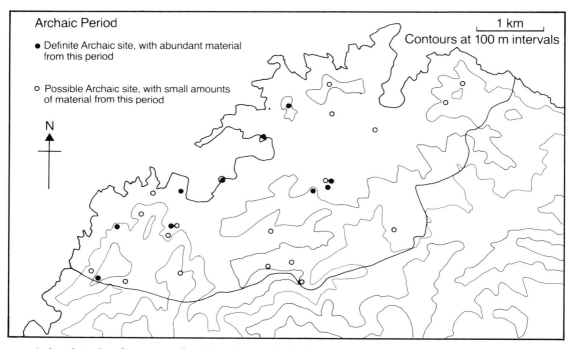

19 Archaeological surface survey of northern Keos in the Cyclades has revealed the way in which the countryside became increasingly occupied during the Classical period, but was then less intensely exploited in Hellenistic times.

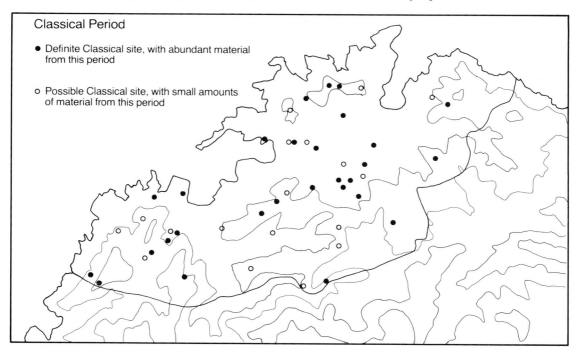

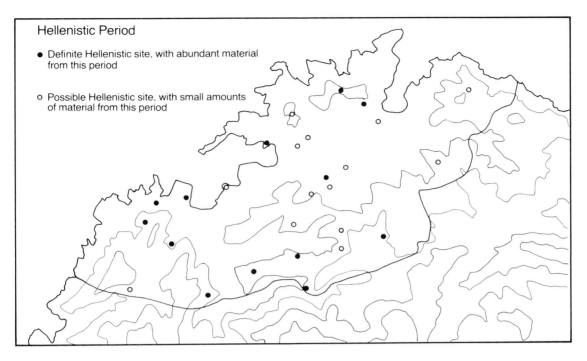

Hellenistic Period

● Definite Hellenistic site, with abundant material from this period

○ Possible Hellenistic site, with small amounts of material from this period

Keos is not very different from Melos in area, but it had a totally different political structure. During the Classical period it supported not one but four cities, and these remained separate settlements even during the brief period when they operated within a single composite political structure. These small cities clearly interacted with their countrysides in a rather different way from that prevailing on Melos. On Melos the scattered settlements are most numerous at the time when it is clear that the settlement at Ancient Melos was politically undeveloped and weak; on Keos scattered settlements are most frequent at the time when political life was at its most active and when the communal organization was complex and all-embracing. Part of the explanation of the difference may lie in the smaller size of the Kean cities: it was much more feasible both to exploit the land intensively and to take part in communal life in these small units that it

was on Melos. That this is not the total explanation, however, is suggested by the fact the Kean pattern is one that recurs in rather more extensive cities on the Greek mainland.

Systematic work in Boiotia, the southern Argolid, and Megalopolis has uncovered a pattern of human occupation over time which is broadly similar to that found on Keos. In all these regions it is the later Classical period (fourth century) which sees the countryside most thickly covered with traces of human activity. This late Classical pattern develops from very different earlier patterns: there is much more early material from the Argolid than from northwest Boiotia, and the Megalopolis area has almost nothing that is pre-Classical. This suggests that the factors which were responsible for the superficially similar late Classical patterns may in fact not be the same, for the way in which the countryside is exploited in a later period cannot be independent of the exploitation of earlier periods. Nevertheless, the nature and density of the Classical remains in all these areas confirm the ineradicable commitment of the Classical city to the production of the countryside.

On the ground today these remains take the form of sherd scatters, which look initially very much alike, but there is no doubt that the sites these scatters represent were anything but uniform. On Melos and Keos the Classical countryside seems to have supported nothing outside the city centre that was larger than a small village. Many of the smaller collections of material may come from establishments which never served as permanent residences, buildings erected as stores or as shelters during periods of particularly intense activity in the fields. On Keos itself in the late nineteenth century there was only one permanent settlement, Chora on the site of the ancient city of Ioulis, but there were a number of scattered houses, especially in the south of the island, which were used as temporary shelters for those tending their vines, oaks, gardens and fields in that area. On the mainland it is clear that, in addition to such small and relatively ephemeral sites, the countryside also supported some large villages which were important subsidiary centres alongside the city itself, and which may have possessed some of the civic structures, temples, theatres and the like, which were the hallmark of urban life. Some of these villages have survived as names as well as as collections of stones and potsherds, and they deserve exploration at greater length.

Askra in northwest Boiotia has just one claim to fame in the literature of antiquity: it was the home of the poet Hesiod, who is unduly rude about the harshness of life there (see Chapter 1). Already in Hesiod's time Askra seems to have been politically dependent upon Thespiai, and by the late fourth century there was a tradition that at some time Thespiai had actually destroyed it. Archaeological investigation has revealed that Askra was a densely occupied village extending over some 15 hectares. The site had been occupied in both the early and late Bronze Age and was probably the first place in the fertile and sheltered Valley of the Muses to be reoccupied after the desertion of the Dark Ages. It remained the most substantial site in the valley throughout the Archaic and Classical periods. There are signs that it received some sort of circuit wall during the Archaic period, and traces of a substantial sanctuary lie just outside the inhabited area. A short way up the valley was the major religious centre of the Sanctuary of the Muses on the lower slopes of Mt Helikon. The very fact that Thespiai thought it necessary to destroy Askra by force indicates that it retained an important role as a centre of local social activity and as a focus for local loyalties. It was thus not simply a place of residence for the farmers who worked the valley; it was a community with a distinct identity.

The literary record of the village of Eileioi, north of Iliokastro in the southern Argolid, is even more slender. It figures only when the traveller Pausanias mentions that there was a sanctuary of Demeter and Kore there on the mountain road from Troizen to Hermione. The archaeological remains are impressive: not only are there circuit walls standing more than a metre high, but there are traces of regular planning in the internal layout of the village. The site has considerable natural advantages and was occupied from an early date. Yet it was not an independent political unit in the Archaic or Classical period, and its walls indicate the amount of public effort which might be expended on subsidiary settlements. Such villages compromise between the social advantages of town life and the practical agricultural benefits which derive from residence on the land which one cultivates.

In one city such villages were built into the political and institutional structure: Athens. Every Athenian was associated by the very name which he bore not with the city as a whole but with one of the 139 village units (demes) spread over the whole territory of Attica. Thus Alkibiades was officially known as Alkibiades the son of Kleinias of the ward of Skambonidai, Euripides as Euripides the son of Mnesarkhides of the village of Phlya. Even the town of Athens itself was treated as an agglomeration of villages for organizational purposes. Many of these villages were densely settled with small dwellings crowded together, and they had a distinct life of their own, with their own officials and public meetings, their own local bye-laws, and their own sanctuaries and calendar of religious celebrations. These villages varied very considerably in size, but some enjoyed social facilities (in the form of theatres, gymnasia and the like) which approached those of the town itself. In the fourth century, at least, there is a lot of evidence that these demes enjoyed a very active political and social life. Even those whose political or other interests led them to spend much time in the town nevertheless kept strong links with their home community. Their land was likely to be centred on that community, and they spent money on the public facilities of their village and were honoured by their fellow demesmen for doing so (see Chapter 6).

In Attica the villages covered the landscape in such a dense network that there seems to have been little need for isolated seasonal shelters on the land. In other parts of the mainland, however, it is clear that villages and smaller sites existed alongside one another, the small sites often vastly outnumbering the villages. Some of these small sites show the stone footings for mud-brick walls in situ, but the vast majority are nothing more than small collections of pottery. On some of the Aegean islands, however, where villages are rare or non-existent, the array of small sites includes a large number of substantial structures known as single towers. There are a small number of comparable sites in Attica and the Argolid, but on some of the Aegean islands they are so numerous that they dominate the archaeological record.

The description 'tower' encompasses monuments of very different scale and type, but certain features are common to the majority of examples known from the Aegean islands. The towers are very strongly built structures, about 10 × 10 m square or of slightly less than 10 m diameter. Today many survive only to a little above foundation height, but there are two examples, one on Keos and one on Andros, which show that such structures could have four storeys and reach more than 20 m in height. It is not likely that all towers attained proportions of this sort, but the monumentality of many tower foundations suggests that we are dealing with something more than casual constructions hastily thrown together by an individual. There has been much debate about the purpose of these towers, but since they must have been as prominent in the ancient landscape as they are in the modern their presence can hardly fail to shed light on the nature of settlement.

Some towers seem to have had a more or less direct association with agriculture. There is literary evidence for towers forming part of more extensive building complexes on landed estates, serving as strong-rooms protecting goods, and on occasions sheltering a workforce threatened by irate neighbours (as in the example at the head of this chapter).

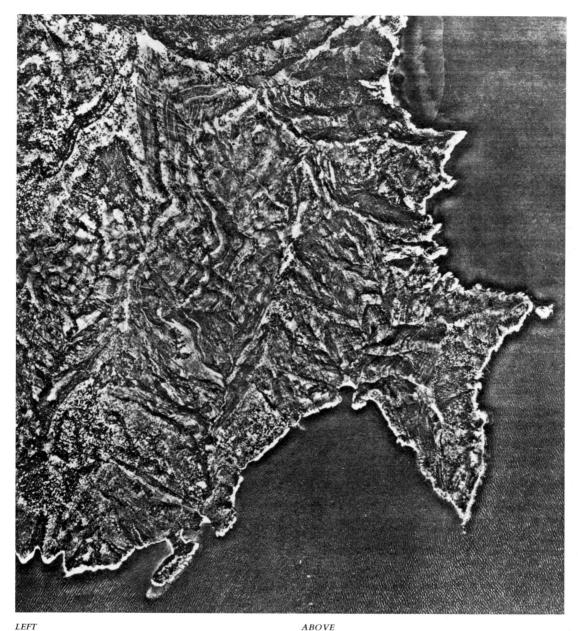

LEFT

20 Remains of towers of uncertain purpose are found scattered over the landscapes of several Aegean islands. One of the best preserved examples is this round tower at Hagios Petros on Andros, some 10 m in diameter and 20 m high, which was constructed in the Hellenistic period.

ABOVE

21 This remarkable aerial photograph of the southeastern part of the island of Thasos well indicates the extremely rugged terrain of the island. The heavily quarried Aliki peninsula is seen projecting from the western part of the south coast.

65

The single towers are often found in good agricultural land, with little else in the way of natural advantages in their situation. Yet it is clear that even in the case of these towers not all served the same precise function. Some of them are surrounded by courts and other buildings, others are completely isolated. Some are in the middle of dense scatters of broken pottery from storage and cooking vessels, which suggest that they were lived in more or less permanently, others are associated with few material artefacts or none at all. Some seem to be independent of other settlements and structures, others are in the middle of more or less extensive villages.

The variety of situations is well illustrated by the 30 or so single towers or analogous structures on the north Aegean island of Thasos [see Figure 24]. One of the towers, small but well built on a rocky peninsula,

obligingly indicates both its date and its purpose by an early fifth-century inscription.

'I am the memorial of Akeratos son of
    Phrasideridas,
Placed on the tip of the ship-steading to give
    safety to
Ships and to sailors. But fare well.'[6]

Four or five other towers on headlands round the island may similarly have warned of dangerous capes. But there are two towers on the coast which are low down in the middle of bays and clearly not markers at all. Both may be part of more extensive ancient settlements,

22 The largest of the towers on Thasos is this example at Thymonia on the south coast which is some 20 m in diameter and dates to the fourth or third century.

and one, at Kalami, is very close to a series of homosexual graffiti carved onto the rocks as they fall steeply into the sea. Some sort of a community clearly passed time here, and the tower does not simply indicate a farmer living on his own in a fertile but remote valley.

The strength of these towers has led to the suggestion that some may have served a military function. Military towers are certainly known from various parts of Greece, and some of the inland towers on Thasos do occupy extremely advantageous positions: from the tower at Amygdaliá the whole of the southwestern part of the island can be surveyed. But position alone cannot prove military function; the tower might be a non-military form of defence, or simply built by people who preferred a good view. The military case is stronger with the exceptionally large and well-placed tower at Thymonia, the most prominent structure of a quite extensive settlement. Towers which have good views can, of course, also themselves be seen, and the same structure is not ideally suited both to being a look-out point and to serving as a refuge. Only one of the Thasos towers seems ideally placed as a retreat from danger from the sea. This tower, known as Stin Trypiti, lies in an area which is agriculturally marginal. It is stoutly built on three levels and lies well up a valley which pursues a tortuous path down to the coast. The sea is visible from the tower, but from that distance the tower itself would disappear into the scrub and native limestone exposed around it.

Individual towers therefore seem to have served different functions, but the decision to expend much time and money on erecting a tower in the countryside for any purpose casts light on the nature and conditions of rural settlement. As the one tower with an inscription shows, even the towers which were coastal markers could be erected to the greater glory of a particular individual. This must have been still more the case with the towers which were built in the middle of small villages, dominating the ordinary structures of rural settlements. The landowner who chose to build a strong-room of these proportions was clearly saying something about what he had to protect when he spent his money so conspicuously. Those who lived in the town were protected by walls built for the common defence, from common funds, on common initiative. Those who lived in the country enjoyed no such public protection – it cannot be proved that any of the Thasos towers were built at public expense, and only in two cases is it at all likely. Rich individuals who built towers usurped for themselves the protective role which communal decisions assumed in the town.

The single towers make manifest the considerable insecurity and need for self-help in the countryside, and some of the reasons why the Thasian countryside was particularly inhospitable will be explored in Chapter 4. The towers also show the implications of this insecurity for rural society. Once the individual is left to look to his own protection, the gap between those who can and those who cannot afford to create private defences becomes apparent. This is a gap which is masked in the town by communal measures. In the countryside the steps which are taken to avoid domination from the outside only reveal the structures of domination within the community. It is a mark of the extent to which the country was undervalued that these towers should so frequently be all that we know of the settlement of the countryside of those islands concerned. Only the wealthy have permanently marked the landscape with their monuments, monuments which are certainly not always at all closely connected with the agricultural pursuits of resident farmers.

It seems to be a general feature of the countryside of all Greek cities in the Classical period that villages and smaller manifestations of human presence co-exist. There seems to be a division, however, between the mainland, where major village centres are important, and the islands, where villages are rare and towers often dominate. Why should the islands be different? The important factor may be physical geography. Mainland cities tend to consist of one or more plain or valley system bounded by mountains or by mountains and the sea. By contrast many islands are effectively just mountains surrounded by narrow coastal plains. Landed communications are more or less unproblematic in a mainland city, but they are often difficult or impossible on the islands. While the central settlement of mainland cities is often at or near the natural geographical focus, an island may

23 The town of Thasos defended itself with monumental walls some 4 km long (below and right), which make use of both major local stone resources—gneiss and marble—and display a wide variety of fine masonry styles.

have no such focus, and the chief settlement may be extremely eccentric. All these factors mean that despite their small size island communities tend to be more fragmented than those on the mainland. Geography prevents the maintenance of efficient networks of communication and hence puts barriers in the way of the organized defence of the territory and of social and political activities which demand that all the people gather together.

The precise local situation will affect the way in which these difficulties are dealt with. The geography of Melos is such that, although an island, it has a natural focus around the bay of Melos. All three major centres of political power on Melos since the Bronze Age have been around the central bay of Melos. It is notable that Melos both enjoyed a highly nucleated pattern of settlement in the Classical period and has no

towers. Keos is also more than a mountain with a coastal plain, but while communications across the island from the centre were possible in the Classical period, the difficulties of communication are reflected in the partition of the island between four separate cities. Despite the improved communications produced by this political fragmentation, Keos is not without towers. Thasos was but a single city, and the town was at the very northeastern corner. The towers here mark the degree to which the countryside was left to its own devices.

Countrysides which have different patterns of building and settlement also tend to have different patterns of agricultural exploitation. Different patterns of exploitation in their turn have different implications for the intensity with which the farming operations are carried on. It seems extremely likely that, the more

numerous the traces of human activity in the landscape, the more intensively that land was exploited. It is less clear, however, that more signs of human presence imply a larger population in the city as a whole. The quality of the archaeological evidence from rural buildings is such that it is rarely possible to demonstrate that two structures were in use at precisely the same time. Similarly it is difficult to determine the exact use to which a structure was put, and it is particularly hard to demonstrate that a building was permanently rather than just seasonally occupied. The evidence of documents which record the conditions on which public land was leased suggests that there were many buildings on the land which were not used for permanent residence. The decision to invest time and effort in building on the land is as likely to be determined by social and agricultural considerations as by a rising or falling population. Indeed, if rising population leads to subdivision of land-holdings it might lessen rather than increase the chances of it being worthwhile to build or maintain a structure on any particular plot.

It has been argued above that dwelling on an isolated farm tends to be linked with exploiting a more or less compact tract of land, living in a village with having a fragmented holding. The advantages of living apart become much diminished if the land farmed is itself scattered. Both partible inheritance systems and the desire to farm land in separate ecological niches (see Chapter 2) will lead to the fragmentation of holdings of farm land, and increase the attractions of moving to a village. Living in a village inevitably leads to uneven exploitation of the land. Pieces of land that are close to the village receive more attention than those further off. This is materially revealed by the 'halo' of potsherds which has frequently been found to surround Classical settlements, both small and large. This halo is almost certainly connected with the practice of collecting animal dung and other refuse from the yard of the house and using it to manure the fields. The fields close by receive more of the manure and hence more of the pieces of broken pottery which come with it. Nucleated settlement and fragmented holdings therefore have both advantages and disadvantages from the point of view of getting most out of the land: in a nucleated settlement pattern the landscape as a whole will be less efficiently worked, but for any individual farmer the land will, in most years, produce more.

Isolated farms are more risky, and they reduce the social contacts and opportuntites of the owner. They do, however, make it possible to hold a block of land and to use a more varied labour force. It is much easier to run a slave workforce where the farmland is contiguous, and has relatively few and clear boundaries, than it is when land is held in ill-distinguished parcels. It is also easier to use the labour of all the members of the family in these circumstances. Isolated residence makes the labour force much less conspicuous, and a farmer who would not want to be seen using the labour of his wife and young children may do so with impunity when they are far from the general public gaze. Anthropological studies carried out in southern Italy have shown that settlement pattern and prevailing morality are very closely linked: women have a position in village society which is much more closely guarded than that enjoyed by women on isolated family farms. This parallel is particularly interesting given the very close constraints upon citizen women in much of Classical Greece, where the women were expected to be just where they are found on the Athenian farm in the passage quoted at the start of this chapter.

The evidence of inscriptions

Archaeological evidence can give little more than hints about the status of the agricultural labour force, and the literary sources offer little implicit, let alone explicit, evidence for the relation of land to residence or of land to labour. But the inscriptions which were so important in informing us about farming practices also give valuable information about the exploitation of particular landscapes.

The estates on Rheneia owned and run by the temple of Apollo on Delos (see pp. 46–47) were leased out for periods of ten years to Delian citizens. Among the extensive documents which record the leasing over a period of almost 150 years from the early third century on are some inventories. These make clear both the mixed farming strategy adopted, with cereals, vines, sheep and cattle, and the presence of quite extensive building complexes: a walled yard is always found, and there are usually a whole series of structures, some more than one storey high. We know enough about the society of Hellenistic Delos to be able to trace the lessees of the estates. Almost all were certainly of high status and will never have had any intention of residing on the estates they leased. Few of the lessees keep the same estate for more than ten years. The way in which they worked the land becomes clear from a document dealing with the problem of exacting rent from defaulters. One clause of this reads: 'If the lessee does not pay the full amount of the rent, first the crops are to be sold, and then, to meet the remaining shortfall, the lessee must sell the cattle, the sheep and the slaves.'[7]

The estates could thus be expected to be run by slave labour, and the buildings will have been occupied by these slaves. The use of slave labour and residence on the land are connected both with each other (the slaves are hardly going to be given the option of choosing to be sociable and to dwell in a community) and with the unusually large size of the estates and their distance from any town.

The more intensely worked land of Hellenistic Thespiai offers a contrast in at least some respects. Most of the land leased is leased in small plots and there are numerous cases of one man taking leases on more than one plot at the same time. Very few of these plots have any structures on them, and when a structure is listed it is simply called a 'yard'. The leases are initially for rather longer than the Delian ones (up to 50 years) and leasing the same land again seems to be common. One reason for this seems to be that men lease plots that are close together and in the same general area as land which they already own and farm. Leased land is an adjunct to their own land rather than the independent exercise represented by the large estates on Rheneia. The lessee himself played a much more active role in the agricultural processes at Thespiai than he did on Rheneia, although he too is likely to have employed some slave labour.

The contrast between Thespiai and Rheneia is not simply a contrast between island and mainland practice. This is made clear by another lease document, from the tiny city of Karthaia in the southern part of the island of Keos. This document seems to be the only list of private leases from the whole of Greek antiquity. Although badly damaged, the stone records some 181 leasing transactions over a number of years. Some 90 distinct individuals, that is, about one third of the citizen population, are involved with land at some 33 locations. We do not know the precise size of the plots leased and cannot locate them on the map, but the names by which they are identified are of great interest. In contrast to the names both of the Delian estates and of the villages of Attica, none of these names are derived from families or human groups, and the vast majority have more or less clear reference to the physical or natural environment. We find 'hollow', 'slope', 'shore', 'peninsula', 'stony place', 'oak', 'basil', 'myrtle', 'brushwood', 'dung', and 'bees'. The only other toponyms whose meaning is clear refer either to secular or religious structures: 'fountain', 'kilns', 'Pythion', 'herm', 'sacred harbour'. Only in a city of very limited size could such names as 'hollow' and 'slope' be unambiguous in their reference, and only in a city with no significant human residence in the countryside could such names prevail, none of which have any reference to man. Whatever structures there may have been in this countryside, residence was clearly firmly centred on the town.

Yet another pattern is found on the island of Tenos, also in the Cyclades. An inscription dating to the very end of the fourth century records transactions involving real property. These take the form of sales, fictional sales (loans), and dowry gifts during a two year period. Here is one of the more interesting entries: 'Artymakhos son of Aristarkhos of Herakleidai bought from Telesikles son of Eukles of Herakleidai the houses and fields in Hyakinthos, all the ones that Telesikles obtained as his inherited portion and those he bought from his brother Kalliteles, the neighbours being Pleistarkhos and Artymakhos, and the lands on the hill-slopes – all that belonged to Telesikles and Kalliteles – and all the water-courses which are on the land, and a quarter of the tower and the storage jars in the tower, and the tiles on the roof, just as belonged to Telesikles, and the house and the garden which Telesikles bought from Euthygenes, and the tiles on the house, and the millstone, for the sum of 3700 drachmas. Sureties: Aratides son of Tykhon of Thestiadai, Artymakhos son of Eukles of Herakleidai, . . . son of Timephenes of Hyakinthos, Euthy-genes and Aristarkhos of Herakleidai, all these being both jointly and individually guarantors.'[8]

The purchaser here already owns neighbouring land and is almost certainly related to the seller. The seller has himself just purchased other land in the area for 2400 drachmas, a purchase that includes a different quarter share in the same tower. It seems inevitable that more is going on than meets the eye or is recorded on the stone. What is particularly interesting, however, is the detailed list of the property acquired. Note the way in which different sorts of agricultural land are referred to with different terms, and the precision with which the contents of the tower and of one of the buildings on the land are specified. It looks as if a significant proportion of the value of the tower and of this building resided in the contents which they housed. About half the transactions on the document which involve land in the countryside have land on hill-slope ('eskhatiai') as well as other land. The care to record this fact is matched by the detail with which some boundaries are described.

'Sosimenes . . . bought the building and all the fields in Balaneion together with the water-courses on the land, the neighbour being Kallikrates as far as the river, where the boundary is the wall which terminates Kallikrates' land, this wall going up to the road, and from the road where it goes round to the fountain, where the boundary is the wall of Melisson which is on the land of Kallikrates son of Melisson, where the wall goes round in a circle and where the gully leads up to Kallikrates' worked fields and where the wall goes round in a circle right to the wall which marks the edge of the half field on the hill-slope next to the gully, which gully leads down to the sea and bounds the worked fields of Mneson.'[9]

Note here the importance of possessing the water-courses, the prominence of field walls, and the way that those walls have a history – one wall is called the 'wall of Melisson', Melisson being the father of the present land-owner. There is little doubt that the countryside of Tenos was being very intensively exploited. Buildings on the land are quite regular, but many of the isolated structures referred to were not residences, and the owners and farmers seem to have lived in the villages from which they took their names. In one case a boundary is given as 'all the area below the road leading from the village to the tower'.[10] All the personnel named in connection with Artymakhos' purchase, barring one surety, are either of Herakleidai or of Hyakinthos (where the property is), and this suggests that this is an exchange of land between men who live in villages close to the land in question.

This inscriptional evidence for a very lively interest in the land reinforces the picture of a late Classical landscape densely occupied and heavily exploited, and it provides the epigraphic equivalent to the archaeological evidence for numerous rural structures. The towers of Tenos emerge as, in some cases at least, joint private efforts, rather than individual displays, offering protection for stores on land over which the owner cannot keep direct surveillance. The evidence from Tenos does not, however, give us any idea of the extent of any individual's landed interests; for this we have to turn to documents other than those recording leases and sales.

A fragmentary Hellenistic document from Hyampolis in Phokis in central Greece appears to list all the lands donated to the city by one Herostratos. The lands are to be leased and the income used for the sanctuaries of Apollo and Artemis. The lands are described in some detail and each plot is defined by its area and by the names of the owners of adjoining pieces of land. These neighbours' names rarely recur, suggesting that the lands were quite spread about, and the preserved figures for plot area show that some plots were quite small: there are six plots of 1 hectare or less (one of these said to consist of wild pear trees), three of about 10 hectares, and only one really large plot of about 30 hectares. At least sixteen plots are listed and no buildings are recorded on any of them, although a tower is mentioned in the opening rubric.

Herostratos' land at Hyampolis seems to have been irregularly scattered over the landscape in plots of varying size. This is the pattern which I have suggested was typical, but it was not a pattern prevalent over the whole of Greece. A puzzling document from the Thessalian city of Larisa gives a list of names followed by areas of land. Many of the areas recorded, especially those listed near the beginning of the inscription where larger plots seem to be grouped, are in units of 25, 50 or 100 plethra (2.5, 5 and 10 hectares). These seem to be single plots of land, and this implies a remarkable regularity in the division of the landscape. There seems no way of knowing whether this regularity was the result of some ancient land division into equal lots, or whether it was the product of the sort of land grant found in some other Thessalian cities in the Hellenistic period. Thessaly, with its broad flat plains, is clearly more susceptible to regular land division than other parts of Greece, and this inscription suggests that its landscape may have had an appearance very different from that of Greece further south. About 400 to 500 hectares of land are recorded in the inscription, and we cannot tell how typical this land is of that of the whole territory of Larisa – it makes a considerable difference whether this is land immediately adjacent to the city or land on the edge of the plain, land long cultivated in these units or newly divided as a piece of social or political engineering. Some names of owners or recipients do recur, but there are some fifty to sixty names which occur only once, and this indicates that the land was, to some extent at least, spread across the whole community.

All these epigraphic documents offer partial windows on particular situations. Because they are partial they must be interpreted with care. Nevertheless, they do something to complement the picture offered by archaeological fieldwork, a picture equally in need of careful interpretation. They suggest that within the Greek world, even perhaps within areas which give a not dissimilar archaeological picture, the use and appearance of the land and the nature and distribution of settlement varied greatly. Rheneia has enor-mous leased estates with isolated buildings housing slaves and cattle; Tenos has a great mixture of villages, small groups of buildings and towers, in an intensively cultivated landscape where provision of water and the precise potential of land evidently mattered a good deal; Thespiai, Hyampolis and perhaps Larisa have lands relatively free of structures, although in the case of Larisa there were regular land divisions which clearly reflected large-scale organization; Karthaia has a landscape that is predominantly natural. This varied picture is partly a product of varied agricultural resources, but agricultural factors alone will not account for all that is happening. The following chapters will explore the non-agricultural resources of the countryside and look at the structure of the society of the Classical city.

4

THE COUNTRY DISRUPTED

The complex geological history of the landscape means that Greece offers enormous ecological variety, but because the rocky skeleton is a predominantly limestone formation the range of minerals available for exploitation is comparatively restricted. Stone suitable for building is widely available, although of varying quality, but metals and precious stones are only found in very restricted areas.

This chapter discusses the mining and quarrying activities of the Greek cities. The presence of both mines and quarries affected the way in which country related to town, but the nature of the effect was very different for each activity. Only mining offered resources that were economically important – and in the case of Athens we can at least begin to measure that importance. The examples of southern Attica and of Thasos are used to show that this economic importance distorted rural society. Quarry-stone had a minimal economic importance and was only sporadically exploited, but despite this its function in terms of display rendered it locally very significant.

The decision to exploit minerals is governed by demand and by social factors. Ores with a relatively low yield of gold or silver tend to get exploited when ores with a similar proportion of iron would never be considered. A poor ore over which a country has control may be worth exploiting even though in economic terms that exploitation is unjustifiable in the face of cheaper imports. This latter factor is particularly important in Classical Greece where the large number of independent cities meant that even meagre sources of iron and copper, from which only a few pounds of metal can have been obtained, were mined.

It is not easy to trace the mines and quarries of Classical Greece. The technology available to the ancient Greeks that was used in extracting stone and metals was basically identical to that which continued to be employed until the nineteenth century and the introduction of explosives. It is frequently not possible to distinguish Classical from later workings on grounds of technique. Worse than that, even when working at a later date can be proved, for instance by the presence of a graffito or a mention in the literature, it is rarely possible to determine whether this later working was the first or whether it continued and itself obliterated earlier workings. Literary accounts referring to the Classical period assist in demonstrating activity in given areas, but they do not enable particular mines or quarries to be identified. Much the same is true of the inscriptional records. On the whole there is more information about quarries than about mines, although the most detailed records relate to the silver mines at Laureion at the very southern tip of Attica.

These records refer to individual silver mines and metallurgical workshops, but not in a way that enables their identification on the ground. With both metals and (to a lesser extent) stones, it is possible by physical and chemical analysis to associate certain finished objects with certain ore sources, but as yet this technique lacks precision and has not been widely enough practised to give anything like a complete picture.

In assessing the part that the presence and working of mineral resources played in the formation and deformation of the Classical countryside, both physically and socially, a distinction must be made between precious stones and metals, which are mined, and building stone and valuable earths (e.g. clays) which are dug or quarried. Such a distinction is in fact already made by Aristotle, who is interested not in the very different economic roles of the two sorts of mineral, but in their formation. Aristotle claims that things that are dug or quarried are produced by the action of the dry or fiery exhalation inside the earth, things that are mined by the vaporous exhalation. Although this explanation is little more than a curiosity for us, it does focus on the fact that both the distribution and the manner of exploitation of metals is determined by the way that they are geologically trapped between much more extensive masses of rock: the early history of the earth continues to exert a controlling interest.

Metals and society: underpinning or undermining?

There is little doubt that the metal of which the Greek city had greatest regular need was iron. Iron was used for domestic and agricultural tools and especially for weapons – swords and spearheads. Iron was not only harder and stronger than bronze, but also more readily available on Greek territory.

Greece had limited copper resources (Corinth was an important centre for copper-working in Hellenistic times), but no native sources of tin. By contrast iron is relatively widely distributed: there is a major iron field in Boiotia, extending through the territories of several cities, and this continues through central Euboia. Deposits of iron are known in various parts of the Peloponnese, particularly from the Malea and Mani peninsulas – territories controlled by Sparta, famous for using iron spits as coinage. Several Cycladic islands yield iron ore, especially Keos, Kythnos, Seriphos and Andros, along with the north Aegean island of Lesbos. The ores of the Laureion in Attica and the island of Siphnos which were exploited for their silver also contain significant amounts of iron, but this seems to have been neglected.

Despite the demand for iron it was nowhere as intensively exploited as were the precious metals. This is partly because silver is less widely distributed. There are basically just two areas of the Greek world where silver is found in significant quantities: the southern tip of Attica and the islands immediately south and east of it, especially Siphnos, on the one hand, and the southern part of the Rhodope massif, Mt Pangaion and the island of Thasos, on the other. Both these sources of ore were discovered at a very early date: the exploitation of the Laureion ores can be traced back to the Bronze Age, and Greek tradition held that the ores of Thasos had been exploited by the Phoenicians before ever the Greeks colonized the island. But in both cases the peak of exploitation is reached in the Classical period, although the mines of Siphnos became inoperable because of flooding after the end of the sixth century. The Pangaion and Thasos mines also yielded gold and were the only significant gold source over which the Greeks had any control.

Because the scale of their exploitation was so much greater than that of other metal mines, and the extraction more thorough, it is the silver mines which have left the most dramatic traces on the modern landscape. On the whole the northern field allowed direct access from the steep hillsides, and the landscape is chiefly marked not by constructions or mining shafts but by slag heaps. In the southern Attic field, however, an immense system of shafts and tunnels was built, following the veins of ore on two levels, and great constructions on the surface created facilities for the processing of the ore on the spot.

Although we cannot be sure of the exact contemporaneity of all the mines or all the workshops, the impression which the remains create is one of quite intense activity, and this is very much confirmed by surviving inscriptional records of the leasing out of concessions in the middle of the fourth century. These records, set up in the agora in Athens, relate to a relatively short period of time, but nevertheless they show that even during that period something over two hundred Athenians took out leases on mines. The record of a typical concession reads as follows: 'Onetor son of Arkesilos of the deme [ward] of Melite [in the town of Athens] registered a working mine called the mine of the god Hermes at Laureion, marked by a stele and having as its neighbour on the north side the wall round the property of Diotimos of the village of Euonymon [on the east coast just south of the city], on the south side the workshop of Diotimos of the village of Euonymon, on the east the road leading from Thorikos to Laureion, and on the west side the road leading from Laureion to Thrasymos. Onetor son of Arkesilos of Melite bought the concession for 150 drachmas.'[1]

Despite the figures that they give for lease payments, these inscriptions do not allow any real impression to be formed of the amount of capital tied up in the mines or the profitability of taking up a concession. A somewhat clearer indication is given by literary discussions which are devoted to or at least touch on mining. One whole speech of Demosthenes revolves around the purchase of a processing installation at Maroneia in the Laureion in the fourth century. This installation is acquired by one Pantainetos on credit for some 10,500 drachmas, and Pantainetos has to pay 12 per cent per annum interest on the money borrowed. On one occasion Pantainetos defaults on his interest payment, but this does not seem to indicate that the operation was not a going concern, for eventually the whole thing is sold outright for almost twice the sum for which Pantainetos originally acquired it, 20,600 drachmas. These are very large sums of money, greater than we know to have changed hands for any piece of agricultural land in Classical Attica, and yet only one small installation is involved.

How this installation may have related to the total exploitation of the region may be gauged from the size of the workforce. Pantainetos' ore-crushing mill employs some 30 slaves. In the late fifth century the general Nikias is said to have had 1000 slaves perpetually on hire in the mines, and Xenophon, who records this, argues that the mines had employed a total of more than 10,000 slaves in the fifth century and that they might conceivably be expanded to employ even as many as 90,000. Pantainetos' slaves had to produce a surplus income of 1260 drachmas per annum simply to enable him to service his loan; if 10,000 slaves produced at that rate, then a surplus income of some 65 talents a year and more would be created. This is the minimum figure, but it is more than twice the greatest tribute that any city had to pay to Athens during the fifth-century empire.

The production of the Laureion mines may, however, have been almost trivial compared to that of the ore of the Rhodope massif. Herodotos could claim in the middle of the fifth century that Alexander of Macedon was getting a talent a day of gold from the mines at Dysoron north of Thessalonika. The still richer resources of the Khalkidike and of Pangaion were not fully exploited until the fourth century: Diodoros can claim in his *World History* that Philip II of Macedon took over mines near Philippi that were scarcely in production at all, and developed them until they yielded a revenue of 1000 talents.

It is not simply that these two areas of gold and silver ore produced revenue on a scale which no other production could begin to rival, and with a regularity which sharply contrasted with the variations in agricultural yield. The magnitude of the operation necessary to extract the minerals was itself unparalleled, both in the total numbers employed and in their concentration. The presence of such resources was bound to have a direct effect on the societies fortunate enough to have them, and more particularly on the countrysides in which they were deposited.

In the first place the presence of such valuable ore concentrates economic wealth in the countryside rather than in the town; secondly it brings a large labour force to an area which is not otherwise central; thirdly it overwhelms the citizen structure with a servile presence. The effect of all this is to divorce the creation of wealth from the political centre, and to separate it off from the citizens who control the political life of the city. In the case of the mines developed in areas under Macedonian control, where the social structure was rather loose, the importance of this separation may have been relatively small; but when mineral exploitation was inserted into the much tighter unit which was the

Classical city, major shock waves can be discerned.

The clearest case is that of Athens. Here the major development of the mineral resources got under way only in the latter part of the sixth century. By this time the settlement structure of Attica was already basically formed and it was to a considerable extent frozen by the political reforms of just before 500 (see Chapter 6). The mining development therefore fell into the interstices of the pattern of agricultural villages, and existed to a large extent alongside them rather than overlaying them, although some mines lay at the very centre of existing villages, notably those at Thorikos. The life of the villages in the mining area was revolutionized by the presence of the mines because of the enormous demands that the presence of the large slave workforce created, because of the amount of capital which was being employed and the amount of wealth extracted, and because of the number of citizens from many parts of Attica who were attracted to the region to take up the leases on the concessions.

The archaeological record reveals the new pressures nicely. In the first place the landscape of the Laureion is scattered with small installations not directly connected with mining. These installations consist of or include a strong building or tower, isolated or attached to another building. Sherds of ceramic beehives have been found close to several of these and some are associated with threshing floors. All of this suggests that they are closely linked to the agricultural exploitation of the rather limited areas of viable soil in the region. Such land is unlikely to have been exploited at all in situations of lower demand, and the building of massive towers, not at all typical of the Attic countryside, shows that the presence of the mining slaves was felt to constitute a major risk to property and security. Small wonder that in one case an inscription cut into the rock on the site informs us that the landowner ran his farm through a bailiff.

A different aspect of the pressure put upon local society by the presence of the mines is revealed by an inscription found in the heart of the mining area. It reads as follows: 'Since Leukios is giving an agora for the demesmen to make, the men of Sounion should immediately choose three men to draw up boundaries for the agora along with Leukios, making it not less than two plethra by one (about 60 × 30 m) in order that the demesmen may have plenty of space in which to do the business of the agora, along with any one else who wants, since the current agora has become completely built over. No one, neither the demarch nor anyone else, is to be allowed to build within the boundaries. The demarch must have this inscribed on a stone pillar and put up in the agora.'[2] The agora was both the political meeting place and the market place of the village, and the volume of business created by mining has clearly overwhelmed the existing facilities.

The presence of the mines and the miners entirely reshaped the local community whose lands were being exploited. The citizens as a whole, however, and in particular those citizens who spent most of their time in or near the city of Athens itself, received much of the benefit of the mining at the cost of much less disruption. In the case of Athens the size of the territory and the strength of the bonds between citizens and their villages prevented any radical expression of this disjunction between town and countryside. This was not true everywhere.

The island of Thasos provides an example of mineral resources at their most disruptive. Renowned today for its verdure, the product of high rainfall and abundant springs, Thasos

made a poor impression on the poet Arkhilokhos, the son of the man who led the colonizing expedition from the Cycladic island of Paros. Arkhilokhos wrote that the island stood out like a donkey's backbone, crowned with wild woodland. Thasian wine production was certainly considerable from at least the fifth century on (see Chapter 5), but the incredible 4 km circuit of city walls, built partly of marble, could hardly have been constructed from the profits of agriculture alone. Mining, mainly of silver, was well established by the early Classical period. At first the chief centres of activity seem to have been down the rugged east coast, but subsequently further mines were established at a large number of places on the west coast. There was even a mine under the very acropolis of the town, but in general the little plain in which the town shelters was not disrupted by miners.

The Thasian situation contrasts with the Athenian in two important respects. Attic silver resources were concentrated in a very small area of the whole territory; the mines of Thasos were spread over a substantial part of the island. Secondly, Thasos lacked the deeply rooted tradition of rural village settlement which was firmly established in Attica before the resources of Laureion were ever developed. The combination of these factors seems to have meant that for the Thasians the countryside was mining country: positively it was the major source of the city's expandable wealth; negatively it was a place of hard labour and servile labourers, the very reverse of the urbane city. In these circumstances it is not surprising that there seems to be no Thasian equivalent of the villages of citizens who run their own affairs as a microcosm of the whole city and take an equal part in public life alongside the residents of the town. Nor is it surprising that the monuments most

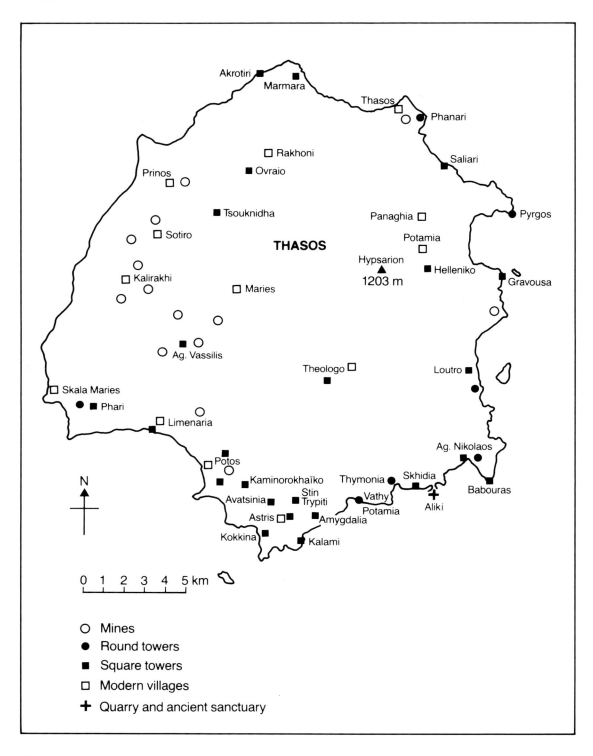

Akrotiri
Marmara
Thasos
Phanari
Rakhoni
Saliari
Ovraio
Prinos
Pyrgos
Panaghia
Tsouknidha
Potamia
Sotiro
THASOS
Hypsarion
Helleniko
1203 m
Gravousa
Kalirakhi
Maries
Loutro
Ag. Vassilis
Theologo
Skala Maries
Phari
Limenaria
Ag. Nikolaos
Potos
Kaminorokhaïko
Thymonia
Skhidia
Babouras
Stin
Avatsinia
Trypiti
Vathy
Astris
Amygdalia
Potamia
Aliki
Kokkina
Kalami

N

0 1 2 3 4 5 km

○ Mines
● Round towers
■ Square towers
□ Modern villages
✚ Quarry and ancient sanctuary

prominent in the Thasian countryside are towers.

Stone and the building of the city

The mining of gold and silver occasionally brought by-products in the way of precious stones: Theophrastos records how a remarkable stone was once found in the gold mines at Lampsakos, from which a signet was carved and sent to the king of Persia because the stone was so odd. Some precious stones were sought after in Greece for their own sake, but Theophrastos notes that stones like the 'anthrakion' of Arkadian Orkhomenos, which was used for mirrors, and the variegated dark red and white stone of Troizen were less valuable than gemstones from elsewhere. Native precious stones can hardly have been of great economic importance for any Greek city.

Stone suitable for building, for sculpting, or for inscribing was a different matter. For basic domestic building, where mud-brick walls were constructed on rough stone blocks and where wooden pillars and props supported tiled roofs, any stones would do, and the native limestone which is widely available could be crudely quarried or picked up as nature had fragmented it. More substantial buildings, and this tends to mean public buildings, whether political or religious, demanded better stone more carefully cut. The local stone might well be unsuitable for such buildings, either because it was too brittle and could not be cut, or because it was too soft and would crumble when worked or when exposed to the weather. In the case of

24 *This map of Thasos shows the distribution of ancient towers and of mineral resources exploited in antiquity. The spread of modern villages contrasts with the concentration of settlement and political activity on the town of Thasos in the northwest corner of the island in antiquity.*

sculptures and inscriptions it is even more true that the local stone would often not do: both statues and lettering require a fineness of detail that is not looked for in straightforward masonry, and marks or natural fissures in the stone, which may not matter at all in building blocks, can ruin the appearance of a piece of carving.

Even in the Archaic period stone suitable for sculpture was transported, often partly worked, over long distances. Here it was not simply that marble was mightily preferred to ordinary limestone, but that particular marbles gained high reputation early on and were sought after even by those with marble resources of their own. Although precise identification of the origin of marbles is not always easy, it is clear that in the sixth century Athens imported marble from the Cycladic islands of Naxos and Paros for the standing male figures known as *kouroi*, which were set up in large numbers as dedications in sanctuaries. This is despite the fact that the Athenians possessed two mountains of marble which themselves were in great demand for sculpture later in antiquity, and from which the great fifth-century monuments of the city of Athens, together with their sculptures, were constructed.

Fashion clearly played a part in these changing patterns in the use of particular stones for sculpture, but for the Archaic period lack of knowledge about available resources may also have been important. The Athenians may not have realized the quality of the stone that was available on their home territory: the Archaic quarries that are to be found on Pendele, which did yield a small number of late Archaic *kouroi*, are not found on the side of the mountain from which the best marble is to be excavated. Since the sculptor seems to have started his work in the quarry when producing one of these standing

25 Even when local stone is good enough for building, it is not always suitable for inscriptions. These two pillars record dedications at the sanctuary at Brauron in Attica (see p. 170 and Figure 56). The photograph on the left shows a sandstone pillar which can now be read only with difficulty; that below shows a pillar of marble whose crisp lettering still clearly informs us that it marks an object which Mnesistrate [wife/daughter] of Theotimides of the village of Anagyrous dedicated to Artemis.

figures, it is not unlikely that particular sculptors and schools of sculptors became closely attached to particular stone resources.

Silver and gold are of high value in relation to their bulk and their transport poses no serious problems, but stone is a very different matter. Many Archaic *kouroi* are over life-size and their transport presented a colossal problem and must have been extremely costly. Transporting building stone over long distances was less problematic, but the costs could become astronomical. From the sanctuary of Apollo at Delphi we have a series of accounts relating to the reconstruction of the temple of Apollo in the fourth century. These make abundantly clear both the costs of transport and the amount of organization which it demanded, as the following excerpts show.

'The city of Delphi further made a second grant when Agesarkhos of Delphi was the magistrate in charge of temple building . . . of 27 mnas 25 staters [1 stater = 2 drachmas]. From this was paid out: to Nikodamos for the machinery at Kirrha [the port nearest to Delphi on the Corinthian gulf] and the construction of a mole, 3 mnas 32 staters $7\frac{1}{2}$ obols; to Nikodamos the price of the sling for the crane mechanism at Kirrha, 51 staters 4 obols; to Onasimos who transported the stone by sea, 21 mnas 25 staters. . . .'

'The city of Delphi further made a third grant when Agesarkhos of Delphi was the magistrate in charge of temple building . . . of 12 mnas 6 staters 3 obols. From this was

26 Large Archaic sculptures were often roughed out in the quarry and might be abandoned if faults occurred or appeared. This unfinished kouros *lies in the Apollona quarry on Naxos.*

paid out: to Onasimos, who transported the stone by sea, we gave an additional payment of 11 mnas 15 staters; to Nikodamos, the price of the pitch and the painting with pitch of the crane mechanism at Kirrha, 10 staters 3 obols.'[3]

Delphi lies in a particularly awkward position. It is high above the Corinthian Gulf, and the climb up from the port of Kirrha is a steep one. The local limestone is not suitable for monumental building, and on a famous occasion in the sixth century the Athenian family called the Alkmaionidai gained considerable publicity by importing not limestone but marble for the façades of the temple of Apollo. The rebuilding of the temple in the fourth century used limestone imported from Corinth. As the extracts show, the handling of such cargoes required the construction of special facilities at Kirrha, both for the docking of the ship and for its unloading. Handling stone was clearly not a regular activity there. Some of those responsible for transport, indeed the two men who received the major payment of 3 talents, came from the Arkadian city of Tegea which had recently faced similar problems itself in constructing its temple of Athena Alea. This suggests that moving stone on a large scale demanded skills which were possessed by few ordinary hauliers. We do not know how much the stone that Onasimos is transporting in the extract quoted cost to quarry. Subsequent accounts, however, allow us to trace four corner cornice blocks from the quarry to the site at Delphi. 244 drachmas is paid for their quarrying, 896 drachmas for their transport from Lekhaion, the port of Corinth, to Kirrha, and 1680 drachmas for their transport from Kirrha to Delphi. The same ratio may not have applied to all the stone, but this example does show very clearly that land transport was much more expensive than sea transport, and that the cost

of the stone itself was almost insignificant compared with the cost of transporting it.

Delphi was the seat of a great oracle and the site of one of the four most important athletics competitions, the Pythian games. This meant that it had the financial resources to meet the costs of importing stone at this price. It also meant that it could not be seen to be cutting costs by using inferior or unsuitable local material. Elsewhere the economic arguments for using what was locally available were not so easily resisted. Even for the great temple of Zeus at Olympia imported stone was used only for the sculptures of the metopes and pediments; the building itself was constructed out of the local stone. This despite the fact that the local stone is of very poor quality, being largely comprised of fossil shells. Such material could only be used at all because the temple was built on an enormous scale, which meant that even the smallest details were quite large in absolute terms, and because of the practice of coating stonework with stucco. Later and less massive buildings at Olympia used imported limestone of better quality. Smaller communities had to make do with the local stone: the fourth-century temple at Mazi across the other side of the Alpheios valley from Olympia makes do with the shelly stone.

Neither Delphi nor Olympia are close to marble sources. When they import stone for building they import limestone, not marble. Athens, by contrast, has access to two large sources of high-quality marble, the moun-

27 *Even monumental buildings at important panhellenic sanctuaries might be built of poor quality local stone. This close-up shows the shelly limestone from which the colossal temple of Zeus at Olympia was constructed in the mid fifth century.*

tains of Pendele (anciently called Brilessos) and Hymettos. On both of these mountains there is a large number of ancient quarries, although many of those on Hymettos seem to date from the Roman boom in that stone. Marble from Pendele is used for the major Athenian religious buildings of the fifth century – the Parthenon, Erekhtheion, and temple of Athena Nike on the Acropolis, the Hephaisteion, temple of Ares, and temple of Artemis on the Ilissos, in or just outside the town walls. It is even used in one or two fifth-century non-religious public buildings, notably the Portico of Zeus in the civic centre known as the agora. But most public buildings in Athens were of limestone, or even partly of limestone and partly of mud brick. When marble is used at all it is used only for details, as for the metopes in the newly un-covered Painted Stoa (Portico) in the agora.

FAR LEFT
28 The major fifth-century public buildings of Athens, including the Parthenon, made much use of marble from the quarries at Pendele in central Attica. Pentelic marble has been heavily exploited in recent times also, and the Spelia quarry is one of the few ancient quarries surviving today.

BELOW
29 Prominently placed on the southern tip of Attica, the temple of Poseidon at Sounion was built in the 430s from brittle marble quarried just a few kilometres to the north.

In other parts of Attica the situation is rather different. Pentelic marble is used as a basic building stone for some work at Eleusis (see Chapter 1), but otherwise the various local sanctuaries around Attica chose to use the local stone. Sometimes this local stone is itself marble, although not the high-quality marble of Pendele. Thus the temple of Poseidon at Sounion uses stone from quarries just a few kilometres to its north, marble that is very white but rather brittle, and the sanctuary at Rhamnous in northeast Attica uses marble from quarries a short distance to the south, which may have been opened especially for the Nemesis temple there. In other cases the local stone is not nearly such a close substitute for Pentelic marble: the sanctuary at Brauron on the east coast uses a sandstone quarried just a few hundred metres away, a stone which is easy to work but undis-

tinguished in appearance, and the temple at Loutsa a little to the north uses the same stone. Private monuments and buildings seem to have been even more closely tied to what was to be quarried on the spot: the so-called Tomb of Sophokles near Dekeleia can afford limestone only for its sarcophagus cover, the tomb itself is built from blocks of a particularly unattractive conglomerate.

It is the Attic rather than the Athenian situation which prevails over most of Greece. The quarries at Doliana south of Tegea are the only good marble source in the Peloponnese exploited in Classical times. Marble from

30 Local stone was not always poor stone. The column drums of the fifth-century temple of Nemesis at Rhamnous, never finished off (probably because of the Peloponnesian war), show off the local stone from which the temple was built to some advantage.

these quarries was used for a small temple close by and for the superstructure, but not the foundations (or stylobate), of the temple of Athena Alea in Tegea. Otherwise it is found only in details of buildings – for column capitals at a hilltop temple west of Asea, for roof tiles at Bassai. The principal building projects at Epidauros in the fourth century did import Pentelic marble for a major part of the superstructure of the round Tholos, as well as for the sculptures of the temple of Asklepios, but otherwise Peloponnesian temples made do with what was to hand. This is even true of such major sites as the games centre at Nemea.

Central Greece suffers a similar dearth of good marble, and here again even major religious sites are at best equipped with buildings of fine limestone. The important sanctuary of Apollo on Mount Ptoon used local stone, of

varying quality, in the buildings of all dates, even though most of the 120 Archaic standing male statues, *kouroi*, were brought to the site from outside sources and set up there as dedications.

A contrasting situation, where good marble is abundant and easily available, prevails on several Aegean islands. Thasos will again serve as a particularly good example. Here marble is as abundant, although not quite as widespread, as the metal resources. The northern part of the east coast of the island, and most of the southern coast, bear heavy traces of marble quarrying in antiquity.

31 The brilliant white marble of the Rhamnous temple (Fig. 30) contrasts strongly with the coarse local limestone used for this temple at Mazi in Elis in the fourth century (compare the stone used at Olympia just a few kilometres to the north, Fig. 27).

The marble was probably most fully exploited during the period of Roman imperial rule, but there is no doubt that the resources were quite heavily tapped in Classical times. Large sections of the wall which ringed the town of Thasos are of marble, a choice of material which must indicate a considerable desire for display, for the gneiss of which other sections were made must have been very considerably easier to work. Large parts of the monumental public buildings were also of marble. Even here, however, it is notable that the lure of the local meant that they even quarried away the top of the acropolis. In the countryside marble was used for certain of the towers and for the Archaic temples on the heavily-quarried marble peninsula at Alikí, but it is not found at all in use in the western part of the island, where even the towers made do with the local bedrock of gneiss. Thasos was a very wealthy island, and the Thasians were clearly prepared to use their marble resources for public display in the town. That they do not make the effort or expend the time or money required to monumentalize the productive countryside is a further indication of the extent to which that countryside was repressed.

Building stone thus rarely moved very far in large quantities, even if it was of the highest quality. Stone for inscribing and particularly for sculpture moved very much further. At Olympia bronze was used for inscriptions rather than importing good stone, but large quantities of marble came in for relief and free-standing statuary. The quantities of stone

involved in sculptures is, however, small, especially after the fashion for colossal statues largely faded with the end of the Archaic period. As a result no stone resources acquire an economic significance which can begin to match that of the silver mines of Attica, the Cyclades, or northern Greece. Demand for any particular stone was very variable, and even at peaks of exploitation no large workforce can have been kept employed for any length of time.

Quarrying can never have changed the face of a society as radically as silver mining invariably did, but it nevertheless did not leave it unmarked. Demand for large quantities of stone came almost solely from public building projects. The sort of demand created by the decision to build a watch-tower or a border fort may not have given rise to a strong bond between the local community which exploited the stone and the community which received it. Forts have no abiding population, and their builders most frequently found their own stone on the very site which is fortified. Decisions to build temples or political meeting places, on the other hand, have a very strong communal aspect. When a central settlement requires stone for its public building projects, the demand may simply make the country community which has the quarry feel increasingly dependent on the centre. This is doubtless particularly the case when the stone is used for the construction of town walls, which create a barrier between the protected community inside and the rural community outside from which the stone comes.

But the need of the central community for stone from its territory may also increase the strength of the bond between town and country. This seems to have been the case in fifth-century Athens, where the massive building programme of the later part of

32 This view of the fourth-century watch-tower at Pyrgaki above the Valley of the Muses in Boiotia shows clearly how stone for such forts was frequently sought locally, the pit formed by the quarrying contributing to the defensibility of the position.

the century conspicuously displayed the dependence of the town on the resources of the mountains: the political life of all the citizens, as represented by the public buildings of the assembly place on the Pnyx and of the agora, and the claim of the city to be self-sufficient, was shown to depend upon Athens being more than a town. The countryside was put at the centre of Athenian public life. When a local community itself undertook a major building project, its decision to use local stone may not have been simply an economic necessity, but also a pointed declaration of the self-sufficiency of that community; through its monumental building activities the community put itself, its strength and its unity, on display.

These various factors are seen most clearly at work in Athens and Attica, but they can be discerned elsewhere as well – in the remote little marble temple by the quarries at Doliana, or in the twin sanctuary at Alikí on Thasos. This latter example has a rather interesting feature. The Alikí temples seem to have been linked to one of the few known Classical villages in the countryside of Thasos by a road supported by a monumental terrace, itself built of marble blocks. The date of the road buildings is uncertain, but its role is clear. It cries out to the visitor to the sanctuary that there is a community responsible which cannot be ignored – even though in the village itself the only noteworthy structure, of which traces remain, is yet another tower.

The exploitation of stone and the exploitation of metals have little in common in ancient Greece. Metals and stone resources were differently distributed across the landscape, and exploited in very different ways and on entirely different scales. Mining was an operation which kept a large workforce continuously employed. Much of the work was hard physical grind, but the running of the metallurgical workshops which separated useful minerals from the mass of ore demanded some skill. Quarrying was only sporadically carried on at any particular site, and, although it required some geological knowledge to be well done, the signs are that it was frequently done rather badly, with no regard for the natural grain of the stone. Once processed, metals were relatively easy to transport; once stone was quarried, the problems had only just begun. Given all these differences it is not surprising that the social impact of silver and of marble resources should be different. But neither of these manifestations of the geological wealth of the landscape left the appearance of town and country or the relations between them unaffected. Temporarily or permanently, mining and quarrying intervened in and deflected the patterns of exchange prevailing within and between Greek cities. But they neither dominated nor replaced those patterns.

5

EXCHANGE AND SOCIETY

The Greek diet relied heavily on cereals. The peasant farmer aimed to grow all the food his household needed on his own land. But rainfall was unpredictable and cereal yields fluctuated enormously. Often, more often in some areas than in others, the farmer's land produced less grain than he needed, and there was no other staple that could fill the gap. As a result no Greek farmer could survive on his own. Irregularly but repeatedly, he had to look to outside sources of food. Sometimes he would not need to look very far; his neighbours had been luckier in the disposition of their lands or wiser in their agricultural strategy. At other times everyone in the area was short and grain had to be procured from another city, near or far.

This chapter explores the nature and consequences of the exchange which the climate made inevitable. The need to buy and to sell in order to live affected a man's relationship with his neighbour and with the local community; it affected the relationship between country and town within a city and the relationship between cities. The grain trade was on a scale far exceeding that of any other exchange of goods, and it had a special character which was largely responsible for the peculiarly low status of those who spent their lives in trade. The trade in grain itself necessitated trade in other goods, but different objects of trade created different social relationships.

Exchanging neighbours

Most Greek farmers, whether they lived in town, village, or on their own, kept all the produce of their fields in their homes. They kept it even if it was more than the household would itself need. From this store those whose crops had done well lent to those who had been less fortunate. Lending to neighbours, relatives and friends was part and parcel of everyday life.

Relations with neighbours depended very largely on their willingness or unwillingness to meet sudden needs, large or small. Those who were tight-fisted were remarked upon. Theophrastos, in characterizing various types of person, says of the rustic that: 'If he lends out his plough, or basket or sickle or bag, he will remember it when lying awake at night and come and ask for it back'[1]; of the stingy man that: 'He will forbid his wife to lend salt or a lamp-wick or cummin or marjoram or grain for sacrifice or garlands or cakes, and will say that these small things grow numerous during a year.'[2]

In a village community lending was closely tied in with success on the farm. The man who was constantly begging because he failed to farm his land properly threatened the structure of social relationships. This is made very clear by the way in which the poet Hesiod chastises his brother Perses: 'This is the law of the farmlands, whether you live by the sea or on rich land in a woody corner far from the noise of waves: strip to sow, strip to plough, and strip to harvest, if you want to bring in a good grain harvest when the time comes. That is the way to get the crops in. If you don't you will be short and be begging at other people's houses. But they won't give you anything. That's how you just came to me, but I will not give you any more, I won't measure you out more grain. Get down to the work which the gods ordained for men. If you don't you will be sorry when you have to seek your daily bread with your wife and children with you from your neighbours, and they ignore your requests. You might get given something a couple of times, but if you trouble them after that you won't get a thing and your words will go to the wind.'[3]

Social relationships in the society Hesiod depicts are oiled by lending and borrowing. But both lending and borrowing may have unfortunate social consequences. Hesiod would rather be a lender than a borrower, but only to people from whom he might himself borrow at another time. For borrowing to meet needs it has to be reciprocal; if it is not the consequences are dire. The man who always borrows finds himself cut off from the rest of society; the man who lends too freely ruins himself; but the man who refuses to lend to those in need brings death. Hesiod makes this latter point particularly graphically when he says that 'not even an ox would perish [from hunger] were it not for a bad neighbour.'[4]

Land distribution was rarely even in Greek cities, and the climate did not choose its vic-tims by rotation. The farmer who had to borrow one year in order to have enough grain to live or to sow again was not always able to repay his loan the next. Small farmers were more vulnerable and became dependent upon those who had larger holdings. Borrowing and not repaying creates an obligation, an informal bond. The society of equal neighbours lending to each other in turn becomes a society with a hierarchy of dependence and ever more clearly marked social distinctions.

In some places at some periods the bonds of dependence between neighbours became formalized: the debtor became the legal slave of the lender. The extent of debt bondage in Athens in the seventh century led to a major social crisis, and the measures taken by the legislator Solon to resolve this have attracted much attention. But concentration on the way in which Solon made it illegal for one Athenian to enslave another has obscured the fact that the nature of the agrarian society made it inevitable that less formal structures of dependence continued to exist. Throughout Classical antiquity, lending and borrowing were important ways in which local communities acquired a clear, if flexible, structure of groups of distinct status. It is arguable that few Greek cities, perhaps none at all, became sufficiently converted to a cash-based economy to replace these ties with the more extensive ties of dependence which money loans make possible. While money loans did become a very important means by which the rich could meet financial obligations without selling off real property, they seem to have played no significant part in the peasant's fight for survival.

Living off the country

Towns had a greater and more regular need for grain from outside sources than country villages did. The majority of those who lived in the towns had land of their own which they farmed, but for many townsmen non-agricultural occupations absorbed all or most of their time. The proportion of the citizen body who needed to acquire grain varied enormously from town to town and was much influenced by factors such as settlement pattern and land-holding.

One extreme situation was that created by the philosopher Plato for the utopian community described in his *Laws*. In this imaginary city every citizen was given two plots of land, one near the city and one towards the borders. Every citizen had to market one third of his produce, but the city 'needed practically nothing' from outside, and the grain on the market was for visitors and resident foreigners. No Greek city in fact enjoyed such an arrangement, although some colonial foundations were constructed with a similar end in view.

In many small cities the vast majority of citizens resided in the town. They travelled out from the town to their scattered holdings of land, often leaving before dawn and returning after dusk. Some had seasonal shelters on their fields but very few resided there permanently. This is still a pattern prevalent in the 'agro-towns' of modern Sicily. As the coinage 'agro-town' suggests, when farmers all reside in the town it becomes difficult to make a meaningful distinction between town and country. But the very fact that most of the town residents were occupied with a country which was itself uninhabited did give the countryside a problematic status. On the one hand the countryside was the town's source of livelihood and sustenance, and on the other the countryside which had no residents had little protection, and was the area in which the city was most vulnerable.

The problems of a town of residence and a country of production are well brought out

by the military writer Aineias the Tactician. Aineias was a native of Akhaia who lived in the fourth century, and his general observations were based on his knowledge of the situation in the small Peloponnesian cities around him. He suggests that the city which is threatened by an enemy at harvest time needs to take special precautions: 'Whenever the territory is full of crops and the enemy are not far off, it is reasonable that many of the men in the city spend all their time in the land nearby, concentrating on the crops. Gather these men into the town in the following way. First make a signal to those outside to go back to the town at sunset. If they are scattered widely over the territory, make the signal through intermediate signal stations in order that all, or at least most, get back to the town. Secondly, once these men have been signalled to return, give those in the town the sign to have supper. Finally give the signal for them to go on guard-duty and take up position.'[5]

The precautions which Aineias suggests are hardly sophisticated, but the danger to a city of having the enemy catch most of its inhabitants out in the fields was real. A number of cities were brought to premature surrender when an invading army caught the best part of the citizen body busy in the fields. But to run and leave harvested crops for the enemy to take was equally dangerous. It gave the enemy the supplies with which to prolong their invasion, and it deprived the city of essential food when under siege. Aineias regards leaving produce in the fields when the enemy invades as treacherous. The Mantineians, in the episode related in Chapter 1, tried to resolve the problem by calling in the men of military age and relying on the old and the young to gather in the crops.

Farming the country from the town knits the city together into an indivisible unit, but it does not stop the country being perceived as separate. The town is directly supplied with grain as the farmers bring their produce back to their own homes, and in good and peaceful years the town is fed without having to buy cereals from elsewhere. But as soon as enemy invasion threatens, or drought hits the land, the country becomes the point at which the city is most vulnerable. When the enemy attacks, the city has to decide whether to try to protect the crops by moving into the countryside, or whether to protect the town and risk the loss of the food supply. The countryside alternately sustains and threatens the life of the town.

In most large cities the town was not the only place of permanent residence. Problems of communication saw to that. Some farmers always resided in the main town, farming the land immediately around it, but the bulk of agricultural activity was carried out from smaller communities, or even from isolated establishments. In this situation the neighbourly exchange which kept the whole community supplied with food in a village or an 'agro-town' was no longer sufficient to feed all those town residents who were not primarily farmers. Even when the territory itself produced sufficient for the needs of the whole population of the city, the exchange of grain involved some degree of commercialization, of buying and selling at a market.

The intervention of the market immediately alters relations between producer and consumer. When the farmer who is short has to go and beg from his relative or neighbour a personal bond is created. When the town is fed directly from the crops reaped by the resident farmers, there is a direct sense that the city is being fed from its own resources. Once any significant proportion of the town residents have to acquire all or much of their

staple food supplies from the market, the direct links are destroyed. The grain on the market might have come from anywhere; it no longer bears any clear mark of being the community's own. That it is a citizen who brings the produce to the market place is no longer essentially significant; he is just another merchant and likely to be held in as low repute as the rest. This was particularly clear in Athens, where we can see the abuse of the merchant turning into the abuse of country life through the abuse of the peasant who must sell his surplus goods in the market. It is a favourite ploy of Aristophanes in his comedies to refer to all whom he wishes to abuse as sellers of something. He uses this ploy partly to trivialize the commercial interests of those who derive wealth from non-agricultural pursuits, but he also uses it in order to make fun of those from a purely rustic background. The poet Euripides is a favourite butt of Aristophanes' jokes, and Aristophanes makes fun of the fact that he came from a village at the foot of Pendele by saying that his mother was a vegetable seller. Attention is turned from the farmer as producer to the farmer as merchant, and the vital produce which the farmer grows and sells becomes mere merchandise. Euripides' bitterness towards women is supposed by Aristophanes to derive from the fact that he grew up among bitter herbs. The farmers' intervention in the market could lead to their being seen to be dependent on an unattractive natural environment.

In the case of Classical Sparta the divorce between town and country was virtually complete. The territory of Sparta, like that of Athens, included both a central town and surrounding villages and smaller establishments. But all Spartiates lived in the town, and the countryside was inhabited and worked by a dependent population, the helots. The helots farmed the land owned by the Spartan citizens, kept a proportion of the produce for themselves, and passed the rest on to the landowner in the town. The Spartan citizen led a communal life, and from the produce from his land he made his contributions to the communal mess in which he was obliged to take his meals. Here town and country residents were separate in status and occupation, and linked by the obligation of the helot to provide food for the consumption of the citizens. This exceptional division between the farmer and the citizen had enormous consequences for the political and military organization of Sparta, consequences which I will discuss in the next two chapters.

In some particular cases the town's need for grain established a special relationship between the town and a particular piece of territory. A nice example of this is provided by two Hellenistic documents from the island of Samos off the coast of Asia Minor. Samos possessed some territory on the mainland opposite called Anaia, on which were some important temple estates and considerable amounts of land belonging to private individuals. During the third century possession of this area was contested. In a rare case of a local pressure group being formed, the citizens who were being deprived of their estates requested the citizen body of Samos to send an embassy to King Antiokhos to resolve the position.

A century later a law about the corn supply passed by the Samians makes it clear what was special about Anaia: '. . . the men who have been appointed in charge of the corn supply shall purchase the corn that is collected from the 5 per cent tax from Anaia, paying the goddess Hera for it at a price not less than the 5 drachmas 2 obols previously fixed by the people. . . . If the people decide to buy more corn they are to make over the surplus money

to the corn-buyer who has been appointed. The corn-buyer shall purchase corn from the territory of Anaia in the way which seems to him most advantageous for the city, unless the people think it more advantageous to buy corn from another source.'[6]

Anaia is clearly a sort of bonus for the Samians. The estates there, both the temple estates and the private lands, provide a source of extra grain upon which the city has first call in times of need, but which can be ignored either when the city is well provided from home territory, or when it can meet its needs more conveniently from elsewhere. Anaia gives Samos an extra resource over which the city is keen to have control, but possession of Anaia is not as keenly contested as that of the rest of its territory. As it is separated from Samos by the sea, attacks on Anaia do not directly threaten the rest of the city, and Samos can exploit it without feeling the same degree of responsibility for its protection. Anaia stands halfway between a city's own territory and an outside source of grain.

Importing corn

All Greek cities sometimes needed to call upon the cereal production of other cities. The Samian corn-law envisages that Samos will not always need even all the grain from Anaia, but it covers every eventuality. Other cities had a more regular need for corn from outside. Procuring grain from other cities in years of shortage was a matter of life and death, and the more regularly outside grain supplies were needed the more obsessed a city became with the supply mechanisms.

The Classical city which had the most regular need for grain from outside was undoubtedly Athens. The question of the corn supply dominated political life. On ten occasions during the year, at every fourth meeting, the assembled Athenian citizen body had a fixed agenda. First it considered the conduct of elected magistrates; next it considered the state of the corn supply and whether any special measures had to be taken with regard to it. This was followed by discussion of national security, of extraordinary crimes to be dealt with by the assembly rather than the courts, and of problems relating to individual cases of property inheritance and property confiscation. These are the sensitive areas of the Greek city: security, property, individual misbehaviour, and the food supply. It is not simply that anxiety about sources of food might be of political importance; the corn supply was *normally* a cause for concern.

This concern made its mark on the institutions of the city. Here is Aristotle's description of the Athenian magistrates with special concern for the corn supply: 'The allotted guardians of the corn supply (*sitophulakes*) used to be five in number for the Peiraieus and five for the city. Now there are twenty for the city and fifteen for the Peiraieus. Their first concern is that corn is on sale properly in the market, and they are secondly concerned that millers sell flour according to the price of barley grain, and that bakers sell bread in accordance with the price of wheat and at the weight which the guardians of the corn supply lay down. The law enjoins them to stipulate the weight. In addition ten men are elected by lot each year in charge of the Peiraieus wholesale market. They see that two thirds of the corn imported into the wholesale market is brought up to the city by the merchants.'[7]

Democratic Athens believed in reducing individual responsibility and therefore regularly used officials in boards of ten. The size of the boards of guardians of the corn supply in the late fourth century indicates the heavy responsibility which they were felt to bear. The forty-five officials listed here who

had special concern with grain were in addition to the twenty others who ran the market in general and looked after weights and measures. Together these officials were probably about one tenth of the total Athenian citizen magistrates.

Athenian regulation of the corn supply was not limited to marketing problems once the grain reached Attica. The Athenians also attempted to control the shipment of grain by law. Athenian citizens engaged in grain shipment were obliged to bring all the grain they carried to Athens. So were those other Greek traders who had made a more or less permanent base in Athens. This regulation tried to prevent grain shippers carrying their cargoes to wherever the price was highest. In doing so it implied that to dispose of corn to anyone other than Athenians was an act of treachery. It had long been prohibited for Athenian farmers to export grain grown in Attica: this law equates grain carried by those resident within Attica with grain grown at home. As we will see Athens was not the only city which effectively extended its territory out to sea when it needed grain, but no other city extended its territory so far.

The close regulation of the grain trade by the Athenians both reflected and produced deep suspicions and divisions within society. Prosecutions of men involved in the grain trade are well represented in the law-court speeches preserved from fourth-century Athens. The orator Lysias makes the following allegations in his inflammatory prosecution speech against corn-dealers who are accused of combining to hoard corn against the public interest: 'Everyone knows that the interests of corn-dealers are not those of other men. They make the biggest profit when they can sell corn at a high price because news of some catastrophe has reached the city. They are happy when they see you in trouble. They are the first to learn of trouble, and they even make up trouble stories – that the ships in the Black Sea have been destroyed, that ships have been captured by the Spartans as they sail out, that markets have been closed or war declared. They are so against us that in these crises they plot against us just as enemies do. When you have greatest need of corn they buy it up and won't sell, trying to make us so desperate that we won't worry about the price but will be happy to go away with our purchase whatever their price. It is sometimes as if we were under siege by them in times of peace!'[8]

The large jury which Lysias is trying to influence will have consisted largely of purchasers rather than merchants, and Lysias plays on their prejudices. The very existence of these prejudices indicates that food supply was an emotive issue at Athens. This was partly because, by ancient Greek standards, Athens had an exceptional need for imported corn.

Athenian demand for corn was not typical, Athens was abnormally heavily populated. Not only was the population very large in absolute terms, about 150,000 (see Chapter 2), but despite the size of the territory the density of population was also high, especially in the town of Athens itself. Athenian territory was rather unsuitable for wheat; barley was safer because less thirsty, but it was less appetizing. Athenian home production must have fluctuated enormously from year to year, but although the territory could have been farmed in such a way as to feed the whole population, there were probably few years in the fourth century when Athens did not need imported corn.

Ancient literary claims, although unreliable, give some indication of the scale on which Athens imported grain. The orator Demosthenes, arguing for the importance of giving privileges to benefactors, discusses the benefit received by Athens because, in return for the privileges he has been given by the Athenians, Leukon, the ruler of the Bosporos, does not exact his usual $3\frac{1}{3}$ per cent tax on exported grain. Demosthenes claims that Athenian records showed that Athens imported some 400,000 medimnoi (about 15,000 metric tonnes) of corn from Pontos. 400,000 medimnoi of corn is sufficent to feed about 80,000 to 90,000 people, more or less half the probable Athenian population, for one year. Demosthenes never actually says that this amount was imported in a single year, and it certainly should not be assumed that this much was imported *every* year, but the claim does suggest that there were some years in which Athens had need of very large amounts of grain. That Athens' needs outstripped those of any other city is illustrated by the distribution of the grain given by Cyrene in about 330 (see p. 34): Athens received 100,000 medimnoi, Corinth and Larisa, the cities which got the next largest amounts, 50,000.

Whatever the scale of the need for imported corn in any particular year, meeting that need was a social and political necessity. Athenian democracy allowed every individual citizen a vote on every issue. Its critics accused it of being maverick in its policies because of this, but despite the accusations Athenian political decisions rarely display any marked leanings towards extremes. The moderation of Athenian policy was only possible because the vast majority of citizens shared common concerns, ideology and prejudices. Particular interest groups seem rarely to have managed to steer the community decision in a way favourable to them alone. In the face of starvation and a split between those who had food and those who had none, such a balance could scarcely have been maintained. Grain imports ensured political stability, and they ensured that the landless residents of the town and those who gained most of their livelihood from non-agricultural occupations were not split apart as a group clearly distinct from the peasant farmers who rarely needed to go far beyond their own or their neighbour's resources in order to survive.

Grain was equally important to prevent undue tension in communities whose need for imported food was less great and less regular than that of Athens. The city of Teos in Asia Minor expressed its concern very clearly in its public curses inscribed in the early fifth century: 'May anyone who manufactures harmful drugs aimed at the Teans as a community or against an individual perish – himself and his family. May anyone who prevents corn being imported to Tean territory by sea or over the mainland, through skill or some device, or who sends it out once it has been brought in, perish – himself and his family.'[9] Interference with the corn supply is here treated as the equivalent of actively poisoning the people of Teos: to stand in the way of importing corn is represented as depriving the community of life itself.

Being in need of corn was a familiar experience in all Greek cities, but getting hold of supplies from elsewhere was not simple. Few cities had the elaborate permanent provision of magistrates whose sole concern was the corn supply which was found in Athens, but most had to appoint such magistrates from time to time (compare the Samian corn law, see p. 97). These magistrates faced two problems: finding another city which had a grain surplus it was willing to dispose of at an acceptable price; and safely transporting that grain home.

No particular city could be relied upon to have a grain surplus available for purchase in any particular year; climatic factors saw to that. In the Hellenistic period the grain trade was so well established that the island of Delos had become a centre of sale and purchase to which cities came from far and wide.

The role of Delos is well illustrated in the following decree of the city of Histiaia on the island of Euboia. Passed in the 230s it honours a citizen of Rhodes: 'The archon proposed that the council should submit the resolution of the people: since Athenodoros of Rhodes has been continually helpful to the people, both privately to any citizen who made requests of him, and to the city as a whole, and since he co-operated with the corn-buyers sent out by the city to Delos, enthusiastically advancing money at no interest and bringing it about that they purchased corn as rapidly as possible, putting the favour of the city before his personal profit, the city should praise him and crown him in order that all should know that the people of Histiaia honours its benefactors and to encourage more men to compete in providing what the city needs. . . .'[10] Delos had no grain of its own, but it served as a convenient place where middlemen like this Rhodian could act as brokers, matching up the needs on one city with corn from another.

There was no equivalent to Delos in the Classical period. Large quantities of corn came into the Athenian port of the Peiraieus, but the Athenians jealously guarded it all for their own use. The magistrates whom a city appointed to buy corn had to make direct contact with a city willing to sell. The way in which it was necessary to shop around is illustrated by the fact that Athens at different times found herself importing grain from Italy and Sicily, the Adriatic, Thessaly, Thrace, various parts of the Black Sea, Cyprus and Egypt. Not one of these areas, still less any particular city, could be regularly relied upon as a source of grain: when drought was not a serious problem, war might be.

When the drought which reduced a city's cereal production was local, the city could try to get grain from a neighbour. This exchange across boundaries must have been very regular, although it was too straightforward in normal circumstances to leave any record in the literary or other sources. The importance of the island of Euboia, in supplying grain to Athens during her struggle with Sparta in the late fifth century, is only recorded by the historian Thucydides when the Spartan occupation of Athenian territory cuts off the normal overland trade route.

However, even getting grain from a nearby city was not without its difficulties. The following historical anecdote told by Xenophon is revealing: '[During the 370s] the Thebans were much oppressed by a short-age of grain. For two years they had been prevented from gathering in the harvest by the war. So they sent men to Pagasai in Thes-saly with two warships and 10 talents (60,000 drachmas) to buy corn. While they were pur-chasing the corn, Alketas, the Spartan in charge of the garrison at Oreos, secretly manned three warships. When the grain con-voy sailed Alketas captured it together with the triremes, taking at least 300 men alive. He imprisoned these on the acropolis at Oreos [Histiaia], which was where he had his head-quarters. Now they say that there was a fine attractive boy who paid court to Alketas and he used to go down to the town to spend time with him. The prisoners noticed this careless-ness, seized the acropolis, and secured the revolt of the city. The Thebans had no trouble bringing in corn after that.'[11]

The Thebans in this story make a public expedition, with naval support, to get grain. Their need is desperate, and the money they

sent will have purchased 500,000 kg of corn, enough to feed 2500 people for a whole year. But despite the precautions the ships bringing back the corn get intercepted.

Thebes and Sparta were at war, but grain ships might be intercepted even by friendly cities. The cities of the Hellespont and the Sea of Marmara were in a particularly strong position to intercept supplies coming from the Black Sea, and a city, which wanted to ensure that the grain it had bought got through, might have to send naval support to prevent attack. Demosthenes relates just this situation occurring in the 360s: 'While the merchants and the shippers were still around the exit from the Black Sea and the peoples of Byzantion, Khalkedon, and Kyzikos were intercepting grain ships because of their private need for corn, you (the Athenian people) saw that corn was fetching a high price in the Peiraieus and was not in plentiful supply, and you voted that the com-manders of the warships should launch their ships and bring them to the pier, and that the members of the council and the heads of the villages should list villagers and raise sailors and quickly make an expedition and give aid in every way.'[12]

Not every city had the naval resources of Athens with which to combat this piratical activity. Athens was particularly prone to have ships bound for her ports intercepted, however, because of her exceptional need for grain and because of her political strength and international influence. Interference with Athenian grain supplies was an effective way of putting political pressure on her. Both the Spartans and later Philip II of Macedon used control of the Hellespont as a means of bring-ing Athens to submission.

The problems Athens faced were not unique in character, even if they were unique in scale. A nice example of the politics of interception played by other cities occurred in the 390s. The Rhodians defected from the Spartans, and expelled the Spartan fleet. Grain ships from Egypt bound for Sparta approached the island ignorant of the change of political allegiance. The Rhodians intercepted them precisely so that they could stock-pile grain in order to withstand the expected Spartan siege.

Imported grain could never replace home supply. Getting grain from outside was an even more risky business than growing it at home, for the threats to crop production posed everywhere by environmental factors were compounded by the dangers of human interference in shipping. No city could free

33 This mid sixth-century Attic black-figure cup shows a merchant vessel with mast, sails, and steersman clearly visible, about to be rammed by a trireme rowed perhaps by pirates.

its farmers from the necessity of trying to grow all the staple food crops the population needed.

A remarkable illustration of the continuing importance of home grain comes from the Athens of the early third century. On two occasions the Athenian citizen body honoured men because they had protected the corn harvest in time of war and ensured that as much of the crop as possible was brought into the city. On a third occasion the people of the Athenian village of Rhamnous passed a parallel decree for the military official in charge of the cavalry at the garrison there: 'He saved the fort for the people during the war, and gathered in the crops and fruits within a range of 5 km and set up covered grain stores in the land, keeping guard himself with the soldiers to enable the farmers to gather in the harvest safely. He also protected

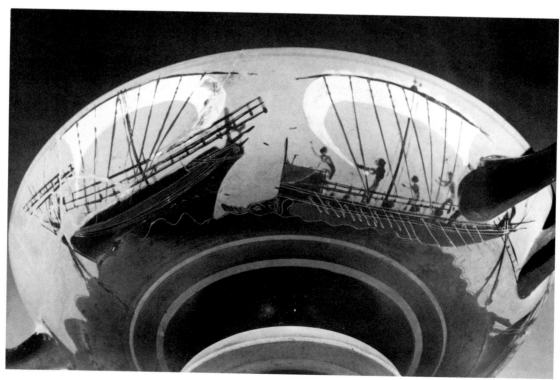

the vines as far as he was able. He imported 500 medimnoi of wheat [about 2 metric tonnes] and 500 of barley, advancing the money himself, and distributed them to the citizens and the soldiers at the usual price.'[13] Imported grain is clearly available to the people of Rhamnous, but what the farmers there are most grateful for is the protection which enabled them to fetch in their own crops. Feeding themselves from their own resources is their first priority.

The subordination of imported grain to home production was a major factor in determining the low status of those involved in shipping grain, and in trade in general. No Greek city wanted to import grain, and doing so implied some failure in home production. As Hesiod's rebuke to his brother shows (see p. 94), being in need of grain was seen by other members of the community as a sign that one had not worked hard enough. Of course all farmers hit bad times and everyone was in need sometime or other, but the man who devoted himself entirely to importing grain was a man who could be represented as contributing nothing to home production, a man who was not even making the effort to subsist. The farmer is a man who tries to be dependent upon no other men; the trader voluntarily puts himself in a position where he is dependent upon other men at every stage of his transactions. First the trader has to hunt for a grain surplus to purchase, then he has to match his goods to a demand, a demand which is at best reluctant, for no farmer wants to have to purchase grain.

Even in Athens trade in staples was left almost entirely in the hands of resident foreigners who were subject to severe disabilities. Resident foreigners had to pay a special tax, could take no part in political decision-making, and could own neither houses nor land. As Chapter 1 showed, Athenians who had sufficient wealth to enable them to engage in trade on a large scale generally chose to tie that wealth up in land, and spent their time producing the food they needed from that land. Imported corn was politically vital to Athens, but bringing it in was left in the hands of men who could play no part in politics and reap no political profit from their actions.

Securing grain supplies was frequently a means of gaining influence within a city. The men who profited were not the traders but those who either protected home supplies (like the Athenians honoured in the decrees referred to above), or secured supplies from outside at a reduced price. Donations of grain are particularly prominent as political counters in the Hellenistic period. One of the most striking cases concerns Protogenes, the man who made himself virtually uncrowned king of the Black Sea city of Olbia. A long decree survives listing all the various benefactions bestowed by Protogenes on his fellow citizens, and these include intervention to secure grain supplies on more than one occasion: 'Again in the priesthood of Pleistarkhos, there was a severe shortage of corn, and grain was being sold at a medimos and two thirds for a gold coin. It was clear that the price would rise further, and in fact the medimnos immediately reached the price of one gold coin and two thirds. Because of this the people were in deep distress and thought it necessary to appoint corn-buyers and to enlist the wealthy to render services for this purpose. When the assembly met Protogenes was the first to promise 1000 gold pieces for the purchase of corn, which he brought and gave on the spot. . . .'[14]

The threat of starvation did more than give an opportunity for a few rich men to win influence by public-spirited benefactions; it threw the whole relationship between town and country into high relief. The community which was pressed into buying corn from outside through the agency of non-citizens was made to realize the extent of its normal dependence upon its own territory. The social disruption produced by shortage underlined the security habitually offered to the city by the agricultural skills of its farmers. Crop failure reinforced the interdependence of the city by showing the town a stark vision of its fate if cut off from its countryside. Neither rich nor poor benefited from dependence upon uncertain supplies from outside the city: the poor faced starvation, the rich the political consequences of a hungry citizen body. The dangers of relying on imported corn were such that they enforced the continuing devotion of the Classical city to an agricultural strategy aimed at subsistence. That subsistence strategy in turn both bound town and country together and imposed low limits on the development of non-agricultural occupations. The under-development of trade and the determination to be self-sufficient in food supplies were closely related one to the other; together they played a large part in shaping both town and country.

The domination of the market

Grain was not the only foodstuff available on the market, and it was not the only foodstuff whose sale was regulated by laws. The following law is preserved from Hellenistic Athens: 'Those who sell Persian nuts, dried almonds, hazelnuts from Herakleia, pine-nuts, chestnuts, Egyptian beans, dates and any other dried fruits that are sold with these, and also lupines, olives, and pine kernels, shall sell them with a measure of a capacity of three half choinikes of grain levelled off [1 choinix = approximately 1.1 litres], selling them with this choinix heaped up, with a depth of five fingers and a width at the rim of one finger. Similarly those who sell fresh almonds, newly

picked olives and dried figs must sell them with a choinix heaped full, twice the size of the previously mentioned one, with a rim three half-fingers wide, and they must use measures made of wood. If anyone sells fresh almonds, newly picked olives or dried figs in any other way or with another type of measure, he must not sell less than a medimnos of grain. If he sells in a smaller type of measure, the magistrate under whose supervision he is shall immediately sell the contents by auction, pay the price to the public bank and destroy the measure.'[15]

Several of the things listed in the law will have been grown locally in Attica, particularly the olives and figs. Most Athenian citizens probably had olive trees of their own, however, and few Athenian farmers are likely to have made more than a marginal contribution to their domestic economy by selling olives, figs or almonds in the market. Nevertheless there are signs that in some parts of Greece, crops other than wheat and barley formed an important part of the agricultural strategy of the farmer, and that selling these crops involved the farmer in the market and created a relationship between town and country which contrasted with that prevailing when agriculture was dominated by cereals.

To illustrate this it is necessary to return to the island of Thasos and its vines. Two separate inscriptions from fifth-century Thasos relate to the wine trade. The first inscription is poorly preserved, but it is clear that it made some provision about trade in wine and in vinegar. The offence involved is unclear, but the penalty had to be paid in kind to the two gods whose sanctuaries on the acropolis dominated the town of Thasos. The law specifically provides that those prosecuted under it may not plead ignorance of the law.

The second inscription is better preserved;

part of it reads as follows: 'No one is to buy grape juice or wine from the crop still on the vines before the first day of the month called Plynterion. Anyone who buys in contravention of this is to be fined stater for stater. Half the fine to go to the city and half to the successful prosecutor. The case is to be tried in the same way as cases of violence. Purchasing wine in pithoi [wide-mouthed jars] is legal as long as the pithoi are sealed.'[16] The rest of this stone contains three prohibitions: wine may not be watered down; Thasian ships may not bring foreign wine into the area between Cape Athos and Cape Pakhys; and small quantities of wine may not be sold from a larger container, whether amphora, large jar, or 'false pithos'.

These various rather mixed regulations are all written from the point of view of the consumer. They reflect and institutionalize the suspicion of the small trader which seems to have been very common in all Greek cities. All have to do with the purchaser discovering that the wine he has bought is not all that it makes itself out to be – that it is vinegar and not wine, or that it has been watered down. The insistence upon sealed containers gives the aggrieved consumer some chance of redress.

Two provisions invite further discussion: the prohibition on trading in a forward market and the prohibition on Thasian ships carrying foreign wine look at first sight like public intervention to control the trade and protect Thasian interests. There is no Classical Greek parallel for the prohibition on trading in a forward market. In its own right such a prohibition might be a piece of bureaucracy aimed at closer control of wine production for fiscal purposes, or it might be a measure against a covert form of usury. The context, however, suggests that it, too, is to do with quality of goods and that it is trying to elimin-

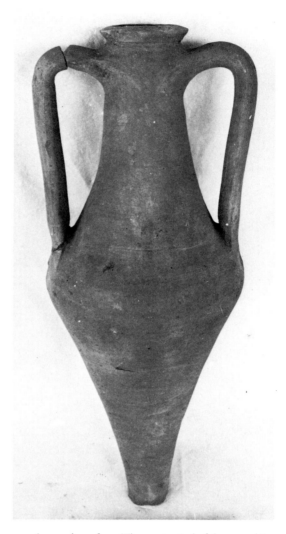

34 An amphora from Thasos, typical of those used in the Thasian wine trade.

*35 Potteries manufacturing amphorae in large
quantities have been found all round the island of
Thasos. This spread of sherds of coarse pottery marks
one such pottery workshop, at Koukos on the south
coast of the island.*

*36 The administration of the city of Thasos in the
later Classical period seems to have demanded that all
amphorae be stamped on one handle. Two examples
of such stamps are shown here, one with a plough and
the other with a kantharos (wine cup). The
magistrates' names, Aiskhron and Heraklei(os),
indicated the year in which the amphora was made.*

ate another possible traders' excuse for the wine they sell not being up to standard. Similarly the control of the wine which Thasian bottoms can carry is probably not an unparalleled piece of protectionism. Rather than forestalling competition from foreign wine, this law may be a rather drastic way of making sure that wine that claims to be Thasian really is Thasian.

The scale of official interference with Thasian wine production and exchange is confirmed by the archaeological evidence. About a dozen kiln sites have now been found all round the island which manufactured the amphorae in which Thasian wine was transported. Throughout the Classical period such amphorae were stamped with a stamp indicating both the potter and the date. Early stamps took a variety of forms, but from the middle of the fourth century the date was indicated by a magistrate's name, and the potter indicated by a symbol which changed annually. The stamp was applied before firing, and it appears on tiles as well as amphorae (not all amphorae, however). The stamp cannot have referred to or guaranteed the content, and no ordinary Thasian will have been able to follow the changing potters' stamps closely enough to determine which amphora came from which pottery. All in all this seems to be a very complicated piece of official control of potting for a very uncertain end. It is indicative, however, of the extent of interference surrounding the wine trade, and may indicate its fiscal importance – on the not unreasonable hypothesis that the stamp represents a tax.

Wine production must have bulked quite large in Thasian agriculture. Farmers no doubt tried to meet their own cereal demands from their land, but they seem also to have produced large quantities of wine for the market. In terms of the economy as a whole

Thasian wine must have made a trival contribution compared with silver, and the various laws are all concerned with home-consumed rather than export wine. The absolute quantities of wine consumed and produced were not trivial, however. The scale of amphora production is enough to show that, and the part it played in the agricultural strategies of the farmers had a profound effect on relations between town and country.

Earlier chapters have argued that geography and geology both encouraged a striking divorce between town and country on Thasos. The wine laws suggest that this divorce was reinforced by the agricultural strategy. The laws on the wine trade were promulgated from the town. The fines in kind paid under the fifth-century law go to the sanctuaries on the town acropolis. The stamps for the amphorae were centrally manufactured and distributed from the town to the potters. But both wine and amphorae were largely manufactured in the countryside. Central control is thus enforced over the production of the countryside. By choosing to grow vines on a fairly large scale the farmers of Thasos make themselves dependent upon the market, and that means upon the town. Wine is not a staple, and the town is therefore free to make its own stipulations. That is what the quality control regulations do. The town which can choose to buy or not to buy wine is in a different position from the town which must buy corn. Whatever the town of Thasos did for *corn*, it asserted its authority over the countryside when it came to wine.

The Thasian situation makes clear the extent to which the political relations between town and country were bound up both with agricultural strategies and with settlement patterns. The countryside which pursued a strategy aimed primarily at its own subsistence and the subsistence needs of the community as a whole was a countryside upon which the town depended and which had to be respected. Once farmers relied on the market on any scale they jeopardized their independence. On Thasos village communities seem to have been few in the Classical period, and what villages there were do not seem to have had any political status. Such a situation minimizes local contacts and local independence and lays the countryside open to control by the town. In Attica the contrasting agricultural strategy is complemented by the contrasting settlement pattern. The villages of Attica were very strong communities which very largely met their own subsistence needs, and which filled local needs by neighbourly exchange.

The near self-sufficiency of the Athenian village community is well illustrated by both archaeological and literary material. Archaeology knows no markets in the whole territory of Athens outside Athens itself, the port of the Peiraieus, and Sounion (see p. 79). That there were other places where regular exchange was carried on is not unlikely, but it is significant that they have remained unknown. In the literature we have one direct denial of local marketing. At the beginning of the Peloponnesian war, after the Athenians had been shut up in the town by Spartan invasions, Aristophanes wrote a comedy named after one of the Athenian villages, the large village of Akharnai. At the beginning of the play the chief character sits in Athens and gazes wistfully at the countryside. He says he is fed up with the town, he wants peace so that he can get back to his village where no one ever shouts out 'Charcoal for sale', or 'Wine for sale', or 'Oil for sale', or anything else for sale. For a country resident to have to buy was, by this token, an unusual exper-

ience and profoundly disturbing. In the Athens of the years of war with Sparta the importance of the market was abnormally magnified. In other towns, not at war and with a lower proportion of the town population employed in non-agricultural occupations, the disregard for the market found in the Athenian countryside must have invaded even the heart of the city.

The luxury of the town

Exchange in Greek cities was not limited to food. Xenophon generalizes: 'When cities are doing well, men have a strong need for money. The men want to lavish expenditure on fine arms, good horses, and impressive houses and furnishings, while the women turn their attention to expensive clothing and gold jewellery. And when cities are in a bad way, either through crop failure or war, which is even more serious in turning the land to fallow, they need coinage for food supplies and mercenary soldiers.'[17] There was a market for luxury goods, but it was a very restricted one. It was highly localized, economically unimportant, socially limited, and dependent upon the existence and state of trade in more vital goods. It was also an urban phenomenon.

The range of goods available in Athens was enormous. The resources of the entire Greek world could be tapped. This range is one of the features incidentally revealed when Theophrastos puts luxury goods firmly in their context in ridiculing the man who: 'buys nothing for himself, but for foreign friends he purchases on commission pickled olives to go to Byzantion, Spartan hounds for Kyzikos, and Hymettan honey for Rhodes. And he tells the whole town about it as he does so. He is a great one for having a monkey and getting a little ape, Sicilian doves, knucklebones made of gazelle horn, oil flasks of the rounded shape from Thourioi in south Italy, walking sticks that have a special twist from Sparta, and a curtain with Persians woven into it . . . .'[18]

Luxury goods were prestige items, the means of conspicuous display. They were irrelevant to the peasant bound up in the countryside of agricultural production. They have only a limited place even in the inventories of the rich landowners discussed in Chapter 1. But for the man who wanted to make an impression on his neighbourhood in the city, or who turned his house into a public meeting place for eminent foreign intellectuals, luxury goods became essentials.

No other city could attract the variety of luxury goods from other places which was available at Athens. But everywhere some goods were available which were conspicuous markers of social distinctions. The most widely distributed of such goods was fine pottery. Most communities of any size produced some pottery of their own. Often local pottery production depended upon the initiative of a landowner who found a source of good clay on his land. The quantity of pottery produced locally might be quite considerable, but the quality was rarely high. This was pottery for use, not for display. The manufacture of fine pottery was far less widespread. In exceptional cases the demand created by a sanctuary, for example, might lead to production of a restricted range of fine pottery in the countryside. This seems to have been the case at the sanctuary of Artemis at Brauron, and it may also have been true of the Kabirion near Thebes in Boiotia (see Chapter 8). But decorated pottery was rarely a product of the countryside.

For most of the Classical period the market for fine pottery was dominated by the output of the potters at Athens itself, where an entire ward (deme) of the town was called 'The Pot-

ters.' Pottery is difficult to destroy, and so the export of Athenian pots is very well documented by their remains. Despite the millions of pots made in and exported from Athens, however, pottery can never have made a significant mark on the Athenian economy. Pots can be manufactured very quickly, even when each is shaped individually, and the evidence for the price of pottery suggests that potters must have worked very efficiently in order to survive. A measure of the trivial economic importance of pottery manufacture is the fact that the number of men involved in making and painting pots at any one time in Athens was probably never more than 200.

Fine pottery is important for its social role. No one needed decorated pottery. The decision to buy an Athenian vase was a decision to display the fact that one had money to spare. It was also a way of showing that one was a man of taste. Some pottery purchase was certainly made in a competitive spirit: a vase that was dedicated to a god stood to be compared with vases dedicated by others; the pots used in burials, whether in or on the grave, were displayed to the community which would measure them by the local standards set by other burials. Purchases of pots did not simply show that one had money to spare; they showed how one chose to spend the money. Little Athenian pot decoration was simply pretty. The scenes painted on pots show considerable sophistication and make demands on the viewer. The subject matter chosen, and its composition, were adapted to the shape of the pot, and scenes often set up serious puzzles for the viewer, demanding that he or she use a considerable knowledge of mythology in the interpretation of what was depicted.

A very simple example will illustrate this. Figure 37 shows two sides of an amphora produced in the very late sixth century at Athens by a man named Phintias. On one side there are four male athletes. One has a discus, two have javelins, and one, dressed and carrying a stick, is a trainer. At first sight this is a simple illustration of how wealthy young Athenians spent much of their time. When we look at the other side, however, matters become more complicated. Again there are four figures, two male on the left side, two female on the right. The central male figure is carrying off the central female figure and is being restrained by the male figure behind him. As on the other side of the vase some of the figures are named, but here the names are of gods not of men: the figure on the left is

37 This Attic red-figure vase by Phintias dates to the very end of the sixth century. On one side (right) it shows the goddess Leto seized by Tityos and about to be rescued by her children Apollo and Artemis. On the other (left) a bearded man in a cloak leans on a stick and watches as three younger men practise with discus and javelins.

Apollo, the woman being carried off Leto. The figure with the bow on the right-hand side is not named, but 'Shame' is written beside her. This scene presents the viewer with a number of puzzles. It is quite possible to get the gist of the story, rape, without deciphering the precise episode involved. The naming of Apollo and Leto steers the viewer in the right direction and together with the attributes given to her prompt the identification of the right-hand figure as Artemis. But if the viewer wants a name for the rapist, he must draw it from his own knowledge of who tried to rape Leto.

The reticence of the artist about the identity of the central figure ties the two scenes on the pot together. By refusing to declare openly that this bearded man belongs to a separate world of myth, the artist prompts the connection of this man with the ordinary Greeks shown on the other side. The vase as a whole can be seen as an exploration of male pursuits. The rape scene provides a quizzical and cheeky answer to the question, 'What are these young men training for?' Each scene stands on its own, but together they constitute a provocative juxtaposition which questions the separation of real and mythical worlds.

Vases such as this demand the viewer's involvement. They require that the viewer is literate and educated. To purchase such a vase and miss its references is likely to be more

embarrassing than not having a decorated pot at all. The vase plays on the urban world: for the peasant farmer the gymnasium was almost as remote as the world of the gods. Virtually no fine pottery makes any reference to the life, occupations or pre-occupations of the farmer (see Chapter 1). In terms of price and availability decorated pottery was not exotic, but the nature of its painted scenes meant that it appealed to precisely the same market as exotic luxury goods.

Luxury goods distinguish town and country just as much as foodstuffs. They do so, however, because they are *not* items exchanged between town and country rather than because they are. The town provides the main market for luxury goods not made in the city; the town is the place where fine pottery is manufactured; and the town is the place where pottery and exotica are consumed. Luxury goods are a mark of urbanity, available to and appreciated only by those whose lives are not tied to producing food for their own subsistence. It is freedom from peasant toil that enables time to be devoted to education, travel, and the cultivation of the body; it is the possession of surplus usable wealth that enables the purchase of non-essential goods; and it is leisure time which enables the formation of social ties which give a forum for effective display of distinction in learning and taste.

Plato, in the *Laws*, says that trade is beneficial because it makes good deficiencies and equals out what is unequal. In this chapter I have tried to show that that statement is both true and false. It is clearly true, in a material sense, of trade in grain, and it is true to a certain extent of trade in other foodstuffs. It is certainly not at all true of trade in luxury goods. It is false in another way even of the grain trade. Town and country were not equated by the exchange of staple foodstuffs; rather, their distinctive contributions were made abundantly clear. The country which meets the town's need for grain establishes its special position in the life of the city. The town which chooses to purchase the wine produced by the countryside establishes its domination over the men who own the vineyards. The town which displays its capacity to purchase and appreciate luxury goods stakes a claim to be culturally distinct.

No city could exist without exchange: both town and country depended on it. But exchange did not leave the city unmarked. The city resolved its problems of supply at a price, the price of bringing into the open the relations of town and countryside, and of displaying the distinctions between them. How far these distinctions became clear depended upon the precise nature of the town and countryside involved. Few towns were as 'urbane' as Athens, few countrysides as repressed as that of Thasos. Exchange is but one determinant of the relationship between town and country, and it cannot be divorced from the others. It is time to look at the way town and country were explicitly related through political institutions.

6

THE POLITICS
OF SETTLEMENT

The variety of the countryside and the way it was settled, the variety of relations between countryside and town and between whole cities and the world outside, all had direct and indirect influence upon the political organization of, and political life in, individual cities. For ancient authors the important variables that determined political arrangements were agricultural productivity and the dominant life-style. Thucydides, considering the early history of Greece, writes: 'When there was no trade, and men did not mix freely with each other either by land or over the sea, but each cultivated his own land only to the extent to which it gave him enough to live off (men had no surplus wealth and did not plant trees because it was unclear when someone else might come and run off with them since settlements were unwalled), men considered that they could muster their daily food requirements anywhere, and so they moved about without thinking twice about it. Because of this they were strong neither by size of settlement nor by any other preparation. The best land, in particular, was always having changes of inhabitants – places such as what is now called Thessaly and Boiotia, and most of the Peloponnese except Arkadia, and the best of the rest of the country. Because the land was so good one group which grew stronger would stir up strife which destroyed the whole community,

and they were also plotted against by people outside. But Attica, which is for the most part a land of thin soil, was free from strife, and has always been inhabited by the same men.'[1]

Aristotle, in a more sophisticated, but equally abstract, piece of analysis, tries to establish the correlation between dominant mode of production and political constitution: 'After the farming community, the second-best citizen body is that where all are herdsmen and live from animals. This community has a great deal in common with the farming community, and besides, these herdsmen are particularly well trained for war by their habits, and can make use of their physical strength and put up with sleeping rough. Almost all the other groups of people who make up the other sorts of democracy are much worse than these. Their lifestyle is mean – none of the things that people who work in crafts and exchange or labouring do requires moral qualities, and yet this is the tribe, so to speak, which comes to the assembly because it is always milling around the city and the market. The farmers, on the other hand, don't meet or need this meeting place because they are scattered around the countryside. It is easy to make a good democracy and good constitution when the countryside is well separated from the city, for then the people are compelled to reside on the land, and one must not hold assemblies in the democracy without the country people, even if there is a mob of men engaged in trade available in the city.'[2]

This chapter takes up the questions raised by Thucydides and Aristotle, and tries to investigate them by a detailed consideration of the political arrangements in a number of individual cities. How close was the correlation between the agricultural regime and the political constitution? How alike were the countrysides of different democratic cities? What difference did the development of the town make? How far were the settlement and the politics of cities affected by what was happening beyond the borders of their territories? But the essential preliminary to answering these questions is an understanding of the variety of the town, for the town was the political centre and had its own political interests which were capable of modifying or opposing the political interests and political force of the farming countryside.

The attractions of the town

'I was with Sokrates when we came upon Euthyphron the seer. Sokrates – you remember, Simmias – started questioning Euthyphron and throwing him into confusion with his jesting as they walked towards the Sumbolon and Andokides' house. But suddenly Sokrates stood still and went silent. He concentrated for a long time and then turned off, and went down the street through the chest-makers, saying to those of his friends who were in front that his divine sign had come to him. Most of those with Sokrates turned off with him, including me for I was near Euthyphron. Some young men of the company, however, went on the way straight ahead to test Sokrates' divine sign and they dragged with them the flautist Kharillos who had come to Athens to Kebes' place with me. As they went through the herm-sculptors by

the law-courts they were met by a whole crowd of pigs, covered with mud, struggling one against the other because they were so numerous. There was no turning off, and the pigs knocked into and knocked over some of them and made the rest thoroughly filthy. Kharillos came home that day with his legs and his cloak all muddy, and we always remember Sokrates' divine sign with laughter and amazement that the god never left or neglected him in any circumstances.'[3]

Ancient Athens presented various faces. This tale throws together the polite society of cultured intellectuals within which Sokrates moved, the public buildings of the law-courts, the craftsmen who made chests, the sculptors and masons who made the stone pillars with bearded heads at the top and erect penises in front called herms, and pigs. The story is very probably not true, but the scene is real enough.

The street of the herm-sculptors has a good chance of being one of the few streets of Classical Athens that has been excavated and published. American excavations from 1939-49 uncovered some $\frac{3}{4}$ hectare of the ancient town to the southwest of the Classical political centre of the agora. One of the ancient streets which was revealed proved to be a small craft centre, with abundant evidence for the working of marble, bronze, and bone. Some of the buildings seemed to be residential, others only workshops. One building stood out for its very much more substantial construction, and may have been a public building in the middle of the muddle of private development.

Finds from the excavation give a very strong impression of the gap between the private and public faces of Athens. From the house called House D, which was a centre for bronze working and some marble sculpting, came two significant discoveries. Beneath the floor of the court of the house was a shallow pit. The bottom and sides of the pit were reddened by the fire that had been burnt in it, and inside were cinders, charcoal and burnt pieces of pottery. This was the scene of the cremation of a small child sometime in the third quarter of the fifth century. In the room at the back of this court was a piece of folded lead. It was inscribed in good fourth-century lettering with the following curse: 'May Aristaikhmos the bronzesmith go to Hades, and Pyrrhias the bronzesmith, and his workshop, and their souls, and Sosias from Lamia, and his workshop, and his soul, and . . . (illegible) fervently, fervently, and Hagesion the Boiotian woman.'[4]

Athens was a cosmopolitan community with high infant mortality. Those facts alone made for tensions such as are displayed in different ways by the home burial of the infant and by the curse. Sudden death, cramped conditions, migrant workers and curses were part of everyday life for many townsmen in Athens, but until dug up and exhibited before us they lie below the surface of our perceptions.

The squalor of Athens even came as a shock to some ancient travellers: 'The town itself is all dry and does not have a good water supply. The streets are narrow and winding as they were built long ago. Most of the houses are cheaply built, and only a few reach a higher standard. A stranger would find it hard to believe at first sight that this was the famous town of Athens.'[5] Although the areas where people actually lived and carried on their crafts were unattractive to this traveller, they were for many part of what made Athens attractive. The migrants who got on one Athenian's nerves had come because Athens seemed preferable to life in Thessaly or Boiotia. Temporary and permanent residents were attracted to Athens from all

over the Greek world: they were also attracted from the countryside of Attica. But Athens had more to offer than simply smoke and din, death and quarrels.

Athens provided facilities for public life on a lavish scale and within a carefully planned space. No other city could match the display of conspicuous expenditure involved in the vast building programme of the middle of the fifth century. This had left the city equipped with the largest and most elaborately decorated temple on the Greek mainland, the Parthenon, built of marble from foundations to gables. It had also extended monumental architecture from the celebration of the gods to the celebration of the routine business of the citizens running the city. Elaborate winged porticos of marble shaped and dominated the public space in which the Athenians carried out their daily business. Athens offered all the services that could be desired: a large market place, cult centres for a whole range of gods and goddesses, gymnasia, a theatre, offices for all the various magistrates, courtrooms, and the space in which the assembled citizen body met to deliberate on political issues. That all this attracted men from other cities was, in a way, entirely just. For the attractions of Athens were in part only possible because in the fifth century Athens could and did draw on the resources of an empire extending well beyond the confines of her own territory of Attica.

Other cities looked very different and had different attractions: 'If the city of the Spartans were deserted, leaving just the temples and the foundations of buildings, I think that in time to come future generations would find it hard to believe that Sparta was as powerful as its fame suggests. Yet the Spartans do indeed control two fifths of the Peloponnese, are leaders of the whole of it, and of many allies outside. It would appear weaker than this because the town is not compactly settled and lacks expensively equipped shrines or private buildings. It is but a group of villages in the old Greek fashion. On the other hand, if the same thing were to happen to the Athenians one would reckon the power of the city as twice what it is from the remains on view.'[6]

Sparta was as extreme an example of a Classical town as Athens. Most Greek towns lay in between, with some striking public buildings and some industrial quarters and commercial centres. But the relative prominence of public and private enterprise varied considerably from place to place. Two examples will illustrate this.

Olynthos, in northern Greece, is one of the Classical towns about which we know most. It has been extensively excavated and it is responsible for much of what we know about the appearance of residential areas in Greek towns. But apart from fountain houses and one or two anomalous structures, we have no clear idea of the provision of public facilities. The excavations uncovered part of the old town of Olynthos, with small irregular houses, and part of the 'new' planned town of the fifth and fourth centuries, laid out in regular blocks of some 300 by 120 Ionic feet (88 × 35 m). These blocks were divided into two rows of five houses, each house being about 60 feet square. Although no two houses were identical all were built up together, with a common network of continuous rubble foundation walls for the whole block. The general appearance must have been quite different from that of the 'industrial' quarter of Athens, but the surface uniformity at Olynthos hid a similar diversity. Many houses seem to have been used only for residential purposes, but others were devoted to productive or retail functions. A number of houses had a small room fronting onto the street which

was not linked directly to the house interior; the number of coins found in these rooms makes it clear that they were small shops. The finds from these shops rarely reveal what was sold, and this suggests that the shops were operated by middle-men who bought in goods ready-made and sold them again rather than producing or processing goods on the spot. Other houses had been more radically altered and had facilities for production. But not all the production was industrial: the eastern half on one house seems to have been devoted to processing agricultural products and was equipped with a full-scale olive or grape press. This press may have belonged to a farmer resident in the town, but the urban location of the facilities would have enabled him to offer them to other town-dwellers on a commercial, or a non-commercial, basis.

The remains of Classical Corinth give an impression very different again. The whole town is dominated by the acropolis of Akrocorinth with its fortifications and temple of Aphrodite, and the lower town by the Archaic temple of Apollo. But other public facilities have left far less of a mark. This is not simply because the Classical market place has not been found or excavated. The Corinthians never inscribed their political decisions on stone, and so political activity was always relatively invisible. What has been well revealed at Corinth is the ancient town as a centre of production and redistribution.

On the very western edge of the town, close to the wall and some 2 km from the temple of Apollo, lay the potters' quarter. The area is well supplied with clay and water. As early as 700 works had been carried out to secure provision of a supply of standing water, and a group of potters must have collaborated to see to this. At the end of the seventh century first one and then a second long building was constructed. These long buildings seem to have been used by a number of potters, but although they shared some facilities the individual craftsmen worked separately. The buildings served as shops as well as places of manufacture. The town clearly offered these potters facilities and a market which they would not have had if working individually in the villages of the territory, but coming to the town certainly did not throw them into the political life of the centre. Their situation contrasts with that of the potters at Athens who were hard by the political centre of the agora and the cemetery of the Kerameikos, which was the scene of much public political display through the public burial of, and monuments to, citizens who died in war.

Much closer to the centre of things in Corinth lay a dramatic example of the town as a centre for redistribution. At the southwest

corner of what was later the Roman forum was a fifth-century building which has been named the Punic amphora building because of the number of these storage vessels found there. The building began life in the middle of the fifth century as a house with some space devoted to stocks of amphorae packed with fish – tunny and sea bream. Rapidly the commercial aspect took over as the building was modified and entirely devoted to the fish trade. When the fish had been sold there seems to have been no use for the amphorae; they were broken up and dumped in one of the rooms. As well as Punic amphorae, there

38 Panopeus in Phokis, whose status as a city is doubted by Pausanias, possesses a fourth-century acropolis wall. This is in a good state of preservation which 'deserves to rank with the best in Greece' (Frazer). The entire south and west sides of the fortification are preserved, stretching over some 400 m.

were an equal number of amphorae made on Khios and a rather smaller number from the Khersonesos. The business did not last for long, but it must have been more or less typical of the sort of enterprise going on all over Greek towns. Only in the town did the demand exist that could justify such specialization by merchants, and only in towns where many other sorts of goods were moving around all the time did the mechanisms of supply exist which made such enterprises possible.

However, the essential services which the town provided were not commercial but political. Corinth was seen by other Greeks as exceptionally tolerant of trade and 'industry.' It was lack of political facilities which put the status of 'town' in jeopardy. 'From Khaironeia you come in 4 km to the town of Panopeus in Phokis – if a place with no political buildings, no place for athletics, no theatre, no market square and no fountains, which is perched on the edge of a violent river, can be called a town. Still the territory has boundary stones with its neighbours, and they send delegates to the Phokian assembly.'[7] Despite Pausanias' remarks Panopeus was a town not entirely without attractions. Its extensive acropolis walls, built in the fourth century, are among the finest of any town in mainland Greece, and it is clear that the city chose to make expenditure on defence rather than on monumentalizing its political activity. This choice was not surprising given the endemic raiding which prevailed in this area of the country (see Chapter 7), but it was a choice which clearly had an important bearing on politics and who ran the city.

Sparta and Athens, Olynthos, Corinth and Panopeus all attracted residents in different ways. The social structure of the towns differed accordingly. But in consequence so did the social structure of the country. The politi-

cal implications of the variations in Classical Greek towns can be fully appreciated only when those towns are reinserted into their countryside. The following sections explore the overall nature and pattern of settlement in a number of rather different Greek cities and look at the political consequences.

Patterns of elite rule

Arkadian Orkhomenos stood on a hill dominating the plain below. Inside an extensive ring of fortifications were a political meeting place (agora) with long open porticos on two sides, a small temple of Artemis, and a theatre. One of the porticos may have been the meeting place for the council. Here religious and political buildings stand next to a theatre used not only for dramatic performances but also for other public meetings. Almost certainly there were no residential buildings within the walls. By the time of the traveller Pausanias the citizens of Orkhomenos lived below the walls on the south side of the hill, where there is today a straggling village.

The countryside of Orkhomenos is not well known. It had some monuments and sanctuaries, but it is less clear how far there were village settlements. Pausanias mentions 'a place called Amilos which they say was once a city'[8] at a point where the roads leading to Orkhomenos from Pheneos and Stymphalos joined. Traces of what may be Amilos have been found, and it may have been part of the city of Orkhomenos. An inscription from the fourth century which records the union of Orkhomenos and Euaimnion makes arrangements about a settlement called Khairiades, and this must have been dependent on either Orkhomenos or Euaimnion. Orkhomenos should probably be envisaged as consisting of a political centre which was heavily fortified, with an adjacent central settlement, and a territory including one or two sizeable communities which merited a name but were not politically independent.

Orkhomenos was ruled by an oligarchy. It was a faithful ally of Sparta during both the fifth and early fourth centuries. Its inscriptions talk of 'the city of the Orkhomenians' rather than 'the people of Orkhomenos.' The most important magistrates were called 'overseers' (*thearoi*), and the year was named after one of these. The nature of the political decisions made by the city is extremely revealing about the interests of those who possessed political power.

The most important political documents from Orkhomenos are the decree about uniting with Euaimnion, a decree defining the borders of Orkhomenos with another city, probably Torthyneion, and a group of eleven

decrees giving citizens of other cities privileged rights among the Orkhomenians. Classical cities frequently passed such decrees, but the identity of those honoured in this way at Orkhomenos is particularly revealing. Eight of the decrees honour men from neighbouring or nearby cities. Two are for men from Kaphyai which shares a border with Orkhomenos to the northwest, and the other six are for citizens, all in Arkadia, of Lousoi, Alea, Megalopolis, and Tegea, and of Argos and Pellene just outside. In one case the decree does not preserve the name of the community from which the man honoured came. In the other two cases the honorific status is used in a different way to deal with special

39 Carved into the side of the hill on which the town stood, the theatre of Orkhomenos was almost certainly the scene of political meetings and dramatic displays.

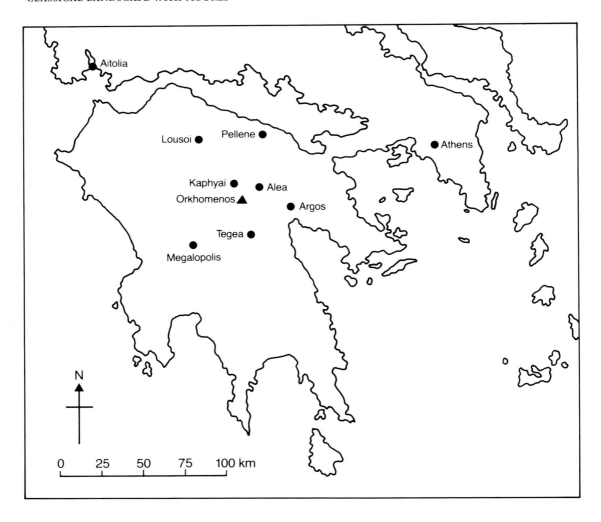

40 *The cities from which those men honoured at Orkhomenos came show the way in which those in power at Orkhomenos bestowed privileges predominantly upon the wealthy members of local communities.*

circumstances which had brought special obligations: one decree honours three Athenian ambassadors, the other four Aitolians.

That the people of Orkhomenos should forge good links with neighbouring communities by honouring their members makes sense. Citizens of Orkhomenos obviously had most to do with people who lived nearby, and these honours are positive ways of asserting their political independence, and are complementary to the laying down of carefully defined boundaries with a neighbour. The honours benefit some parts of the community more than others, however. The men honoured were men of high status in their own communities – there is, after all, little point in cultivating good relations with men who have no clout at home. These men are given the right to own land, pasture sheep, and in one case gather wood, in the territory of Orkhomenos. When given to Athenians or Aitolians these are merely generous honours. When given to members of nearby communities they are very real privileges, privileges which the recipient will feel obliged to repay with further benefactions towards citizens of Orkhomenos. The men who are most likely to benefit from these continued attentions are men who themselves move around the neighbouring cities – the same men of high status who were themselves likely to be honoured with a special relationship by one of these other communities. Honouring rich men is a way of attracting honours for one's own wealthy men. But the Orkhomenian peasant farmer does not have much to rejoice about. As a result of the privileges granted to these foreigners he will now face still greater competition for grazing and wood-gathering.

Political activity in Orkhomenos was divorced from daily life; political decisions were taken in a space which was not the space of residence, trade or manufacture. No citizens lived within the wall which enclosed the political buildings, and a fair proportion may have lived in villages in the countryside. The restriction of political activity in space was closely related to its restriction to the hands of relatively few of the citizens. The city provided lavishly for political activities with buildings which have left substantial remains visible today. Political decisions were inscribed and prominently displayed on stone pillars. But politics did not involve the citizen body or invite involvement. Politics was managed by the few and presented to the many as a *fait accompli*, to be admired but not questioned. Politics was thus both divided off and divisive. Those in power used that power to control access to and use of the land of Orkhomenos. They thereby strengthened their bonds with the men of high status in neighbouring communities and reinforced their own status and political control in Orkhomenos.

The situation at Orkhomenos, about which we are well informed, was almost certainly not uncommon in Arkadia. The other Arkadians given privileged status at Orkhomenos will have found the political situation there quite familiar. Both the prominence and the isolation of the political buildings would have been paralleled in their communities, and they themselves would have indulged in the same game or political honours. This is not, however, the only pattern of elite rule.

In Orkhomenos residence close to the political centre was not forbidden; there was simply little to make it attractive. In Sparta, on the other hand, the settlement of the landscape was strictly regulated. Spartan citizens had to reside in Sparta itself. The dependent workforce of helots had to reside on or close to the land that they tilled. The other communities of *perioikoi*, dwellers-around, had no political rights to attract them to Sparta, and no reason to want to live with the helots. They resided in their own villages. This divorce between town and country is one of the pervasive organizing features of Spartan society.

All Spartan boys received a common education from the age of seven onwards. This inculcated obedience and a competitive spirit, and produced highly disciplined citizen infantry. No Spartan engaged in any craft,

41 This late seventh-century votive terracotta statuette of Artemis Orthia comes from the sanctuary at Sparta which was the scene of much competitive display in the education of young Spartan boys.

trade, or agricultural activity. His food was produced from his land by helots whom he controlled but did not own. The countryside was essential to every Spartiate as the source of the contributions they were obliged to make to the communal mess, but all a Spartan ever did in the country was fight. He fought both openly on the battlefield in military struggles against other cities, and secretly in the continual war declared on the helots themselves (see Chapter 7).

The helot was condemned to the countryside. In some ways helots differed little from ordinary peasant farmers. They could own property, form families, and keep a proportion of the produce of the land they tilled. But they had no independence and

were compelled constantly to display their subordinate status by wearing rough animal pelts and dogskin caps. For the helot there was effectively no possibility of improving his status, and no possibilty of an active community life.

The few services the Spartan soldiers required were provided by the *perioikoi*. The villages of *perioikoi* were the places where craftsmen lived who met the Spartan need for metal goods (especially weapons), textiles, and the like. The *perioikoi* had their own land and were effectively self-governing, although they had no possibility of initiative in foreign policy. The Spartan treatment of *perioikoi* was generous compared with that of the helots, but there was no way a member of a perioikic community could become a Spartan citizen.

Spartan society was rigidly stratified: the undifferentiated body of Spartan citizens at the top; the *perioikoi* in the middle; the equally undifferentiated mass of helots at the bottom. Spartan settlement was equally stratified: the Spartan town, the perioikic villages, and the helot settlements (possibly villages, possibly farmsteads). In theory the town ruled the countryside as Spartiate ruled helot. In practice all the strata were confused. Spartiates were not all equal – some were rich, some poor, some lost citizen rights and formed a group that was neither citizen nor perioikic. The town was the town least distinct from the countryside of any town in Greece: it did not even have the massive walls which distinguished Panopeus. There was almost nothing in the way of monumental architecture to display the activities of the citizen body. More fundamentally the hierarchy was reversed in vital ways: essentially, the country ruled the town. The helot population represented a constant threat to their Spartan oppressors. The Spartans could not live without them, but it could not trust them either. Because of this fear the Spartans were compelled to live together as a group in the town. They were compelled to maintain higher standards of military preparation than any other Greek city. And they were compelled to draw a cloak of secrecy over their political activities. For the Spartan citizen the attractions of the town had to be regarded as distractions; the town that was divorced from the countryside had to avoid the political display and involvement with trades and services which elsewhere marked out the urbane life of the town.

The cases of Orkhomenos and Sparta illustrate in different ways that oligarchy was as divisive of settlement as it was of the citizen body. In Orkhomenos political activity is separate from residence and the men with power exploit the countryside for their own ends. In Sparta the whole citizen body is divided off from the countryside, but in order to oppress that countryside effectively it has to divorce the town as political centre from the town of commerce and manufacture. In democracies, on the other hand, although the ideology of the undivided citizen body reintegrates the town, it does not always reintegrate the country.

Democracy and the hierarchy of settlement

In Classical Thasos the countryside was oppressed by the town even though the political regime was democratic. Democracy was deeply rooted on Thasos. In 411 those who were responsible for the oligarchic revolution at Athens forced the Thasians to change to an oligarchic constitution, but the Thasians preferred to revolt from the Athenian empire and restore democracy rather than to remain loyal and accept oligarchy. Later legislation shows the Thasians taking active measures against home-bred oli-

garchic sympathizers. Although much smaller than Athens, Thasos too elected a very large number of annual magistrates. At the top were the *arkhons*, the '*theoroi*' (overseers) and a body known as the 300. In administrative capacities we find men known as '*karpologoi*', '*demiourgoi*', 'regulators of the women', 'regulators of the market', 'receivers', 'supervisors', 'sacred registrars', 'accountants', 'generals' and 'men in charge of the gymnasium'.

All the administrative personnel were concentrated on the town. The town monumentalized the wealth of the city – through the town wall, through the enormous number of sanctuaries both on the acropolis and in the lower town, and through a spacious agora. The town possessed the only harbour which the city thought it fit to regulate by law. The most concentrated residential centre on the island, the town was the place of political decision-making, military defence, public religious activity, and the exchange of goods. But it was the mineral and agricultural wealth extracted from the countryside which made all this possible.

Geography and the pattern of settlement combined to undermine political equality on Thasos. In theory there were apparently no obstacles to full political participation by all Thasian citizens. In practice the people of the town exploited those of the country. Communication over the mountainous island was slow and difficult. Effectively the only way to move from one side of the island to the other was by sea. Journeys to the town became major expeditions and could not be undertaken with any frequency. Services were concentrated in the town. The only features of the countryside recorded on a signpost inscription found at Alikí are two sanctuary sites. Those who were not compelled themselves to labour in the fields or mines or quarries for their living, but could afford to oversee from a distance the exploitation of the resources they owned, could yield to the attractions of the town and take advantage of its facilities. Those engaged in actually extracting the surplus from the land could not. Because villages were underdeveloped in the Thasian countryside, no other centre could offer anything like the range of services available in the town. Since there were no centres for local loyalties to focus upon, it was inevitable that both political and social arrangements would undervalue the labouring countryside.

The very different nature of the social organization in a landscape where villages are well developed is nicely illustrated by the situation in Elis in the western Peloponnese. Elis was always a rather odd city. It had the panhellenic sanctuary at Olympia in its territory, and this was a source of local strife within the city. Elis was made up of the distinct regions of Hollow Elis, Pisatis, and Triphylia, and almost all we know of the early relations between these regions is that there were repeated struggles over control of Olympia. Only in the fifth century were the regions united as a single city: Diodoros in his *World History* dates the union of the earlier smaller cities to 471 BC. The union was not accomplished without a struggle: Herodotos says that in his own time the Eleians had sacked many of the cities of the area.

The formation of a new city in the fifth century seems to have had little major effect on settlement. Archaeological investigation has made it clear that the town of Elis itself was by no means a new foundation of the

42 A view of the panhellenic sanctuary at Olympia in Elis, looking up the valley of the river Kladeos and showing something of the landscape of central Elis.

Classical period. The site had been occupied in the Bronze Age, and it was reoccupied in the Geometric period and continuously inhabited from then on. It is equally clear that other major settlements in the territory of the new city were not deserted after the union. What happened was a change at the organizational level.

Something of the organization of Elis in the Classical period emerges from inscriptions on bronze preserved at Olympia. The most remarkable is a document of 450–25, which apparently regulates relations between the village of Skillous and two officials who seem to be officers of Elis. The relations between Elis and this village in its territory are likened at one point to relations between Elis and the quite independent city of Mantineia. That the villages of the territory should be able to negotiate with the magistrates of the city in this way, acting almost as independent political units, would be unthinkable in any other city. Yet this may not be an isolated case. Another inscription, written in the Eleian dialect, is an agreement between two communities which are otherwise unknown. It is not certain that the two communities involved are in Elis, but the active part played by the sanctuary at Olympia in the agreement makes this quite likely.

These inscriptions suggest that Elis had a very loose political organization, and that the separate villages had a strong degree of independence. This picture is further substantiated by the description of Elis given by the historian Polybios, writing in the second century: 'The land of the Eleians was particularly thickly inhabited. It supported a larger population and more rural establishments than the rest of the Peloponnese. Some of the inhabitants were so enamoured of country life that they, being sufficiently prosperous, had not taken any part in politics for two or three generations. This came about because those who were involved in politics had taken great thought and concern for those living in the country. They had made provision for disputes to be settled on the spot and ensured that those in the country did not lack the necessities of life.'[9]

The settlement pattern of Elis reflects the strength of the village centres and the wide variety of services which the villages were able to provide. In the area around the modern town of Makrysia, which is almost certainly the site of ancient Skillous, there have been extensive finds of Classical material over a wide area. The land immediately round the village was clearly heavily occupied. The same appears to be the case in the one area of Elis which has been systematically surveyed. This is the area around Eleian Pylos (modern Armatova). Pylos itself was certainly an important centre from the eighth century on, but much of the Classical population nevertheless chose to have a base in the countryside around. Some of these Classical sites are very close to Pylos itself. The famed prosperity of Elis may in part have been a product of this pattern of exploitation: the naturally rich soils encouraged intensive exploitation, and the political arrangements enabled men to live out on the land and devote themselves to farming. Because the villages were only loosely linked together, and because they retained a high degree of independence, they had a very strong sense of community identity. The village itself made many of the decisions which affected the lives of local people, and it did not simply act as an administrative unit enabling the city to run its own institutions effectively. Because of this men could continue to dwell for all or part of the year outside the village centre, without losing touch with the group which made the vital decisions.

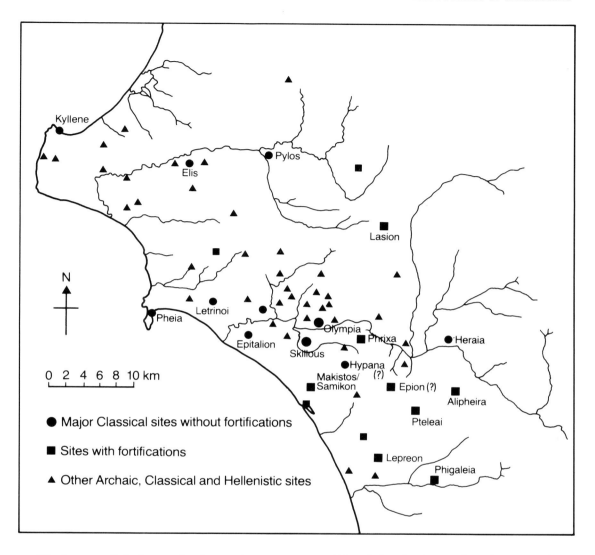

The loose political organization and strong villages of Elis show one way in which city organization could be carried on while respecting the integrity of the countryside. But there was a price to be paid. The independence of the local community was extremely advantageous for the running of day–to–day affairs at home, but it stood in the way of efficient decision-making on matters of foreign policy. It is in part the greater prominence of relations with other cities that

43 Although there has been no intensive systematic survey of Elis, it is clear from chance finds and upstanding monuments that the countryside was thickly settled and heavily exploited in the Classical period.

characterized Athens which accounts for the contrasts between the organization of Eleian and of Athenian democracy.

The political organization of Attica was the most complex of any city in Classical Greece. Fortunately it is also the organization about which we are best informed. Athens is one of the few places on the Greek peninsula where continuity of occupation from the Bronze Age through the Dark Age to the Geometric period can be demonstrated. During the Bronze Age the countryside of Attica had supported a considerable number of settlements, but most, and possibly all, of these were subsequently abandoned. The settlement history of the Geometric and Archaic periods is one of a new colonization of the countryside from Athens. By the sixth century there was a large number of flourishing villages, and there is some sign that regional interests exerted an influence on Athenian politics. At the end of the sixth century there was a major political reorganization, and the democratic organization of Classical Athens was created. The population which had previously been divided into four tribes was now divided into ten. Each of these new tribes was artificially constructed from discrete groups of citizens from different parts of Attica. One third of each tribe came from the area round the city, one third from a coastal area, and one third from an inland area. Every tribal area (trittys) was made up of one or more village (deme). Recognition by the village replaced membership of a kinship group as the criterion for citizenship. All citizens, from whatever village, had the right to assemble in Athens to take political decisions. There was a council which arranged the agenda for these public assemblies and carried out the decisions of the citizens. This council had 500 members drawn from all the villages: the number of representatives sent by a village

was broadly determined by the population of that village.

This organization created a complex network of political bonds. Every village was linked in the first place to the other villages of the same tribe in the same area, in the second place to the other villages of the same tribe in different areas, and in the third place to all the villages of all the tribes in the assembled citizen body. These connections were primarily administrative: the villages and the tribes were convenient units for the preselection of candidates for various magistracies and offices and for army organization. From the point of view of political organization the groups of villages were solely a product of administrative convenience.

The villages were living communities, not artificial creations for political purposes. As the villages varied in size, so they offered varying services to their members. At the top end of the scale were the very large villages like Eleusis or Thorikos, which had theatres, major sanctuaries, military forts, and harbour facilities. At the bottom end of the scale were tiny hamlets which were nothing more than a collection of dwellings. The very large villages certainly provided services not only for their own members but also for those from smaller settlements in the lands around who did not wish to travel in to Athens. All the villages had a political life of their own. Part of their political life simply facilitated the political administration of the city as a whole, but the local community also had its own interests and independent concerns. Villages had their own religious calendars, saw to their own finances, and honoured their own benefactors.

The political reorganization of the late sixth century both recognized the independent existence of local communities throughout Attica and gave those communities a direct role in the running of the whole city. The villages of Attica and their residents were politically empowered by the reform. Men living in distant villages had to contribute to central political life: every village had to provide representatives for the Council of 500. This was no trifling duty either for the villages or for those they sent. The rules for service on the Council were such that every village must have sent well over half its members who survived to over thirty to serve for at least one year of their lives. Councillors had to attend frequent meetings throughout the year, and for one tenth of the year they had to be on constant duty and effectively resident in Athens itself. Putting the village into the centre of political life was a keystone of the democratic extension of political power to all the citizens.

In their independence the villages of Attica resemble those of Elis. But the links between the villages and the central administration of the city were very different. This difference is reflected in the settlement pattern. In the sixth century Attica, like much of mainland Greece perhaps (see Chapter 3), was a countryside settled in village communities rather than isolated establishments. By and large it remained a countryside of villages throughout the Classical period. The spread of small settlement sites around the village, which appears to be common in Elis, is never a feature of the Classical Athenian landscape. In Elis the villages provided services to their members; in Attica the villages provided some political services, but they also demanded further political services for the city as a whole. A man of Elis who chose to live on his land could still keep in close touch with all the political activity that mattered – the activity of the village. The Athenian who removed himself from the local life of the village would have no hope of maintaining an active interest in the central political decisions of the city. In Elis there was no great encouragement to take part in the central politics of the town; in Athens new representatives for the council were demanded from every village at least every other year.

The need for the citizens of Attica to live in villages for political reasons was a powerful conservative control over the settlement pattern. As far as we know the settlement pattern found in Attica in the sixth century was not closely determined by political factors. But after the democratic reforms had given the villages an important role in the political organization of Athens, any change in the patterns of residence had political overtones. When the system was revised and reformed in the late fourth century the changes that were made were very minor. Effectively the political revolution of the late sixth century had imposed a freezing hand over settlement in Attica and had inhibited change. Yet it is precisely during the period from 450 to 300 that fundamental changes in settlement patterns are to be seen in almost all the other areas of the mainland and islands about which we possess detailed information.

The almost static settlement pattern of Classical Attica was combined with considerable changes in society and economy. The town of Athens itself was transformed, not simply by the monumentalization of the political centre and of the Acropolis, but also by the immigration into the town of a large number of Greeks from other cities, and by the increase in the number of Athenians with residences in the town as well as in their home village. The Peiraieus had not even been the main port for the Athenians in the sixth century. By the fourth century it was a centre for exchange quite unlike any other in Greece: a fourth-century writer, Isokrates, claimed that the Peiraieus had 'so much abundance that the things which it is difficult to procure individually from other cities can all be had readily from the Peiraieus.'[10] The silver mines were much further developed during the fifth and fourth centuries, after a lower seam (the so-called 'third contact') had been discovered soon after 500.

All these changes had little effect on patterns of residence. As long as the political organization made it unattractive to leave the villages, the agrarian structure necessarily, as we have seen in Chapter 2, remained wedded to subsistence strategies. Although the Peiraieus offered a new concept in exchange, it is notable that markets are one facility that the large villages of Attica do not pride themselves on possessing (see Chapter 5). The villages had 'agoras', but these seem rarely to have been more than political meeting places (for an exception see p. 79). The services developed in the countryside are more manifestations of the independence of the local community than means of integrating that community with a wider exchange network. Theatres, gymnasia, religious buildings and forts are the monumental additions to the villages during the Classical period, conspicuously displaying civic pride and self-sufficiency. Ironically, it is precisely because of the radical recognition of the countryside as integral to the political machine of the city that settlement in Attica remains unchanged and conservative throughout the Classical period.

44 The monumentalization of the political centre of Athens in the middle of the fifth century also monumentalized the routine activities of ordinary Athenians. The frieze of the Parthenon displays a procession of all Athenians, and it is a procession which has the basic cult activity of animal sacrifice (see pp. 174–184) at its centre. At the east end of the south side, shown here, cattle are led to slaughter.

Thasos, Elis and Athens were all democratic cities, but their democracies worked in very different ways. On Thasos a democratic town virtually ignored the people of the countryside, although it relied on their production. In Elis the democratic village communities were but loosely tied in to the city and the countryside ran itself without central interference. In Attica the town was the place where the major political decisions were made, but the participation of the countryside in those decisions was enforced by the carefully structured political organization. Of course some men in Elis did move in to the town in order to exert greater political influence, especially over relations with other cities. Of course many Athenians who lived far from the town took but a small part in the decisions made there. Nevertheless the contrast between Athens and Elis was almost as great as that between both those cities and Thasos.

The different sorts of democracy correlated with different patterns of settlement. On Thasos and at Athens the shape of the democracy was determined by the nature of the settlement of the countryside at the time democracy was established: lack of villages repressed the Thasian countryside; the presence of villages was a cornerstone of the equality of town and country in Athens. In the case of Elis democracy was built on the pre-existing pattern of village communities, but it enabled the development of that pattern, as the degree of village independence and self-sufficiency encouraged men to move into the country around the villages. In no case was the settlement pattern inevitable. This is most clearly demonstrated in the case of Thasos. In antiquity the town of Thasos was the largest settlement by a very long way, and was the only place in which important decisions for the island were made. In the past

few centuries on the island, however, matters have been very different. Several different settlements in turn have been the seats of island government. The population has not been concentrated on any single settlement, but split between half a dozen or so, more or less equally large, communities. Geography does create problems of communication on Thasos, but the Classical solution to these problems is not the only one. It was a solution adopted not least, it seems, for political reasons.

The pressure of external forces

For some cities political decisions outside their own control were as important as their own choices. Every city aimed at self-sufficiency, but few succeeded. Many cities needed not just food from outside, but also military help and protection from or against more powerful neighbours or imperial cities. These needs created pressures which were reflected both in the political organization and in the settlement pattern.

In the fifth century one major source of such pressures was the Athenian empire. After the great war against the Persians the Athenians took the lead in a League of Greek cities who were determined to drive the Persians out of Asia Minor as well as Greece. In order to pursue this campaign the Athenians extorted first contributions of ships and soldiers and then contributions of money from the allied cites. Cities which resisted were brought to heel by military pressure. Athenian imperialism influenced all the islands of the Aegean: islands in the empire needed a strong administrative structure in order to extract the tribute required from their citizens; islands not in the empire required an equally strong administration in order to secure their continuing independence.

The demands created by the Athenian empire may have influenced settlement on both Thasos and Melos (to take two examples already discussed in this book). Certainly the primacy of the town in Classical Thasos, and the enormous administrative superstructure bases there, were well adapted to meeting Athenian pressure. The town-biased democracy of Thasos was much more suited to the requirements of membership of an empire than the country-biased democracy of Elis. Melos was not a member of the Athenian empire, but it was not exempt from the pressures. The maintenance of independence may have been one of the factors which encouraged the increasing dominance of the settlement at ancient Melos over the rest of the island. Ancient Melos certainly acquired massive fortifications in the Classical period, and these may well mark the insecurity of an island trying to retain its independence in the face of Athenian pressure. Melos in the fifth century needed to be able to make rapid decisions on foreign policy, and such decisions were much facilitated by the concentration of the citizens in a single settlement.

The effects of a partial dependence upon outside political developments can be seen even more extensively in the case of the Boiotian city of Thespiai. The cities of Boiotia were already loosely connected with each other in the late sixth century, when they occasionally fought wars together in the common interest. In the middle of the fifth century the Boiotian cities got together in a formal confederacy, partly to strengthen themselves against Athenian imperial ambitions. The cities contributed eleven officials, known as Commanders of the Boiotians, and Thespiai with the dependent communities of Eutresis and Thisbe provided two of these. No single city provided more than two in the original arrangement.

Thespiai seems to have been a city with a relatively liberal constitution inclined to pursue an independent line. When the Thebans had supported the Persians, in the Persian wars, Thespiai had taken part in the Greek resistance and had her town burnt down as a result. Sometime (perhaps shortly) afterwards Thespiai took the unusual step of enrolling outsiders as citizens. This may well imply a very open political outlook as well as a demographic crisis. During the long war of the Spartans and their allies, who included the Boiotians, against the Athenians at the end of the fifth century, the perceived independence of Thespiai led to a major reverse. In 424 the Thespians suffered heavy losses at the hands of the Athenians in a battle at Delion. The Thebans took advantage of Thespian weakness, accused the Thespians of Athenian sympathies, and razed the walls of the town. The Theban action and the way in which the Thespians honoured those who died in 424 strongly suggest that Thespiai, unlike Thebes, had a democratic constitution at this time.

Thespiai continued to be very much under the thumb of Thebes for the rest of the fifth century and for the first 30 years of the fourth. Changes in the federal arrangements had meant that Thebes provided four of the 11 Commanders of the Boiotians rather than two and that she had a preponderant influence. When hostility between Sparta and Thebes became intense in the 380s and 370s, Thespiai ended up being the base for a Spartan garrison. The results were disastrous: Thebes again razed the walls of Thespiai and this time proceeded to form a second confederacy in which Thespiai had no independent part. The Thespians were so insecure that in 371, when the Thebans faced and decisively defeated the Spartans at Leuktra, in Thespian territory, the Thespians are said to have fled the city to a natural stronghold called Keressos.

Thespiai only regained political freedom after Thebes was destroyed by Alexander the Great in 335. The third confederation which the Boiotian cities formed in the late fourth century took a very different form. The centre was not now Thebes, but the neutral and uninhabited site of the sanctuary of Poseidon at Onkhestos. All the cities of Boiotia were now separately represented in the federation, and although some magistrates were more regularly provided by large cities than by small the member cities were of more

equal status. Votes were taken by city, and a more extensive federal administration gave the participating members considerably more say in the decision-making process.

The history of Thespiai is the history of a city which in the course of 250 years passes from complete independence, through a period of voluntary limited dependence, to complete subordination, and back to independence, within broad limits, again. The city was not without internal factional strife, but it seems generally to have encouraged citizen participation in politics.

The history of settlement in Thespiai shows a distinct correlation with this political history, demonstrating the way in which political independence encourages centralized residence in order to facilitate participation, and how the loss of an independent political

45 At some stage, perhaps late, in the fourth century, Thespiai provided her only point of access to the Corinthian gulf with major fortifications. Ancient Kreusis (modern Livadhostra bay) can never have been a major harbour, but it did offer a possible landing site for hostile forces.

life encourages a flight to the countryside. During the Archaic period there seems to have been little residence outside the town of Thespiai itself and the major villages such as Askra and Eutresis. The villages may have had a recognizable political life of their own: an inscription of the early fifth century talks of 'the Thespians and those with them'. The involvement of the citizens in political life, coupled with the demographic crisis of the second quarter of the fifth century, meant that there was little pressure on the land, little reason to cultivate land not within easy reach of a major settlement, and good reason to live in the town. Aristotle is quoted as saying that the Thespians regarded it as so base to learn a skill or spend time farming that most of them were poor and heavily in debt to the thrifty Thebans and this may well relate to the fifth century. From the late fifth century, when Theban domination of Boiotia increased, there is a major reversal. Numerous small sites, of various types, appear in the countryside, some of them at no great distance from the town. Not all these sites will have been residences, but all provide good evidence that the population of Thespiai had become outward looking and was no longer concentrating its efforts on the town. From about 300 onwards the situation changes again. The small sites disappear. In the Hellenistic period the countryside of Thespiai was relatively free of structures.

Hellenistic Thespiai had an extremely active political life. An enormous body of public decrees is preserved from this period, and they reveal immense civic pride in the activities of being a citizen. One inscription listed all the magistrates for the year on a stone displayed for all to see. One third-century writer went out of his way to comment on the competitive spirit and ambition which he found in Thespiai. Not all Greeks, however,

saw the intense concentration on home politics as healthy. In a famous and much debated passage the historian Polybios complained that the cities of Boiotia had thrown themselves into military activities to the neglect of the administration of justice, and that men had given up leaving property to relatives and instead were bequeathing it for feasts and drinking parties. Polybios' accusation that the courts had not met can be straightforwardly disproved, and it seems that in fact the backlog of cases which he observed was a product of extreme litigiousness. His accusation about the way men were bequeathing their money is still more interesting. There certainly was an increasing number of charitable foundations during this period. These foundations sometimes encouraged conspicuous consumption in memory of the deceased, and sometimes provided for the founding of schools, the free supply of oil to the gymnasium, and so on. In any case they were more a sign of the vitality of city life than that it was moribund. Polybios may have made a connection between such foundations and the derelict countryside which he observed. There is little doubt that the move away from isolated residence and back to town life led to a reduction in the intensity of agricultural activity, even perhaps to a reduction in the area farmed. There may well have been plenty of ruined structures in the countryside. To a casual observer this might look like a withdrawal from agriculture and a sign that sons were not able to succeed to their fathers' estates. In fact the land leases from late third-century Thespiai show that although a great deal of land was in the hands of public bodies there was an active demand for that land, a demand which came from men of high status who were already farming land in that area (see Chapter 2).

Politics was obviously not the only factor

in any settlement history. Nevertheless the changing residential preferences at Thespiai illustrate the way in which relations with other cities and external politics could combine with internal politics to play a major part in determining the settlement pattern of a countryside, and profoundly affect the way in which that countryside was exploited. The changes in human occupation, of which the archaeologist observes the traces here, correspond to very great changes in the structure of society.

The individual cases I have discussed in this chapter show something of the variety of ways in which political and social relations between town and countryside were constituted. In Sparta the countryside was ruthlessly and unquestioningly subjugated to the town. At Orkhomenos the political privileges offered by the country were, perhaps cynically, exploited by those in power. On democratic Thasos the countryside was left outside politics, while at Athens it was included in a radical way which made it the basis for the political organization. At Elis it was left with an enormous degree of independence. The different alignments of the countryside in turn affected political life and political decisions. Thespiai, Thasos and Melos all seem to have had their settlement patterns influenced by political decisions made in other cities. The political decisions made in Sparta (or Orkhomenos, or Athens) were influenced by the settlement of the countryside. This is a complex web of influences and counter-influences. One more important strand must be dealt with immediately: war.

7

THE FIELD OF WAR

At the very end of the fifth century, shortly after the successful conclusion of their conflict with the Athenians in the Peloponnesian War, the Spartans invaded Elis.

'The Spartans had long been angry with the people of Elis both because they had made an alliance with the Athenians, the Argives and the Mantineians, and because the Eleians were keeping the Spartans from competing in the athletic and equestrian competitions at Olympia, on the grounds that a judgement had gone against Sparta. Not only were these complaints sufficient in themselves, but when the Spartan Likhas gave his chariot to the Thebans and they were announced as victorious, the Eleians had Likhas whipped and chased him away when he mounted the chariot to be garlanded, despite the fact that Likhas was a member of the Spartan Council of Elders. Later, when Agis, the Spartan king, sent to make a sacrifice in accordance with some oracle, the Eleians prevented him from making prayers for victory in war, saying that it had been customary from of old that the Greeks should not seek divine support for war against Greeks, and so Agis had to go away without sacrificing. For all these reasons the authorities and the assembly at Sparta decided to teach them a lesson.

'The Spartans sent ambassadors to Elis to say that those in power at Sparta had decided that it was proper that the Eleians should let the local communities be autonomous. When the Eleians said that they would not do this because they held these cities as legitimate prizes of war, the Spartan authorities raised an army. King Agis led the army and invaded Eleian territory through Akhaia via Larisos. When the army was only just in enemy territory and was ravaging the land an earthquake occurred. Agis thought this a divine sign, left the territory, and disbanded the army. This made the Eleians much more bold and they sent ambassadors to all the cities which they knew to bear grudges against the Spartans.

'In the next year the Spartan authorities again raised an army against Elis, and all the Spartan allies, including the Athenians, except the Boiotians and Corinthians, joined the expedition. Once Agis invaded via Aulon the people of Lepreon immediately revolted from the Eleians and came over to him, and so did the Makistians and then the Epitaleis. As he crossed the river the Letrinoi, Amphidoloi and Marganeis came over. From there he came to Olympia and sacrificed to Olympian Zeus, and no one tried to stop him. After sacrificing he marched to the city of Elis, cutting and burning the territory, and took an enormous number of cattle and an enormous number of slaves from the land, with the result that, when they heard, many Arkadians and Akhaians voluntarily joined the campaign and shared the booty. This expedition was, as it were, a source of food for the Peloponnese. When Agis got to the town he did a lot of damage to the area around and to the very fine gymnasia; they thought he was unwilling, rather than unable, to take the town, for it was unwalled.'[1]

Sparta and Elis were both, as we have seen in Chapter 6, relatively peculiar cities. The war itself goes on to develop in an interesting way, as we will see later. But this opening episode of hostilities reveals very nicely what many Greek wars were like. The war is between neighbouring cities. It is fought over the status of border territory, which becomes an issue not for its own intrinsic importance but because the aggressive city has other grudges. Warfare takes the form of unresisted raids carried out during relatively brief summer campaigns. The raids concentrate on the countryside, and are not aimed at conquest – Agis ignores the chance to take the political centre – but at gathering booty. The main control on hostile activities is religious scruple. In all this the countryside is central: a particular piece of country provides the excuse for fighting; the whole country is fought in; the agricultural year regulates the hostilities; and agricultural wealth and products provide the prizes of war.

This chapter explores the way in which the countryside is, in every sense, the field of war. The centrality of the countryside to warfare had considerable effects on the nature of the Greek cities, their social structure, and the way in which town related to country. In the Classical period the nature and importance of the countryside determined the way in which wars were fought and the composition of the army. Because of this the countryside shaped the ideology of the citizen and the way in which this was expressed through the education and training of young men. Decisions on

military strategy had profound implications for the relationship between town and countryside, and the way in which citizens perceived the countryside changed as attitudes towards defence and fortification changed.

Traditional Greek warfare

Most fighting in Archaic and Classical Greece was between neighbouring cities in disputes over border land. Much of this fighting was not so much warfare as piratical raiding not intended to threaten human life. One extreme situation is described in the following historical anecdote, not necessarily true.

'In early times the area of Megara was settled in villages, and the citizens were divided into five parts. ... When the Corinthians, who were always plotting to get Megara under their own influence, stirred up the Megarians to war against each other, the Megarians nevertheless fought fairly and gently, as befits relatives. No one harmed the farmers at all, and those who were captured had to pay a set ransom, which was received once they were set free. They did not exact it at once; instead the person who had taken a prisoner took him home with him, gave him salt and a share of his table, and sent him home again. The man who brought the ransom was praised and continued to be the friend of the capturer, calling him "spear-friend" rather than "spear-captive". The man who defaulted gained a bad reputation as unjust and unfaithful among the citizens as well as among the enemy.'[2] In this story the

46 The density of fortified sites in Phokis and Lokris in central Greece is a token of the continued tradition of petty raiding in this area. Most of the fortifications seem to date to the later part of the fourth century.

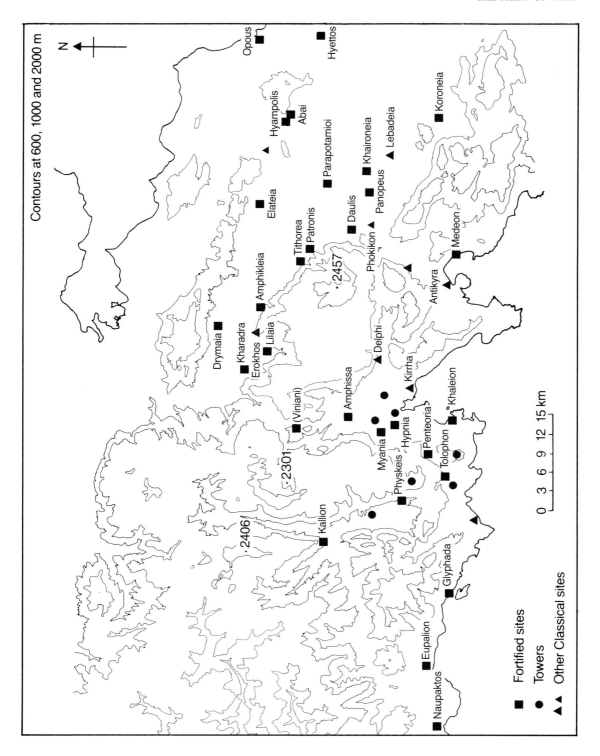

Contours at 600, 1000 and 2000 m

N

Opous
Hyettos
Koroneia
Hyampolis
Abai
Parapotamioi
Khaironeia
Lebadeia
Panopeus
Elateia
Daulis
Tithorea
Patronis
·2457
Phokikon
Medeon
Amphikleia
Antikyra
Kharadra
Erokhos
Lilaia
Delphi
Drymaia
Amphissa
Kirrha
(Viniani)
·2301
Khaleion
Penteoria
Tolophon
Myania
Hypnia
Physkeis
Kallion
·2406
Glyphada
Eupalion
Naupaktos

0 3 6 9 12 15 km

Fortified sites
Towers
Other Classical sites

139

raids are between villages not cities, but the pattern of conflict is very like that of much inter-city warfare.

For Thucydides, the historian of the great conflict between Sparta and Athens, such raiding was a feature of early Greek history prolonged only in backward areas: 'The Greeks used to make piratical raids on each other by land too. Even up to the present time many parts of Greece are inhabited in the old manner – as in the area round the Ozolian (Western) Lokrians, the Aitolians, the Akarnanians, and the mainland there. Those men have kept the custom of carrying arms from that old raiding. It used to be the case that the whole of Greece carried arms because settlements were undefended and travel from one place to another insecure: living in arms was as usual for them as it is for the barbarians.'3

Thucydides wants to make the contrast between old Greek warfare and the war whose history he is writing as great as possible. In fact it was not just on the edges of the Greek world that war remained essentially raiding. But raids on a neighbour's territory in the Classical period were different in one respect from those of earlier times. The network of political alliances was such that minor border raids could quickly involve large numbers of cities, and the conflict could rapidly increase in scale.

In the middle of the 390s a major conflict involving the four most powerful Greek cities, Sparta, Athens, Thebes, and Corinth, was sparked off by a border raid. 'There is a piece of land near Mt Parnassos which is disputed by the Phokians and the Western Lokrians. They had fought about it on occasions even before this. Each side often uses this land as pasture, and whichever side happens to find the other doing this collects a large force and raids the sheep. Many such raids had

occurred before, and they always resolved them for the most part by discussion and judicial proceedings one with another, but on this occasion the Lokrians made a counter-raid to snatch back sheep in return for those the Phokians had run off with, and the Phokians immediately invaded Lokris under arms. As their land was being ravaged the Lokrians sent ambassadors to the Boiotians, accusing the Phokians and saying that the Boiotians ought to help them – they were always friendly towards them at that time. . . . When the Phokians heard the news from Boiotia they retreated from Lokris again and sent ambassadors to Sparta straightaway, saying that the Spartans should warn the Boiotians not to enter Phokis.'4

Although this particular incident was unusual in its consequences, this account makes it clear how frequent the raids themselves were. These raids do not try to gain control of the disputed territory; they aim directly at the agricultural wealth of the region. The border dispute provides an excuse for a sheep-raid.

Warfare like this, consisting of raids, was the perfect complement to farming. Gaining agricultural supplies by raiding was an alternative to farming, a way of making up deficiencies in one's own supplies. The burden of the raid falls upon the farmers who lose the product of their work and have their continuing livelihood threatened. It is up to the farming community to make the counter-raid. The whole community was indirectly threatened by the reduction in its food supplies, but it was the individual farmer who faced a complete loss of livelihood. Those who farmed the land were the ones most directly interested in defence, and it was their own agricultural land that they were most concerned to fight about. Aristotle claims that: 'In some communities there is a law that those who live right next to the border should not take part in the debates about going to war with neighbours, on the grounds that their own private interest prevents them from giving good counsel.'[5]

However much individual interests had to be discounted, the farmer had to be central both to political decisions and to military activity. As we have seen previously (see p. 98), the matters that topped the agenda of the Athenian assembly ten times a year were the corn supply and the defence of the territory. Both these issues put the countryside at the centre of the political stage. In both cases the farmer is the most important actor: the city which depends on the farmer's production must also see to his protection. Warfare was a way both of supplementing home food supplies and of securing them, and as long as this remained the case the farmer was himself obliged to turn soldier. In many cities the possession of full citizen rights was limited to those who both owned land and performed military service.

To be a soldier in a Greek city was essentially to be a heavily armed infantry man, a hoplite. Specialist light-armed troops and archers were associated with the margins of the Greek world and with barbarians. The hoplite's equipment was made up of a metal helmet which offered virtually full facial protection, a bronze or leather cuirass which covered the whole of the torso, front and back, down to the hips, bronze greaves pro-

47 Part of the remarkably well-preserved western fortification wall at Drymaia in Phokis, built in the fourth century of squared but not entirely regular ashlar masonry and strengthened by frequent square towers.

tecting the calves, a round shield made basically of wood but with a bronze rim, which
was held by one strap round the the forearm
and by one handle gripped with the left hand,
and a heavy wooden spear with an iron head,
in all some 2 m long. This armour afforded
a very high degree of physical protection,
which is one reason why casualties in Greek
battles were rarely heavy. But the armour was
also very expensive and suitable only for specialized employment. Hoplite armour pre-
supposed warfare in pitched battles, for a
man so armed could not fight alone. The
heavy armour made rapid manoeuvring
impossible, and the hoplite shield protected
only the left side of the body. The hoplite
spear could only be used at close range to
make a thrust, not at long range to throw.
The hoplite had to operate in close ranks in
a phalanx where he could shelter his right side
behind his neighbour's shield and could use

FAR LEFT

*48 This white-ground funerary lekythos (oil flask),
with a partly equipped hoplite taking leave of his wife,
displays clearly the helmet and shield of the Classical
infantryman. It was painted in the middle of the fifth
century by one of the most important painters of white-
ground lekythoi, known to scholars as 'the Achilles
Painter'.*

ABOVE

*49 Although the frieze of the Parthenon is dominated
by cavalry, some heavily armed 'apobatai' also appear.
These were men who, wearing the standard hoplite
armour, took part in a competition at the Panathenaic
games which involved leaping onto and off moving
chariots. The figure on this slab from the north frieze
is about to mount a chariot.*

his spear safely against an enemy threatening from close range. In hoplite battles the heavily armed soldiers advanced against each other until the front ranks actually met. The soldiers at the front thrust with their spears and attempted to penetrate the defences of the opposing hoplites, and the men behind pushed and tried to keep their line moving forward in order to force the opposition to retreat and make it difficult for them to maintain their line.

Hoplite warfare has great advantages but also great disadvantages. The strengths and weaknesses are well brought out by the historian Polybios in his account of the Roman conquest of Greece in the late third and early second centuries.

'What was the reason why the Romans were victorious, and what was the defect of those who used the hoplite phalanx? Basically it was that in this war there was no control over the times and places for battles, and that the phalanx has only one moment and one kind of place in which it can operate to its own advantage. If the opposing sides had to come together at times and in places suited to the phalanx when they were on the point of deciding a conflict, then it was reasonable, given what we have just said, that those who used the phalanx always carried off the victory. But if it were possible to change the form of battle, and to do so easily, then how could the arrangement of the army just described induce any fear? Everyone knows that the phalanx needs flat plains free of trees, and with nothing in the way – no ditches, ravines, banks, confluences or river streams, for all these are enough to get in the way and break up the ranks. It is pretty well impossible to find places without any of these obstacles over a space of 5 km or more, or at least it is rare, as anyone would agree. Even supposing that such places can be found, if the enemy do not

come down and join battle in such places but march around ravaging the cities and territories of the allies, what is the benefit of the phalanx? By staying in places suitable for its operation it could neither help its friends nor save itself. For the enemy will easily prevent the bringing in of vital supplies once they get control, without any struggle, of the open country, and if the phalanx wants to leave the suitable places and buckle to it will be easily handled by the enemy.'[6]

Hoplite warfare can easily be presented as an absurdity once the aims of fighting become the conquest of the town and the incorporation of its whole territory. The hoplite force cannot deal with an enemy which does not concern itself primarily with the plains. But as long as raids for agricultural booty lay but thinly concealed behind the military activities of Greek cities the plains were what was at issue. Hoplite warfare was perfectly adapted to the defence of the plains.

Just as the aims of traditional Greek warfare were limited, so was its scope. Routed enemies were not pursued far, truces were immediately offered for the recovery of the dead, and the conflict was governed by complex informal rules which in time came to seem ridiculous. Polybios again: 'The Greeks of old did not even choose to defeat their enemies by deceit, supposing that there was nothing glorious or even secure in successes unless one killed those drawn up against one by fighting in open battle. For this reason there was an agreement not to use unseen weapons or weapons which struck from afar against each other, but they supposed that only hand to hand combat in massed ranks was a true decider of events. For this reason they made public declarations to each other about wars and battles in advance, when they decided to risk them, and even about the places into which they were about to advance and draw up their lines.'[7] Traditional Greek warfare did not aim at annihilation; it settled scores and amassed booty. Look again at Plutarch's story about Megara (p. 138).

As warfare was restricted in its scope, so were peace treaties. Until the fourth century peace treaties were always made for a limited period of time. The peace concluded between Athens and her allies and Sparta and her allies in 445/6 was for thirty years. The treaty which ended the first phase of the Peloponnesian War in 421 was for fifty years. In the wake of this peace of 421 the Spartans and the Argives made a separate treaty whose clauses are particularly revealing. Argos and Sparta had repeatedly had disputes over the piece of border land called Kynouria. In 420 the Argives wanted to go to third-party arbitration about this land but the Spartans refused. The peace which both sides finally agreed has an important clause covering the conduct of future conflict. Provided that the other side is not already at war or suffering some epidemic, either city can at any time challenge the other to fight about Kynouria, but whichever side is victorious may not continue the pursuit beyond the borders of the other city. This treaty ensures that claims to border territory are not given up, but it prevents the border conflict escalating to threaten the core area of the city.

To non-Greeks, the endemic but petty nature of these border raids was incomprehensible. After the Ionian revolt at the beginning of the fifth century, the Persian administrators attempted to impose some order on the Greeks of Asia Minor: 'Artaphernes, the official in charge at Sardis, sent for messengers from the Greek cities and compelled the Ionians to make agreements one with another that they would submit to arbitration and not raid and pillage each other. He compelled them to do this and then he had their territories measured by parasangs – the name the Persians give to a unit of 6 km – and drew up the boundaries for each which they continue to have from that time down to my own time.'[8]

Almost three centuries later the Roman general Metellus tried to discourage the raids by the imposition of fines: 'The Thebans had to pay a fine to the Phokians, at Metellus' first arbitration, for invading Phokis by force of arms, and another to the Euboians, at his second, for ravaging the Euboian countryside, and a third to the Amphissans for ruining their countryside when the corn was ripe.'[9]

Border conflict was one manifestation of the peculiarity of the Greek city. The fragmentation of the landscape into so many independent political units multiplied borders. The attempt to subsist on home resources of food magnified the importance of the peasant and his fields. The citizen body was closely identified with the territory, and threats to that territory were threats to the political integrity of the city. The citizen was trained as a soldier to defend the countryside and maintain its borders, and the soldier as citizen made the political decision to fight.

The countryside of training

The pressures created by traditional warfare had a profound influence on society. The vital need to defend the arable land put the farmer at the heart of the army and of the political system. It organized the city around military conflict in a way which generated aggression as much as defence. Hoplite warfare demanded special skills which could only be acquired by training. In his works on household management and on hunting Xenophon is at pains to point out that farming and hunting are an ideal background for fighting because they promote endurance, physical fitness, and an ability to work with others. *Faute de mieux* it was fortunate and appropriate that farmers should be naturally predisposed by their daily activities to be good soldiers. But fitness was no substitute for training in a corps, and farming provided neither the competition nor the specialized practice in arms which hoplite fighting demanded.

Some sort of military training of young men is widely attested from many Greek cities. Few cities could control the education of the young completely in the interests of producing efficient hoplites, and some of the training was indirect. Young men were encouraged to take part in athletic competitions. A competitive structure pervades much Greek communal activity, and war was seen as the ultimate contest. Cities set a good deal of store by success in the great panhellenic athletic competitions, as the opening story of Sparta's grudges against Elis shows. Men who were victorious in such competitions received great public honours in their own community and were frequently able to make their athletic prowess the basis for political influence. Some Greek towns, like Elis in the passage quoted (and see p. 63 on Athens), seem to have been ringed by gymnasia, and the high value put upon success and distinction there encouraged the young to submit to a rigorous training in sport.

Many cities supplemented athletic activities by a period of intensive training in war for young men as they came of age. Abundant evidence from late Classical and Hellenistic Athens shows that at least a large proportion of citizens between the ages of eighteen and twenty there went through a closely controlled training in military and civic duties. They were taught to fight as hoplites and some of the skills required by light troops – use of the bow and the sling and the throwing of javelins. They served as garrisons for the forts and watch-posts in the countryside.

They had major parts to play at many of the most important religious festivals. The assembly frequently lavished honours both on these young men (ephebes) themselves and upon those who had charge of them.

This military training set apart a socially restricted group for military activities, and it defined their role in terms of the countryside. The oath taken by the ephebes at Dreros in Crete in the late third century brings out the nature of their concerns very clearly.

'The ephebes, those who had put off all childhood garments, who numbered 180, took the following oath. I swear by the Hearth in the civic centre and by Zeus of the Agora and by Zeus Tallaios, and by Apollo Delphinios, and by Athena who holds the city, and by Pythian Apollo, and by Leto and Artemis and Ares and Aphrodite and Hermes and the Sun and Britomartis and Phoinix and Amphione and Earth and Heaven and heroes and heroines and fountains and rivers and all the gods and goddesses that I will never on any occasion be well disposed towards the people of Lyttos, by any means or device, night or day. I will effect what harm I can to the people of Lyttos. No lawsuit or action will be bound by oath. I will always be a lover of Knossos and I will not betray the city of Dreros, not the guard-posts of Dreros or of Knossos. I will not betray men of Dreros or of Knossos to the enemy. I will not initiate civil strife and I will oppose any man who promotes such strife. I will not form conspiracies in the city or outside the city nor join any conspirator, but I will report it to the body of magistrates if I learn that anyone is conspiring. If I do not keep to this word of mine may all the gods and goddesses by whom I swore be mad with me, and may I perish with the most despicable death, myself and all my possessions, and may the earth not bear fruit for me, nor women give birth naturally nor flocks. But if I keep my word may the gods by whom I swore be kind to me and give me many good things. I swear by the same gods that I will report the magistrates to the Council . . . if they do not exact the same oath which we swore from the herd of the ephebes when they put off their garments.

'These are the outlines of the ancient territory of Dreros for each group of young men who put off their boyhood garments, and this is the oath which they swear and keep. And the Milati invaded the city of Dreros at the time of the new moon for the sake of land about which we fight. The winner from the herd of ephebes . . . and each plant an olive and show that he has cultivated it. If he refuses to plant he is to be fined fifty staters.'[10]

Crete was one area where armed border conflicts continued to be endemic into the Hellenistic period. Polybios wonders at one point whether one should talk of the beginning of hostilities in Crete at all: 'Wars between peoples are so continual there and their cruelty to one another so excessive that the beginning and the end are the same in Crete, and this that would be a paradox elsewhere, that the beginning and the end are the same, is there something repeatedly observed.'[11]

Endemic warfare lies close to the surface in the Dreros oath. It was inevitable in a community whose young people swore perpetual enmity with another city. The final note reveals that the ephebes of Dreros actually faced an incursion from another city. The constant threat of war is one reason why the ephebes have to be committed to the border forts; but it would be wrong to see the ephebic countryside as simply the space of conflict.

The ephebic connection with the countryside is with the countryside as the place of production as well as of destruction.

The divinities by which the ephebes swear include a wide range of natural powers and forces, earth and sun, rivers and fountains. The ephebes are made to stake the reproduction of their own household and flocks on their loyalty to their oath. The slightly incoherent final lines of the inscription link martial success with ephebic agricultural activities and the ephebic commitment to the cultivation of the olive. The country to which the ephebes are bound is the country as the farmer's field. The young men acquire their first political rights at the same time as gaining their first military duties, and they are made to affirm their political loyalty. The terms in which they do so involve accepting that the city is territory as well as community, and that political status is inseparable from a stake in the farming of the land.

The ephebe was not, however, either an ordinary citizen or an ordinary hoplite, and his relation to the countryside was a very special one. The ephebes at Dreros begin their term of service by putting off the clothes of childhood. This ritual marks the fact that they are no longer boys. But the ephebe does not become just another citizen at a stroke. The body which the ephebe enters is not the citizen assembly but the 'herd' of young men. The ephebe stood in a peculiar relation to the citizen body which was marked in different ways in different communities. At Gortyn in Crete these young men formed a special court, that is they had additional rights. At Athens they were almost completely debarred from judicial activity: they could appear in court only for cases involving disputes about inheritance or heiresses.

The activities of the ephebe were a training for hoplite warfare but they were not the activities of the hoplite. The continuous service of ephebes as garrison troops stationed on the frontier in forts is quite the opposite

50 *This sixth-century jug by the Amasis painter shows a bearded hunter with his dog returning to the city. The fox and hare which he has caught are displayed for the elders to observe.*

of the brief summer campaigns fought by hoplites in the cultivated plains. Ephebes went on hunting expeditions alone at night using nets; hoplites hunted in a group and attacked their prey with a lance. This opposition is dramatically expressed in the myth by which the Athenians 'explained' to themselves their festival of the Apatouria at which the youth was recognized as a member of a descent group and as a proper Athenian immediately before he became an ephebe. According to this story there was a border conflict between the Athenians and the Boiotians which it was agreed to settle with a duel. The Boiotian king, Xanthos (the Fair one), faced the Athenian Melanthos (the Dark one). During the combat Melanthos shouted out that Xanthos had someone helping him, and when Xanthos turned to look he killed him. In this story all the values of the hoplite are inverted: the border is no place for hoplite battle; hoplites cannot fight alone; hoplites do not use trickery. Service as an ephebe was the necessary preliminary to joining the hoplite ranks, but the activities of the ephebe were anti-hoplite. The young man who was to enter the ordered line of hoplite battle had to pass through a period of carefully controlled disorder. Before a youth could be recognized as a full member of the community he was made to experience life as an individual.

The world of the ephebe was not the real world of the hoplite or the real world of the farmer. The ephebes were made to live out a fantasy. This fantasy, which all experienced, had a profound effect on the perception of reality. In some versions the myth about Xanthos and Melanthos was localized at Panakton, a fort on the edge of the Skourta plain in northern Attica. The Skourta plain was virtually a no-man's land on the border between Athens and Boiotia. The fort at Panakton was the subject of a special clause in the Peace of 421 between Athens and Sparta and her allies. It was agreed that this fort, which had earlier been taken by treachery, should be given back to the Athenians. In the event the Boiotians gave it back, but they did so only after they had demolished it; they claimed that there were 'ancient oaths about it that neither side should live in the place but that they should graze it as common land'.[12] The Athenians who brought their young men up on the story that showed the borders were places of treachery and inverted values were made to experience that same treachery and challenge to accepted values in real life.

The city which used the frontiers to inculcate the virtues of the citizen soldier into its youth committed itself to taking those frontiers seriously in its military policy. The citizen farmer was central to the political life and political decisions of the Greek city. Military policy was firmly based on the protection of the plains. But the protection of the plains demanded the preservation of the borders; training the citizen soldier involved stressing the importance of the marginal land at the edge. Because the borders figured so prominently in the life of the incipient citizen, disputes about borderlands were not simply disputes about the definition of the territory but about the definition of the whole citizen body.

In its military arrangements Sparta stands out as exceptional. In most Greek cities, as in Athens, the period during which the young men were trained was the only period in their lives when they were on permanent military service. The citizen army was an army of farmers. It was not a specialist army and it had to be levied specially whenever the need arose. In Sparta things were different. Not two years but the whole of childhood and adolescence from the age of seven was spent in a strictly controlled programme of training and education designed to produce good hoplites. Once their training was complete the Spartan citizens formed a standing army. Spartan men led a life of leisure and training designed to maintain their fitness and *esprit de corps* and to nurture the next generation of hoplites. Numerous small local festivals were held throughout Spartan territory which involved games. One fifth-century inscription records that a man named Damonon won over thirty victories in horse races at festivals all over Spartan territory. The fact that all Spartans were always soldiers and nothing but soldiers had a profound social and political effect. In other cities military needs affected political arrangements; in Sparta military and civic organizations were inseparable.

Many Spartan institutions can be paralleled to some degree in other cities, but the Spartans turned these institutions to radically different ends. This is well illustrated by the Spartan parallel to ephebic service: the secret service (*krupteia*). The following brief description gives the essential flavour of this institution: 'What they call the secret service . . . was as follows. Those in charge of the young men after a time sent out those who seemed to be especially on the ball into various parts of the countryside, with daggers and some supplies but nothing else. By day they hid themselves, scattered about in places that were altogether obscure, but by night they came down onto the roads and slaughtered any of the helots they caught. Often as they went about the countryside it was the strongest and most powerful helots that they killed.'[13]

For the Athenian ephebe the field of operation for his covert deceit is the borderland, the area disputed by the enemy. For the Spartan in the secret service the field for his confidential mission is the whole countryside, the enemy are the very helots on whom Spartan agriculture depends: the whole territory has become a marginal area, perpetually subject to dispute.

The different military arrangements of Sparta are rooted in a different relationship between town and country. I have argued above that in the Greek city generally the farmer was the keystone of the military effort and the heavily armed hoplite was the backbone of the army because agricultural production was central to the life of the city but vulnerable to warfare that was essentially raiding. In Sparta the situation was different. The Spartans were not farmers. Spartan territory was not subject to raids from without. In Sparta the enemy was within: it was the enemy which farmed the land. Sparta, alone of Greek cities, divorced the farmer from the soldier. Doing so meant bringing war within the boundaries of the city and defining the citizen by contrast to the farmer at home rather than by contrast to the raider at the border. Sparta alone had a standing army because in Sparta alone war was continuous. Every year when the chief Spartan magistrates took office they declared war on the helots. Aristotle remarks in the *Politics* that the provision of a separate force of specialized full-time soldiers is bound to lead to the loss of political rights and oppression of the farmers. In Sparta the need to oppress the farmers made a standing army inevitable.

The Spartan soldiers were not farmers, but they were not independent of the countryside. It is true that the Spartans were less tied to the rhythms of the agricultural year than other Greeks, but since the Spartans rarely fought alone without their more conventional allies' armies this was a limited advantage. In 428 the Spartans invaded Attica in the spring when the corn was getting ripe and then withdrew. When the city of Mytilene, which was trying to revolt from the Athenian empire, asked for support the Spartans proposed to make a second invasion of Attica: 'The Spartans . . . told their allies who were present to go quickly to the Isthmos of Corinth with a two thirds levy in order to make a second invasion of Attica. They themselves got there first and prepared troop ships at the Isthmos to offer transport from Corinth to the sea near Athens, so that they could attack by land and sea at the same time. The Spartans made these preparations energetically, but the other allies were slow in mustering. They were involved in bringing in the harvest and were fed up with campaigning.'[14] The expedition is in the end called off. The Spartan flexibility was undermined by the agricultural commitments of the allied soldiers.

The need to repress their own countryside also kept the Spartans from making long expeditions abroad. They were not able to exploit the freedom from the agricultural year which dependence on the helots gave them. When the Spartans did undertake major expeditions abroad they were reluctant to commit their whole army and they went to extraordinary lengths to prevent trouble at home while the expedition was away. The clearest example of this came in the late 420s when Sparta sent a force to campaign against Athenian allies in northern Greece and Thrace. In an unprecedented turnabout 700 helots were armed to fight as hoplites. In an equally unprecedented increase in the oppression, some 2000 other helots were annihilated. Both these unique actions were occasioned by the fear of a helot revolt, a fear heightened by the fact that the Athenians had established a base on the coast of Messenia from which they could encourage helot trouble. In the face of heightened fears of hostility in the

countryside, the Spartans chose to export or kill some of their constant enemy.

The Spartan action in sending out an army consisting partly of helot hoplites to campaign for more than a single season in a distant part of Greece is an indication of the way in which the long conflict between Sparta and Athens at the end of the fifth century questioned the traditional ways of fighting a war. The innovations in warfare which were made at this time have profound implications for the relations between town and country.

Changing strategies: changing countrysides

The continuation of the story of the Spartan campaign against Elis with which we began (see pp. 137–138) illustrates the changes which were happening in Greek military strategy.

'Then when Agis departed and crossed back over the River Alpheios, leaving a garrison force at Epitalion near the Alpheios with Lysippos as commander and exiles from Elis, he disbanded his army and himself went home. For the rest of the summer and the following winter the territory of Elis was plundered and ravaged by Lysippos and those with him. During the following summer the Eleian leader Thrasydaios sent an embassy to Sparta and agreed to demolish the walls of Pheia and Kyllene, to give up the cities of Triphylia called Phrixa, Epitalion, Letrinoi, Amphidoloi, and Marganeis, and in addition also to give up Akroreia and Lasion which were claimed by the Arkadians. The Eleians claimed that they should keep Epeion, the city between Heraia and Makistos, on the grounds that they had bought the whole territory from those who held the city for a price of 30 talents, and had paid the money. But the Spartans compelled them to give this up too, considering that buying by force from a weaker party is no more just than confiscating by force. But the Spartans did not deprive the Eleians of the presidency of the temple of Zeus at Olympia, even though this had not belonged to them of old, for they thought that the rival claimants were but country people and would not be able to manage the presidency. After this, peace and an alliance was made between the Eleians and the Spartans. So ended the war between Sparta and Elis.'[15]

The war had begun in the old manner, with summer raids reaping much booty. It was transformed into a very different exercise by the establishment of a permanent garrison in the territory. Rather than ending in simple glory and booty for one side, embarrassment and shortage for the other, it ended in a radical revision of political and territorial alignments.

In traditional Greek warfare minor raids might be ignored or they might be reciprocated (as in the story of Phokis and Lokris on p. 140). Serious raiding was normally resisted. The sequence of events when the Athenian general Tolmides made a raid on Sikyon in the middle of the fifth century is typical. Tolmides landed and ravaged the countryside. The people of Sikyon offered battle. The Athenians broke through the Sikyonian line and pursued the army back to the town. The Athenians then withdrew. If a city that was invaded did not offer battle this was seen to be something that had to be explained, and it was often taken as a sign of weakness: 'The Athenians from the thirty ships that were sailing round the Peloponnese first destroyed some garrison troops at Eilomenon on Leukas by ambush, and then later came to Leukas with a greater force. This force included all the Akarnanians who had joined the expedition in full force, except for the people of Oiniadai, and the Zakynthians

and Kephallenians and Corcyrans with fifteen ships. The people of Leukas kept quiet although the land inside the isthmos, where Leukas itself and the temple of Apollo are, as well as the land outside, was ravaged; for they were too vastly outnumbered.'[16]

The people of Leukas in this example chose not to come out and fight because of the scale of the enemy operation. The traditional pattern of Greek warfare was a pattern dependent upon wars being fought by forces of limited size which had limited aims. Thucydides, in his survey of wars in early Greek history notes that: 'On land there was no united war from which any sort of empire was built. As many wars as there were, were against those who shared a border, and the Greeks did not go far from their own land in foreign campaigns to overturn others. For they had not joined together as subjects of the greatest cities, nor did they themselves make common campaigns as equals, but neighbours fought against each other individually.'[17] Meeting the enemy in open battle was a realistic way of regulating relations with neighbours. Fighting a hoplite battle was less well advised when the enemy aims went beyond raiding and redefining the city.

From an early date the Greeks realized that fighting against non-Greeks new strategies might be necessary. Herodotos claims that the Milesians chose not to fight a pitched battle when faced with attacks from the very much stronger power of Lydia in the sixth century.

'Alyattes fought the Milesians, taking over the war from his father. He drove the Milesians back and besieged Miletos in the following way. When the crops were full grown in the land, then he used to put in the troops. They campaigned to the sound of the pipes, the strings, the fife and the flute. When they came to Milesian territory, they did not pull down the buildings on the land, nor burn them nor tear off their doors, but they left them standing throughout the country. When they had destroyed the tree crops and the arable crops they went home. The Milesians had control of the sea so that there was no point in the army investing the town. The reason why the Lydian did not pull down the houses was that he wanted the Milesians to use them as bases for the continued working and sowing of the land, so that when he invaded he had something to destroy. The war went on for eleven years with the Lydians doing this, and in this time the Milesians experienced very considerable damage in two areas, both in their own territory at Limeneion and in the plain of the Maiander.'[18]

Changes in the pattern of war between Greeks began only after the great war against Persia. The continuing campaign against the Persians led to new structures of alliance within the Greek world, and to wars which were no longer simply glorified raids. The Athenians ignored the countryside when they campaigned against recalcitrant allies in order to secure their continued commitment to the anti-Persian campaign. Athenian attacks focused strongly on the town, the political centre. By contrast with the Spartans, who do not even try to take the unwalled town of Elis, the Athenians insisted that allies whom they subdued should pull down their town walls. Traditional hoplite warfare spares human life because it is interested in the countryside; the Athenians on occasion executed the adult males of the cities they reduced and sold the women and children into slavery.

The changing aims of warfare altered the priorities for defence. The hoplite army was a good defence in wars that were aimed at the countryside and its products. When wars had openly political aims the defence of the town, the political centre, had to come first. When wars, like the later phases of the Spartan war against Elis, aimed to take over large tracts of territory and to incorporate their settlements, new methods of defending the whole landscape had to be found. In early Greece hoplite battles are relatively frequent, sieges rare. From the fifth century on siege operations became frequent and towns had to build ever more sophisticated defences to cope with them. Notably it was the Athenians who were thought of as the people who knew most about siege warfare in the middle of the fifth century.

Traditional war strategies did not die out overnight, and the extent to which a city could ignore the ravaging of its territory varied considerably from city to city. Not all cities enjoyed the happy position of Miletos, which was fortunate enough to control the sea while the enemy controlled the land. The whole history of the Peloponnesian War, however, was shaped by the fact that Athens did enjoy such a position.

Athens itself was by no means on the coast, but in the middle of the fifth century the Athenians built the so-called Long Walls which linked the town to the sea. These Long Walls were not at all sophisticated defence works, but they were more than sufficient against siege techniques which depended on starving a community out rather than breaking down its stone defences. Because of these walls Athens was able to abandon the countryside in the struggle with Sparta without risk to the community. As long as Athens' navy controlled the sea, the Athenians could keep themselves supplied without needing to enjoy the products of Attica itself, and this meant that the Athenians could refuse the Spartan challenge to fight a hoplite battle in the field.

No other city was in Athens' position. No

other city had a navy that could begin to match the Athenian. Athens encouraged various allied cities to follow her example and link themselves to the sea by long walls, but their capacity to abandon their countryside was heavily dependent upon Athenian willingness to help them secure supplies by sea. Because Athens controlled the sea, the Athenians could ensure that other cities could not cut themselves free of their territory as Athens herself had done. In attacking other cities the Athenians employed the traditional strategy of invasion and devastation which was no longer of any use against Athens. Athens refused to fight for her own territory but the Athenians regularly used invasion in order to challenge other cities to fight hoplite battles.

Whether a city could ignore the invasion of its territory depended also on the length of time the invasion lasted. In the Spartan campaign against Elis, Elis is able to ignore the invasions while they only last a short time, but once the Spartans set up a permanent base the Eleians are quickly brought to an agreement. Long invasions not only meant much more complete destruction of the crops and buildings in the countryside, they also posed a great threat to the unity of the citizen body. Long invasions created internal pressures, partly because they did not affect all alike (farmers were hit harder than those without land, and some farmers were hit harder than others), and partly because in a city under siege there was considerable scope for treacherous action and suspicion of treachery. Most Greek cities suffered some degree of political disunity. In the normal course of traditional warfare this did not much matter: in hoplite battles even the general can do very little once battle has commenced, and there is little scope for effective treacherous action. When a city is under siege political differences within the citizen body acquire a military importance, and, because of this, cities split by faction were reluctant to let themselves come under siege.

The pressures in a city facing siege are well revealed by what happened when, during the long war between Sparta and Athens at the end of the fifth century, a Spartan army under the General Brasidas invaded the territory of the Athenian colony of Amphipolis.

'Brasidas set out from Arnai in the Khalkidike and marched with his army. At evening he arrived at Aulon and Bormiskos, where Lake Bolbe flows out to the sea, and having had a meal he went on during the night. It was winter, and it snowed. Brasidas was all the more eager to press on because of this, wanting to escape the notice of the Amphipolitans except for the traitors . . . . The town itself was at some distance from the river crossing and walls did not extend down to it as they do now. The guard at the river was small. Brasidas easily overpowered it, both because of treachery and because it was winter and he had fallen upon it unexpectedly. He crossed the river. Immediately he held all the possessions of the Amphipolitans who live all over the territory. Because his crossing came as a sudden surprise to those in the city, and because many of those outside had been captured and others had fled to the fortifications, the Amphipolitans got into a great panic, particularly because they were suspicious of each other. It is said that it seemed that Brasidas could have taken the town if he had been willing to restrain the army from plundering and go against it at once. As it was, he settled his army down, and, when he had overrun the parts outside without any of the opposition he expected, he kept quiet. Those opposed to the traitors had enough influence among the people that the gates were not opened straightaway, and they sent a message with Eukles, the general who was with them from Athens and in charge of the security of the countryside, to the other general in the Thracian region, Thucydides. . . .

'Brasidas, fearing the arrival of help, hurried to take the city first, if he could, and proposed a surrender on reasonable terms, announcing that any of the Athenians or Amphipolitans in the city who wanted could remain, sharing similar and equal rights, and that those who did not want to stay could leave the city taking their property with them within five days. The majority changed their minds when they heard this, particularly since the proportion of Athenians in the population was small, most of the population being of mixed origin, and there were relatives in the city of those who had been captured outside. Compared with what they had expected they considered the offer to be just. . . .'[19]

The citizen body at Amphipolis was split in various ways. It was split in its residence: a significant proportion of the citizens lived out on the land even during the winter. It was split in its origin: a colonial foundation, it included not only men from Athens but also others from other communities. It was split in its sympathies: there was an Athenian general based in the town, but there were also those who had more sympathy with the Spartan cause (those whom Thucydides calls traitors). In the traditional pattern of warfare all these splits would have been masked. Invasion would not have occurred in the winter. The enemy would not have arrived at night. The country residents would have been joined in the fields by many who lived in the town. A political meeting would have been held to decide whether or not to fight a hoplite battle. If a battle was not fought the people of Amphipolis would have had to sit out a short period of ravaging, but there

would have been little question of the town itself being threatened, let alone surrendering.

The new war strategy demanded new physical defences. A city which expected to meet an enemy invasion by marching out with its hoplite army needed nothing more than a city wall as an ultimate defence following defeat in the field. The nature of the town wall depended on the site of the town. This is neatly illustrated by the varying defences of cities in Arkadia. At one end of the scale lie cities like Tegea which were little more than a collection of villages on a more or less flat site. Tegea had a wall but it was very long and offered no serious protection. Sparta, a similar type of town, had no defences at all in the Classical period. At the other end of the scale are the hilltop fastnesses such as Teuthis (modern Dimitsana) and Brenthe (modern Karytaina). Neither type of defence was enough to serve alone against the new war strategy: Tegea could not stand a serious battering of its defensive circuit, a hilltop site could not endure a long siege. Amphipolis built additional walls to link it to the river crossing after the Brasidas episode.

The need for new defences was not limited to the towns. The countryside needed new defences also. There were some fortifications in the Greek countryside in the fifth century, especially where raids were frequent. But these were rarely more than watch-towers. Watch-towers are referred to in the ephebic oath from Dreros, and they seem to have been particularly frequent in Crete, which is not surprising given the frequency of petty wars there. Forts which could house and protect a substantial force seem to appear first in Attica. On the western part of the border with Boiotia there were forts at Oinoe and Panakton operative before the beginning of the great struggle with Sparta, and during that struggle the Athenians added coastal

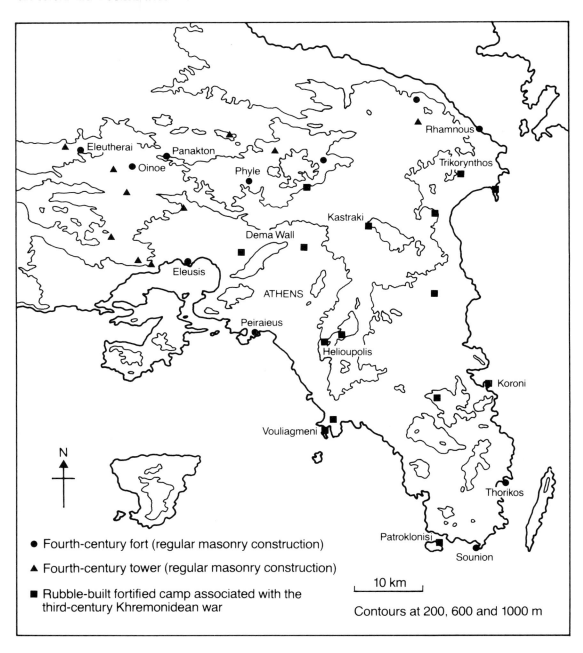

Eleutherai

Panakton

Oinoe

Phyle

Rhamnous

Trikorynthos

Kastraki

Dema Wall

ATHENS

Peiraieus

Helioupolis

Koroni

Eleusis

Vouliagmeni

Thorikos

Patroklonisi

Sounion

N

● Fourth-century fort (regular masonry construction)

▲ Fourth-century tower (regular masonry construction)

■ Rubble-built fortified camp associated with the
third-century Khremonidean war

⌞ 10 km ⌟

Contours at 200, 600 and 1000 m

*51 This map shows the development of a system of
fortifications in Attica during the fourth century, and
the very different pattern of forts needed in the conflict
of the Khremonidean war of the third century.*

fortifications at Sounion and Thorikos. Even in the territory of Athens systematic defence in the form of a series of forts covering all possible points of enemy access was only undertaken in the fourth century.

Attica was not the only place where the developments of the Peloponnesian War had their effect. The different expectations of fourth-century Greeks about the course of warfare are well illustrated by the work of Aineias the Tactician called *What to do about a siege.* Aineias does not assume that invasion will be followed by a hoplite battle. He envisages considerable obstruction of the invading force through the prior occupation of strategically important positions and the use of some light troops. He advises that extremely careful precautions be taken to ensure that the town is secure against a siege, both in terms of its physical defences and in

terms of internal solidarity. These new assumptions are reflected in the increased provision of fortifications in the countryside and in more and different city walls.

A totally new concept of town defence appears in the fourth century. This is the wall which encompasses not just the urban nucleus but also a considerable chunk of countryside. Such a wall had two advantages. It could be placed in the strongest possible natural defensive position, and it protected agricultural land as well as residences. These walls represented a considerable investment, for they were much longer than traditional town

52 When Messenia, comprising the entire southwest quarter of the Peloponnese, was liberated from Spartan overlordship in 370, a new city was founded on Mount Ithome. The curtain walls and elaborate gateways of Messene (below and overleaf) are the finest surviving examples of sophisticated fourth-century town defences.

walls, but once built they were relatively easy to defend. The enemy could not hope to put pressure on all parts of the wall at once, and the defenders in the town could concentrate themselves at whichever point was most heavily under attack. This type of fortification was used in the Peloponnese at the newly founded cities of Megalopolis and Messene and at the older city of Phigaleia. The walls at Phigaleia and Messene are well preserved. They are very similar in general principle, but contrasting in details. The wall at Phigaleia is a plain circuit, with simple towers and no elaborate gateways. Its masonry is fairly regular in coursing and block size, but it is not very finely finished. The wall impresses most by the way it strides out over the undulating green countryside. The defences of Messene are the finest of any Greek city, and for part of the circuit they are preserved to a considerable height. The towers are lofty and the gates elaborate, exhibiting limestone masonry of the finest quality, with delicately tooled faces to the blocks.

The new fortifications of the countryside are concerned with controlling enemy access to the territory more closely. In small cities the new fortifications take the form of new and better watch-posts. Thus in the territory of Mantineia a small watch-tower was built on a height called Stavromyti which offered extensive views over all the passes into Mantineian territory from the northeast. In larger cities, and cities with a coastline, watch-towers were not enough; it had to be possible to station troops at the borders to offer preliminary defence. Both Athens and Sparta ringed themselves with defences. The various perioikic communities on and near the borders of Spartan territory seem to have been encouraged to defend themselves in the fourth century. A large hilltop fort at Belmina watched the route into Lakonia

from Megalopolis, and all round the coast of the Malea and Mani peninsulas perioikic towns either fortified their own position, as at Epidauros Limera, or a nearby height, as at Teuthrone. In Athens the fourth-century ring of forts was still more extensive. The Boiotian border received a further major fort at Eleutherai, and Phyle, Panakton and Oinoe were rebuilt. On the eastern part of the frontier forts were built at Katsimidi and Agia Paraskevi and on the coast at Rhamnous an acropolis which had long been defended was turned into a full-scale fort. The other coastal forts at Thorikos, Sounion and Eleusis were maintained.

The concern to control enemy incursions into the countryside led to the development of one type of fortification which is totally new in this period. This is the field-wall. When invaded by the Spartans in the 370s, the Thebans erected a palisade with a trench some distance from the city in order to allow some agricultural activity to continue. On an unknown occasion sometime in the fourth century Athens made a similar sort of defence in stone. Across the low and relatively level ground between the northern mountain range of Parnes and the minor range of Aigaleos immediately north of the town of Athens, the Athenians built a long wall of rubble stone. The wall was very carefully designed with numerous small gates through which the Athenian defensive force could conveniently make sorties against the enemy invader. The wall involves the Athenians using light-armed troops rather than hoplites, and it would have been unthinkable in the fifth century. Much less sophisticated but much more extensive is the less-well-built rubble wall which runs across the hilltops which border the small coastal plain of eastern Boiotia facing Khalkis in Euboia. This wall is designed to prevent that coastal plain being

attacked from central Boiotia. It was probably built for some specific circumstance rather than as a permanent defence, and it may date to the third century.

The new war strategy and the new fortifications that went with it had major social implications which profoundly affected the relationship between town and country. The decline of the traditional strategy represented the beginning of the decline of hoplite warfare. The hoplite was not trained or equipped for besieging fortified sites, he could not operate in mountainous terrain, and he was not even very effective at ravaging the countryside. The new strategy demanded more light troops, who needed to be very thoroughly trained in a wide variety of military skills, and it demanded specialist troops who could set up siege works quickly and effectively. The farmer who was limited to short campaigning seasons when he was not busy on his land was not the man for the new sort of warfare. The citizen soldier certainly did not die out overnight, and major wars continued to be decided most frequently by hoplite battles, but the development of fortifications and sieges undermined the farmer's position at the centre of the army and because of this it undermined his position in the centre of politics.

The displacement of the farmer hoplite changed perceptions of the countryside. The countryside of hoplite battles was the agricultural countryside. The countryside of fortifications and garrisons was mountainous and hostile. The final aim of the fortifications was to prevent the enemy penetrating into the

53 One of the forts developed on the north border of Attica during the fourth century is this one at Gyphtokastro (probably ancient Eleutherai), which guards the pass to Boiotia. The walling of the east side is exceptionally well preserved.

productive countryside, but in achieving that aim the new strategy brought the wild countryside much more to the forefront of citizen perceptions. Once the defence of the farmland was removed from the hands of the farmer it came to seem much more of a chore. Neither manning solitary forts nor paying mercenary troops with special skills were attractive propositions. Political debates about defence are virtually unheard of in the fifth century; in the fourth century they are one of the dominant strands in the historical tradition. The unity of town and country had been cemented by the service of the farmer as hoplite. In the traditional strategy war never came near the town. In the fourth century war threatened the town as well as the country. Whether they were garrison troops at border forts or non-citizen mercenaries, the soldiers who decided the issue were more and more removed from the political debate. In that debate the farmer no longer had a special voice. The scope for political divisions arising between town and country was enormously increased.

In the event the new strategy in warfare was itself overtaken by further developments. The methods of Philip of Macedon in his conquest of Greece took warfare directly to the town. Philip had no interest in the countryside, only in the incorporation of cities. The defeat of the Greek cities in the battle at Khaironeia in 338 led to the whole of Greece coming under Macedonian suzerainty. The cities were left with a nominal independence, but they no longer had scope for the pursuit of individual foreign policies. Warfare from now on was either the parochial settling and resettling of old scores with neighbours, or it involved full-scale revolt against Macedonian control.

When old scores with neighbours were settled it was more frequently by diplomacy than by force. Petty raids and ritual battles are replaced by complex settlements inscribed on stone. In the late third century the city of Epidauros twice called in arbitrators to re-define its borders with its neighbours. One of the redefinitions concerns the border with Hermione, the other the border with Corinth.

The agreement with Corinth gives the tone of these arbitrations well: 'When Aigialeus was general of the Akhaians and Dionysios was priest of Asklepios in Epidauros, the Megarians made the following decision for the Epidaurians and the Corinthians about the land which they were disputing and the area of Sellanus and Spiraion. They sent 151 men to decide following the resolution of the Akhaian court. The arbitrators went to the territory itself and judged that it belonged to Epidauros, but the Corinthians disputed the line of the boundary and so the Megarians sent 31 men to draw up the boundary according to the resolution of the Akhaians. These went to the land and decided on the following boundary: from the peak Korduleion to the peak Halieion; from Halieion to the peak Keraunion; from Keraunion to the peak Korniatas; from Korniatas to the road on the ridge of Korniatas; from the ridge of Korniatas to the ridge on Aneia above Skolleia; from the ridge above Skolleia under Aneia to the peak over the waggon road leading to Spiraion; from the peak over the waggon road to the peak at Phaga; from the peak at Phaga to the peak at Aigipura; from the peak at Aigipura to the peak of Araia; from Araia to the peak under Petra; from the peak

54 During the Khremonidean war of the 260s when Egyptian-led forces invaded Attica, both the Athenians and the invaders rapidly constructed a number of fortified camps. The rubble walling of one of the Ptolemaic bases, at Koroni peninsula on the east coast of Attica, is shown here.

under Petra to the peak at Skhoinous; from the peak over Skhoinous to the peak by Euorga; from the peak over Euorga to the ridge over Sukousia; from the ridge over Sukousia to the peak over Pelleritis; from the peak over Pelleritis to the peak of Panion; from Panion to the ridge over Holkos; from the ridge over Holkos to the ridge of Apollonion; from the ridge of Apollonion to Apollonion.'[20]

The dispute between Epidauros and Corinth clearly did not involve much territory. What land was involved was rough terrain, not prime land. Prime land had long since ceased to be the subject of dispute in neighbourly conflicts. The countryside was not important for itself, but for the political charge that it carried. Local pride was at stake. Macedonian overlordship reduced the Greek cities to playing at politics, and it was the politics of territory and of the borders of territory that they played.

In the major conflicts between the Greek cities and Macedon the countryside was utterly devalued. This is abundantly clear from the so-called Khremonidean War, when a coalition of southern Greek cities supported by Ptolemy II Philadelphus of Egypt challenged the control of Antigonos Gonatas in the 260s. This conflict left a mark on the countryside of Attica which is still visible today in the form of rapidly constructed forts. The assisting Egyptian troops occupied the little island of Patroklonisi near Cape Sounion, and various points on the east and west coasts of Attica, notably Koroni, Kynosoura, and Vouliagmeni, from which they seem to have advanced on the city of Athens (there are further forts at places such as Helioupolis and Kastraki). The interest of these forts lies in the way that they were built

with no regard at all for the settlement of the Attic countryside – they are placed with a view to military strength and neither pose a threat to nor offer defence of the villages and their inhabitants. Play wars quibbled over desolate countryside; real wars no longer looked twice at the fields through which the troops passed in their advance to victory or defeat. The spoils of victory were the control of the town.

The changes in military strategy altered the very nature of the Greek city. The traditional strategy of hoplite warfare had been developed because of the fundamental importance of the productive countryside. The city which depended upon hoplites for its defence was a city in which the residents of the countryside could not be ignored in the political decisions made in the town. When the military aims of warfare altered and wars began to be fought, in some cases at least, for reasons independent of the production of the fields, the hoplite lost his central place, and the town and the country became distinguishable in military planning. The Classical city provided a paradigm for the independent unit of mutually dependent town and country. Already questioned by the developments of the late fifth century, this mutual dependence was destroyed by the Macedonian conquest of Greece. The city which in the fifth century had fought for its fields and had maintained its identity through border disputes and the military training which they involved, in the third century was reduced to having a quibble about the unproductive mountains settled by a third party in a piece of diplomatic play-acting. In a process of gradual separation warfare became divorced from the farmland and from the farmer, and the Greek city lost its essential identity.

8

THE COUNTRY OF THE GODS

The last chapter showed how developments in military strategy during the Classical period involved a change in the status of the countryside. Traditional warfare put the farmer at the centre of the stage and was fought for and in the farmers' fields. The new strategy operated by some cities in the fourth century changed things in two ways: fighting was increasingly in the hands of specialized professional troops rather than those of the farmer. The country of military service was increasingly not the fields but the wild countryside of the borders.

The changing status of the countryside can also be seen in changing religious practices. Temples and shrines were found all over the territory of the Greek city; there were sanctuaries in and around the town and throughout the countryside. The rituals at these shrines celebrated every aspect of human life and activities. But whatever the specific festival was, the rhythm of the religious year and the central religious actions were dominated by agriculture. It was the agricultural year which determined the calendar of religious festivals. At the same time animal sacrifice made the agricultural countryside central to religious ritual, just as the hoplite battle made it central to military ritual. Through sacrifice and the religious calendar the structure of Greek religious behaviour was rooted in the countryside, but in other ways cult practices

became increasingly divorced from the productive farmland. The objects which men dedicated suggest that they came to think of their relationship with the gods less in terms of the animal world than they had before. New cults exploited the countryside as a wild place rather than as the seat of farming.

Anyone trying to understand and interpret Greek religion faces enormous problems. We are not short of evidence for Greek religious practices. There is plenty of material evidence for the form and siting of temples and shrines and for the nature of imperishable dedications. There are more or less explicit pictorial and literary accounts of what happened at various religious ceremonies. There are numerous literary versions of the stories told in connection with religious actions and festivals, and sometimes these stories are presented as 'explanations' of particular features of those actions or festivals. But we have virtually no discussion by any ancient writer of why temples were built in the form they were, why animals were sacrificed in the way they were, or why certain objects were dedicated to the gods and not others. Any attempt to make sense of all this information must impose a framework of interpretation from the outside.

This chapter takes a partial view of Greek religion. It is based on the assumption that Greek religion made sense. Examining the structure of religious activities and exploring what is common and what is peculiar, continuities and discontinuities, helps to show that Greek religion can validly be seen as 'problem solving'. By his religious actions man reconciled himself to the natural and human environment. Religious practices and the stories told in connection with them created a framework within which man could comprehend the changing world. Because of this, men's reactions to political and social changes were shaped by their religious experiences. Equally, however, new developments in the secular world altered and expanded the religious framework which tried to comprehend them.

The gods of city and country

Temples and sanctuaries were to be found in both town and country. The monumental buildings of holy places frequently dominated both settlements and the unsettled landscape. The structures devoted to cult worship provided the chief man-made landmarks in the countryside. Pausanias' *Guide* to the Greece of his day, the second century AD, is in parts little more than a list of cult places. Here is part of his account of Arkadia in abbreviated form.

'What is left of my account of Arkadia is the road from Megalopolis to Tegea . . . . Among the remains of the city of Oresthasion, on the right of the road after Haimoniai, are some columns of the sanctuary of Artemis . . . . On the straight road from Haimoniai is Aphrodision and then another place called Athenaion, on the left of which is a temple of Athena with a stone statue in it. Just two and a half miles from Athenaion lie the ruins of Asea . . . . Half a mile from Asea is the head spring of the Alpheios with a roofless temple of the Mother of Gods with two stone lions. There is a way up from Asea to

the mountain called Boreion. On the peak of the mountain there are traces of a sanctuary which Odysseus was supposed to have built for Saviour Athena and Poseidon on his return from Troy. . . . At Pallantion is a temple with stone statues of Pallas and Evander, a sanctuary of Demeter and Kore and on the hill above the city a sanctuary of the Pure Gods. . . . On the right of the road to Tegea is a small mountain called Kresion on which is a sanctuary of the Abundant God.'[1]

From this account it is clear that the landscape of Arkadia was littered with religious monuments. Some of these were in towns or former towns, others were at places distinguished by their natural position, at a fountain or on a hilltop. The archaeological record supplements Pausanias' account and makes it clear that the impression which he gives of a countryside dominated by temples is not simply the result of his own particular interests.

No particular god or goddess was worshipped solely in a town or solely in a country environment. In the short excerpt from Pausanias, temples of Athena are recorded both in a former town and on a mountain. Similarly a map of cult distribution in Classical and Hellenistic Attica shows quite clearly that all sorts of gods were worshipped in all sorts of places. Although town and country naturally provided different environments for cult activity, neither town nor country had a monopoly on any particular type of cult place. Monumental Classical temples of marble were to be found in towns, in villages, and in isolated sites. Cave shrines were to be found on the Athenian acropolis and the acropolis of the large village of Eleusis as well as in the mountains. Hilltops frequently attracted cult activity, but this was as true of small hills within or beside towns as it was of mountains in the countryside. But this does not mean that the natural landscape and the human landscape had no influence on the nature of religious activity.

Religious cults exploited the natural countryside, and they also exploited the political countryside of human settlement. The following account of two simultaneous festivals at Sparta brings out some of the ways in which particular religious activities needed different natural and human contexts.

'The Cleaver is a dinner of a special sort. When they hold the Cleaver they put up tents beside the temple (of Apollo at Amyklai), and put wooden couches in them. They spread

55 This small temple of Saviour Athena and Poseidon lay at the top of a pass between Asea and Pallantion on the main route from Sparta to Tegea. It was said by Pausanias to have supposedly been built by Odysseus.

rugs on these and entertain anyone who comes and reclines on the benches, not only natives but also any strangers who are visiting. At the Cleaver they sacrifice only goats, and they give pieces of meat to all, along with small cakes like honey cake but rounder in shape. Everyone who takes part is given a green cheese, a slice of paunch and sausage and dessert of dried figs, broad beans and green beans. Any Spartan citizen who wants to may celebrate the Cleaver. They celebrate the Cleaver in the town, and at the same time they celebrate the Tithenidia or Nurse-Festival for the children. On this occasion the nurses bring the male children into the country, and at the image of Artemis Korythalia they celebrate the Cleaver in a way very like that already described. But they also sacrifice milk-fed sucking pigs and they have oven-baked bread at the feast. The sanc-

tuary of Artemis is by the fountain called Tiassos in the parts towards Kleta.'[2]

In this account it is explicitly stated that the Cleaver which is for citizens and visiting members of other cities takes place in the town, while the Tithenidia takes place in the country and involves those without political rights, the young Spartan boys and their nurses. Both festivals clearly have very strong connections with the agricultural countryside whose products are abundantly provided in the celebrations, but in the second case the additional sacrifice of sucking pig and the setting at a fountain stress the natural fertility and abundance of the countryside and its connections with young life. Ironically the geography of Sparta was such that, although Amyklai counted as 'town', it was almost certainly further from the rest of the 'town' of Sparta than the site where the Tithenidia was held in the 'country'.

Town and country provided distinct religious contexts at Sparta. They did so to an even greater degree in cities where urban and rural life were more clearly distinct. The sanctuaries of the central town were bound up with political activity both because of their position and because of their rituals. The divinity most frequently associated with the town was the goddess Athena. Athena had the epithets Polias (Goddess of the City) and Promakhos (Goddess who fights for us). Her most prominent attribute was the Aegis, a sort of shield. Athena was the most important town goddess not just at Athens, but at Thasos, Sparta, Miletos, and Tegea. At Athens it was the festival of Athena, the Panathenaia, which provided the major excuse for the whole city to parade its military and political strength.

The activities of the town as a community were often reflected in the sanctuaries found immediately outside the town. We have most information on such sanctuaries for Athens. Here several sanctuaries were closely associated with the gymnasia where youths and adult males kept themselves fit for military service. There was the sanctuary of Apollo Lykeios, which was the training ground for both hoplites and cavalry in the Classical period and then became the seat of Aristotle's school (the Lyceum), and the sanctuary of the hero Akademos, which became the site of Plato's 'Academy'. At the sanctuary of Artemis Agrotera a massive goat sacrifice was held annually in memory of the victory in the battle of Marathon. The sanctuary of Heracles in Kynosarges had a gymnasium. In the fifth century this became famed as the meeting place of the sons of Athenian fathers and foreign mothers who lost Athenian citizenship by a change in the law in the middle of the century. All these suburban sanctuaries acquired much of their character by being adopted by one or another social group. Some of these groups were parts of official groups (as the military men who met at the sanctuary of Apollo Lykeios), but they were not essentially so. The sanctuaries outside the walls provided religious foci which were not constrained by the political space within the town. These cults provided the space in which the citizen could be social without being political.

The sanctuaries of the countryside exploited a landscape that was natural, cultivated and also political. Different sanctuaries exploited these different aspects in different ways. A good example of the way in which sanctuaries drew on the cultivated and productive countryside of the farmer is provided by the cluster of sanctuaries in the Attic village of Phlya, northeast of Athens. That village had altars to Dionysos-given Apollo, Artemis the Light-bearer, Flowery Dionysos, the Ismenid Nymphs, Earth, Demeter who sends up gifts, Athena Tithrone, Kore the First-born, and the Holy Ones. The deities and their epithets here make clear the connections with cultivation and the vegetable production of the earth.

Cults developed their natural setting in various ways. One remarkable feature of cults in Boiotia is the way in which a similar natural setting, with a more or less dramatic mountain backdrop and a good water source, is consistently found to be combined with the presence of a cult which gives oracles and which is associated with two divine figures, a hero and a nymph. The archetypal example of this is the sanctuary of Apollo on Mt Ptoion, but cults all over Boiotia fall into a similar pattern. In all these cases the features of the cult seem to have been formed in relation to the natural setting rather than simply to the patterns of human activity in the area.

The political aspect of cults in the countryside is most clearly seen in the cult places frequently found at or near the borders of territories. Such sanctuaries were often the focus of the major religious festival of the city, and on that occasion town and country may have been linked by a procession out to the shrine. By its control of and interest in the cult, the city marked out its possession of its own territory. One very clear example of such a sanctuary is that of Hera at Argos. This sanctuary lies on the northeast border of Argive territory, some 9 km from the town of Argos itself. The sanctuary lies on an acropolis which has extensive views over the whole territory of Argos. Possession of this place was essential to the security of the city of Argos. The development of the sanctuary, which involved building work on a very large scale, occurred at the very end of the eighth century, and cult activity is found here virtually as early as it is found in the town itself. There is little doubt that the develop-

ment of the sanctuary of Hera is to be related to the formation of the city of Argos as a recognizable political unit. Building up the sanctuary was a way of marking out the borders of the city and expressing a commitment to the countryside of the plain as well as to the town site.

The relations between the natural countryside, the agricultural countryside, politics and the siting of cult places were clearly complex. Two examples will show how the simplified picture drawn above was confused in reality.

The goddess most closely associated with agriculture was Demeter (Mother Earth). Her most important Athenian shrine was in the village of Eleusis, but there was also a major shrine in the centre of Athens. The chief festivals of Demeter at Athens had both rural and urban aspects. The festival called the Thesmophoria began outside Athens. It was a festival limited to married citizen women, and after their preliminary celebrations they marched into the town, where they celebrated the way in which their productivity was essential to the continuation of the Athenian citizen body. The other festival was mainly celebrated at Eleusis, but in the course of it there were important processions from Eleusis to Athens as well as from Athens to Eleusis. Because the fertility of the land cannot be divorced from the fertility of its human inhabitants, festivals of Demeter cannot be devoid of political content. This is not true merely of Athens. The Thesmophoria is the festival most widely attested in Greek cities, and the sanctuary at which it was celebrated is almost always close to the city, very frequently in the immediate environs of the city wall. The civic side of the cult is particularly well brought out on Thasos, where a number of altars were found in the sanctuary of Demeter and Kore just outside the city wall. These had been dedicated to the divinities who presided over the phratries, the descent groups into which the citizen body was divided. Here the suburban situation stresses the fact that the women who alone celebrated the festival of the Thesmophoria had no part to play in political affairs. But at the same time the altars recognize that the women are essential to the continuation of the descent groups on which the society is founded.

Artemis had very different associations. The contrast is clearly brought out by considering the festivals of Artemis at Athens. These festivals did not simply happen outside Athens; they were celebrated on the very margins of Attica. The festival of Artemis Mounykhia took place at the shrine of Artemis in the port of the Peiraieus; the Tauropolia took place on the east coast at

Halai Araphenides, around a temple recently uncovered in the sand dunes; and the Brauronia took place at the isolated sanctuary at Brauron, near the mouth of a river in marshy land just a few kilometres south of Halai Araphenides. The Thesmophoria was a festival for citizen wives. The Brauronia, in contrast, focused upon girls entering puberty, and prepared them for the dangerous wild period between the arrival of womanhood and what the Greeks considered the 'taming' of marriage. Artemis Brauronia was the god-

56 This view over the valley of the Erasinos in eastern Attica shows the estuarine site of the sanctuary of Artemis Brauronia. The site was flooded and silted over in antiquity, and the portico in the shape of the Greek letter pi has been reconstructed since the sanctuary was excavated in the 1950s and 1960s. (See also Figure 25.)

dess who received dedications of clothing from adolescent girls with menstrual problems and from mothers who had just given birth. Demeter is appropriated by the city because her associations are primarily cultural; Artemis is banished to the margins because her world is the world of nature.

The case of the cult of Artemis at the small city of Kaphyai in Arkadia shows that the relegation of Artemis to the area outside the town was not simply something that happened at Athens. At Kaphyai, as at Athens, there was a sanctuary of Artemis inside the town, but we know nothing about the cult there except that it involved some mystery rites. Two hundred metres outstide the town, however, was another sanctuary of Artemis, situated in a grove. This Artemis had the cult title 'Strangled', for which Pausanias gives the following explanation: 'Some children playing round the sanctuary found a rope, tied it round the neck of the cult statue and said that Artemis was being strangled. The people of Kaphyai discovered what the children had done and stoned them to death. As soon as they had killed them the women contracted a disease, and their children dropped out of the womb unborn, until the Delphic oracle told them that they must bury the children and burn annual offerings to them because they had died unjustly.'[3]

The children had died unjustly because Artemis was rightly called 'Strangled', for strangulation, for the Greeks, meant shedding no blood, and Artemis is the virgin goddess who presides over childbirth but does not herself bleed, either in defloration or parturition. The story of strangled Artemis focuses on the same areas of life and the same problems of menstrual and lochial blood which dominate the Brauron sanctuary. At Kaphyai as at Athens problems of wild nature are relegated to the wild nature outside the town.

The countryside was not simply the place of farming and of wild nature, it was also a space which was passed through, the emptiness between communities. Just as the seasonal threats to the growing crops are faced in the worship of Demeter, and the life crises of women in the cults of Artemis, so the insecurity of the traveller too needed to be comprehended in religious terms. In the countryside of Attica this was done in a striking way. Along all the roads from the town, half-way between the town and a village, were placed statues of Hermes, pillars with a bearded head on top and an erect phallus in front. On one side of the pillar was an inscription recording that the herm stood half-way to some particular village. On the other side an inscription gave some moralizing advice, such as 'Don't deceive a friend', or 'Pass by, thinking just thoughts'. Hermes was the god associated with transit: he was the god who guided men's souls to Hades after death, and he was the messenger between gods and men. The traveller in Athens was assured by his presence of the possibility of making a safe journey, and he was reminded that his safety depended upon his own honest behaviour. The herms provided a link between the town and the countryside by overseeing the safe passage of the citizen from the fields to the centre and from the centre back to the fields.

The countryside of agriculture, the countryside of wild nature, the countryside of political borders, and the countryside of isolation – religious practices exploited and tried to comprehend all these aspects of the landscape. Individual festivals looked very different and were organized in very different ways, but at the heart of all religious activity was always the productive farmland. For the organization of the religious year and the sacrifice of animals centred all religious activities on the farm.

The agricultural heartland of religion

The religious calendar A society's holy days are also its holidays. The citizen of a Greek city had his life shaped by the festivals to the gods. Those festivals were also feasts, and many poor citizens must have looked forward to festivals for the roast meat which they provided. But as well as giving physical recreation for the body through food and, often, games, the festivals also recreated the community, as those who took part in the feast were drawn together in a common cause. The fact that both the distribution and the nature of the major festivals were largely determined by the farming year therefore had a profound effect on the citizen's perception of agriculture and of the countryside.

The only Greek religious calendar which it is possible to reconstruct in detail is that of Athens. Although a certain number of days each month were set aside for regular festivals to particular deities, the major annual religious festivals were far from evenly distributed through the year.

The Athenian civic year began in July (Hekatombaion), when the new set of annual magistrates took office. This month was marked by two major civic festivals, the Panathenaia and the Synoikia. The Panathenaia was a great carnival, a religious procession of sacrificial cattle combined with a display of military and civic might which included a parade of cavalry and the trundling along of a warship. This was a festival which highlighted the actions of the Athenians as a political body and exhibited their preparations to face the outside world. The Synoikia was more of an inward-looking affair, the celebration of the legendary unification of Attica by Theseus.

The agricultural year began in September/October with a group of festivals of a very different kind. The festival of the Proerosia at Eleusis explicity celebrated the acts of ploughing and sowing. The 'bean festival' of the Pyanepsia, after which the month was named, put the wealth of agricultural produce on display and explored the relationship between continuing plant and continuing human life. The fertility of the citizen wives was celebrated in the Thesmophoria; the important initiation of the growing youth into the social unit at the Apatouria (see p. 149); and the display of young men as ephebes at the Oskhophoria.

The Oskhophoria is described in the following way by an ancient lexicon: 'Oskhophoric songs are what the Athenians sing. Two young men are taken from a dancing group, dressed as women, and put in charge of the feast carrying a branch of a vine laden with fine grapes (the branch is called '*oskhe*', which is where the songs get their name from). The Athenians hold a procession from the temple of Dionysos to the sanctuary of Athena Skiras. The dancing group follows the young men and sings the songs. The ephebes from each of the civic tribes hold a running competition with each other. The one who gets there first tastes from what is called the "fivefold cup", which is a mixture of olive oil, wine, honey, cheese and barley.'[4] This festival links the ripening of fruit with the ephebes' change in status. Agriculture provides the model and the means for the understanding of human physical and social development. Together, the festivals of September/October picked up the moment of ploughing and sowing and used it to celebrate the physical and social beginnings of human life.

The following month, a busy one in the fields (see pp. 13–14), had no major festivals. The two winter months, December and January, saw two major dramatic festivals and also the winter solstice festival of the Haloa. Although the details of this festival are not well attested, it is clear that it involved a feast of both food and ribaldry, when model sexual organs of both sexes made out of pastry were set out on tables. This was a women's festival, and is best understood in relation to the Theogamia in the following month. The Haloa took place when the seed corn had yet to sprout, the Theogamia when it first appeared. The Haloa celebrates the sexual potential in nature, the Theogamia (Divine marriage) the harnessing of that fertility in marriage.

February and March saw two festivals which explored the limits of personal identity. The Anthesteria was the festival at which the new wine of the previous vintage was opened. But the festival was not just a chance to get merry; the opening day of joy and drunkenness was followed by a day marked by rituals to keep evil at bay. The festival celebrates and regulates the power of wine for joy and for madness. The second festival was the Dionysia, the festival named after Dionysos, the god who was most closely associated with wine (see p. 189). The Dionysia was the occasion of the tragic festivals when dramatists competed with sequences of plays which explored the power of man to become other than himself through conscious imitation as well as through inebriation.

April, the season of warfare, and May, which saw the beginning of the harvest, had no festivals which lasted longer than a single day. June, the last month of the civic year, had three important festivals, the Dipolieia, the Arrephoria and the Skira. The Dipolieia explored the interconnection between agriculture and sacrifice and will be discussed at greater length later (p. 179). The Skira and Arrephoria both involved secret rituals and were interdependent and linked to the Thesmophoria. The Arrephoria managed the

57 *This fourth-century terracotta statuette of a female figure holding a pig, which comes from Tegea, almost certainly represents the goddess Demeter. (See also Figure 15.)*

173

transition of the young girl who had been shut away in the women's quarters into the productive wife who weaves and has children and who is central to the Thesmophoria. The Skira seems to have been closely connected with the putting away of the newly harvested grain into storage bins. It celebrated both the production of the dead corn and its reproductive capacity as seed. It appears that pigs were 'buried' at the Skira which were then retrieved at the Thesmophoria.

The agriculturally dead period of July and August is the period of the civic festivals of the first month of the new year, and of the festivals of the Demokratia and the Genesia in the following month. The Demokratia was a celebration of democracy, and the Genesia was a festival of the dead at which the Athenians remembered all those who had died fighting during the year and celebrated the city for which they had died. This burial of the dead soldiers was immediately followed by the festivals of the beginning of the agricultural year which celebrated and produced new soldiers and new citizens.

The agricultural year shapes the religious year, both because the farmer's activities were themselves of vital importance and because they provided a paradigm for the understanding of other aspects of human life. The annual pattern of sowing, cultivation, and harvest provided a framework for the understanding of events of long or uncertain periodicity. The life of the farm provided a model of growth, change, maturity and death; human birth, development, labour and death could be thought about using that model, and because of the regularity of crop development the uncertain human events could be seen to be part of a larger pattern. Farming directly provided livelihood and sustenance for the majority of Greeks. It also provided a way of ordering their lives.

Sacrifice The central action in all Greek festivals and in all Greek worship was the sacrifice of an animal. The more pious the people, the greater the number of animals slaughtered. The gods were considered to judge the holiness of men from the amount of smoke from the burnt thigh-bones of sacrificial animals: 'Of all the cities of men on earth which lie beneath the sun and the starry heavens, the holy city of Troy and King Priam and the folk of Priam of the ashen spear are most dear to my heart. For never does an altar there lack a seemly feast for me, a libation and savoury smoke; and we receive the honour.'[5]

One of the fullest ancient descriptions of the ritual when an animal was sacrificed is provided by the parody of a sacrifice in Aristophanes' play called *Peace*.

'*Trygaios*: Come on. Get the sheep and bring it as quick as you can. I'll provide the altar on which we'll make the sacrifice. . . . Here's an altar by the door. We've got the basket with the special barley grains and the garland for the victim and the knife. There's a fire here, nothing is missing except the sheep. Come on, take the basket and the holy water and go quickly clockwise round the altar. . . . I'll take the torch and dip it, and you, sheep, get on and shake your assent. You, slave, offer some of the barley grains and sprinkle the holy water. Let's make a prayer quickly: "O most holy royal goddess lady Peace, mistress of dancing, mistress of marriages, receive our sacrifice. . . ."

Slave: Take the knife and see that you slaughter the sheep like a good butcher.

Trygaios: But it's not allowed. . . .

Slave: Why?

Trygaios: Peace hardly takes pleasure in slaughter, does she? Her altar doesn't like blood. Bring the sheep inside once dead, cut out the thigh-bones and bring them out here.

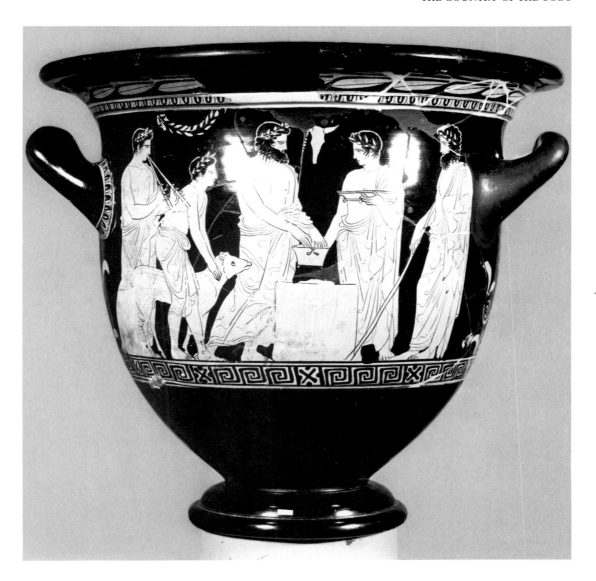

That way we'll have plenty of lamb for the man who put on the play.

    Slave: Take the two thigh-bones and put them here. I'll go for the entrails and the sacrificial cakes. . . .

    Trygaios: Roast them well now. . . . Keep still while you're doing the roasting and mind the chine. . . . Cut out the tongue. Bring the wine to pour a libation.'[6]

58 This crater (mixing-bowl), painted perhaps in the 420s, shows the sacrifice of a young ram. The ram is led to the altar to the music of the double aulos (a reed instrument). The priest is about to sprinkle the ram with purifying water and with barley grains, after which the animal's throat will be slit.

*59 The excavation of the sanctuary of Demeter and
Kore on Akrocorinth recovered hundreds of little flat
model offering trays, and a smaller number of model
winnowing baskets (illustrated here), with assorted
fruits and cakes made of clay. These seem to be of
sixth-century date.*

60 The scenes on the shoulder of this
hydria (water-jar), recovered from the
Etruscan cemetery at Caere, show a
sacrifice to Dionysos. All the stages of
the ritual are shown, from the jointing
of the carcass to the roasting of the
entrails, the boiling of the meat and
ritual ablutions. Sacrifice as butchery
could hardly be more clearly
presented.

The sacrificial victim was led to the altar, induced to nod assent to its own death by being sprinkled with water, and then further sprinkled with whole grains of barley. A knife was taken from the basket of grain and the animal's throat slit. The blood spurted over the altar. The butcher carved up the beast, giving the thigh-bones to be burnt for the god and the entrails to be roasted for the priest and his helpers to eat immediately. The rest of the carcass was boiled. Wine was poured onto the burning bones and sacred cakes for a libation. The sacrifice concluded with a communal feast.

Greek sacrifice was not the killing of any animal. With very rare exceptions the killing of a wild animal did not constitute sacrifice. Sacrificial victims must all be domestic animals, and in particular cases the type of domestic animal was still more closely limited. Two separate stones from the same sanctuary in Rhodes give the following instructions:

'On the sixth of the month Theudaisios let a pig without blemish be sacrificed to Poseidon the god who nourishes.'[7]

'On the twenty-first day of Agrianios, a kid to Dionysos.'[8]

A regulation from Thasos controls by prohibition:

'To the Nymphs and Apollo the leader of the Nymphs, a female or male animal, whichever you wish to sacrifice. It is not allowed to sacrifice a sheep or a pig. No singing. To the Graces it is allowed to sacrifice a goat but not a pig.'[9]

The sacrifice of a farm animal was accompanied by ritual use of other farm produce. This is particularly clearly indicated in the following fourth-century document from the island of Thera: 'Boundaries of the land of the Mother of the Gods. To the good fortune of the good spirit. The sacrifice established by Arkhinos. From the first year sacrifice an ox, a medimnos of wheat, two medimnoi of barley, a measure of wine, and the other first fruits which the seasons bring. Do this on the fifth of the month Artemision and the fifth of the month Hyakinthion.'[10]

Sacrifice reproduced the work of agriculture. The animals that had been bred and the crops that had been grown so that men might live and eat were taken and converted into food. The killing of the animal was made sacred by the presence of a priest, but in other ways sacrifice was not distinguished from secular animal slaughter. The Greeks used the same words to refer to sacrifice, the sacrificial victim, and the man who cut up the animal, as they used of the abattoir. What happens in the slaughter house and what happens at the sanctuary were not verbally distinguished. The sacrifical feast was prepared by the same man as the secular feast and it was prepared in the same way. 'To sacrifice' was simply 'to act' or 'to make [the bones] smoke'. This use of non-specific terms was partly euphemistic, as Plutarch recognized: 'Because they were disturbed and afraid they called it "to do" or "to act", since they were doing something important in sacrificing a living animal.'[11] More importantly, the fact that there is no special vocabulary for sacrificing emphasized that when they sacrifice men only repeat in a dramatic way the action that is the heart of agricultural activity.

The intimate link between sacrifice and agriculture was explored at an early date by the poet Hesiod. In his poem *Works and Days* Hesiod makes explicit the link between arable agriculture and the practice of burning the thigh-bones of sacrificial victims to the gods. He links this practice with the myth of how Prometheus tricked the gods into thinking that thigh-bones wrapped in fat were more attractive than meat.

'The gods have hidden away the corn that is life for men. If they had not you could so work in a single day that you would have enough for a year even if you were idle. You could hang your ship's oar above the fire and there would be no need for the toil of oxen and mules' enduring of labour. As it is, Zeus has hidden corn away, angry in his heart because wily Prometheus tricked him. That is why he devised painful cares for men. He hid fire. But Prometheus the good son of Iapetos stole it back again for men from Zeus the counsellor, hiding it from Zeus who loves thunder in the hollow stem of fennel.'[12]

Prometheus hid thigh-bones, and not meat, in fat. In return Zeus hid the corn. This mythical tit-for-tat links sacrifice with agricultural labour. Men must labour to grow corn if they want to keep domestic animals for meat. Arable farming depends upon there being cereal crops that are distinct from weeds; similarly sacrifice depends upon there being animal victims which are distinct from wild creatures. Man's control of his environment is essential to farming and to sacrifice. Both depend not only on the breeding of plants and animals, but also upon the possession and control of fire. If fire is not under control its raging threatens the countryside with its animals and crops. If man cannot keep and use fire he cannot cook and cannot consume either cereals or meat. Without fire he cannot sacrifice. Agriculture, cooking and sacrifice are the activities which distinguish man from his wild ancestors, and distinguish man from the beasts.

Sacrifice and the labour of the countryside were intimately linked, but their relationship was problematic. The problem is most clearly expressed in the 'explanation' for the ritual at the Bouphonia (Ox-slaying) during the mid-summer festival of Zeus of the City (the Dipolieia) at Athens. The following account is preserved in Porphyry's treatise on vegetarianism, written in the third century AD but depending on a good fourth-century BC source.

'Of old, men used to sacrifice the fruits of the earth, and not living creatures. They did not use the sacrifices for their private consumption. The story is told that when there was a communal sacrifice at Athens, one Diomos or Sopatros, who was not a native but did farm in Attica, had the sacrificial cakes and biscuits laid out on the table in the open in order to sacrifice them to the gods, only to have one of his oxen come in from its labours and wolf down or tread on the lot. Sopatros was so angry with what had happened that he snatched up a whetted axe which was nearby and struck the ox. The ox died. When his anger had cooled and he reflected on the deed he had done Sopatros buried the ox and decided of his own accord to flee, because he regarded himself as impious. He fled to Crete. Drought gripped the land and there was a terrible crop failure. The Athenians consulted the god. The Pythian oracle replied that the exile in Crete would solve matters, and that once they had punished the murderer and resurrected the corpse it would be better for them if they ate the meat in the sacrifice in which the animal died and did not refrain. An enquiry was held and Sopatros was found out. Sopatros thought that he would be freed from the ill-feeling surrounding him for being accursed if they were all to do the same action, and he said to those sent to fetch him that an ox should be axed by the city. They were at a loss as to who would strike the blow, and Sopatros said that he would see to this for them if they made him a citizen and so shared in the murder. They agreed and returned to the city and arranged the action in the following way, which continues to be their practice even now.

'The Athenians chose maidens to carry water jars and bring water to whet the axe and the knife. When the sharpening is done one man delivers the axe which will strike the ox, and another slaughters it. After this, when the flaying has been done, all taste the ox. They then sew up the ox-hide, stuff it with straw, and stand it up again, in the same form as it had when alive, and yoke it to a plough as if it is working. They hold a murder trial and summon all who have been part of the action to defend themselves. The water carriers blame the men who did the sharpening as more guilty than them; they in turn blame the man who passed on the axe; he blames the man who did the killing, and he blames the knife. Since the knife has no voice they condemn if for murder.

'From that time until now the same parties always sacrifice an ox in the same way at the festival of Zeus of the City on the acropolis at Athens. They put a cake and barley scones on the bronze table and then lead farm oxen around. Whichever ox tastes the cakes is killed. There are now families from the actors involved: all those descended from Sopatros who struck the ox are called Ox-Strikers (Boutupoi), those from the man who brought the ox Goaders (Kentriadai). They call those descended from the slaughterer Carvers (Daitroi), after the feast that results from the division of the meat. They stuffed the skin, and when they were brought to trial they sunk the knife in the sea.'[13]

The labouring ox is at the very centre of this rich account. The ox which is sacrificed was the agricultural beast par excellence – it could even be claimed that the ox was the poor man's slave. The ox draws the plough and makes arable agriculture possible. But the ox also consumes part of the grain it helps produce: keeping cattle through the winter involves stall-feeding. If the ox is not to be consumer of the grain it must be killed and itself consumed. The peasant's dilemma is that he needs the plough ox but cannot bear its appetite. The ritual of the Bouphonia creates the fiction that it is possible to have a plough ox that is not a consumer by stuffing the hide of the ox which has itself been consumed.

The killing of the ox involves the whole community in the peasant's dilemma. The peasant who has killed his own ox acts as if he had killed a man; he buries the corpse and flees. His act is even more serious than that: by not eating the ox he has upset the delicate balance of nature, and drought ensues. Not eating the ox undermines the productive capacity of agriculture. But eating an ox is not within the capabilities of a single man – it is a feat reserved for those of heroic stature. Killing an ox must be a communal act because its consumption demands a group of people. The city ends up sharing the guilt for the killing because it shares the meat.

Public sacrifices reinforced and displayed the social structure of the city. By sacrificing the products of agriculture the city reaffirmed the central importance of its territory as a source of food. By dividing and distributing the sacrificial meat the city showed and repeated its social priorities. When the animal was carved up, the entrails which were roasted were consumed by those intimately involved in the sacrifice, but the rest of the animal was jointed and boiled for public consumption. The division and distribution of the meat publicly expressed the extent of the citizen body and the relations within it. This is very clearly brought out in a long decree from the city of Koressia on the island of Keos. The inscription dates to the third century.

'The chief magistrates who are in office are to pay the person who has undertaken the duties 150 drachmas for sacrificial victims.

Whoever takes on the duty is to provide a surety acceptable to the magistrates that he will give the feast as prescribed by law. He must sacrifice one mature ox and one mature sheep. If he sacrifices any pig it must not be older than eighteen months. A feast is to be provided for the citizens, for those invited by the city, for resident foreigners and freedmen and for all that pay taxes to Koressia. Supper, wine, fruit and nuts, and all the rest are to be well provided along with an amount of meat per person not less than 2 mnas in raw weight, and a part of the entrails which the sacrificial beasts have. The chief magistrates and the financial officer and the herald must examine the beasts and weigh the meat and preside at the sacrifice. The supper is to start in the evening, and good wine must be provided until sunset. If the feast meets with the approval of the magistrates, the financial officer is to give the rest of the money to the person who has undertaken the duty on the following day. If not he is to deduct 20 per cent from the sum he hands over.

'The chief magistrates are to arrange for games at the festival at 65 drachmas expense. A gymnasiarch is to be elected along with the other magistrates, a man younger than thirty years of age. He is to arrange a torch race for the young men at the festival and look after the other events in the gymnasium and provide training in throwing the javelin, using a bow, and using a catapult, three times each month. The strongest of the young men who is present is to be in charge of exacting fines of up to 1 drachma. The chief magistrates shall give prizes to the winners: to the man who wins the archery competition, a bow, a quiver of arrows, price 15 drachmas; second prize, a bow, 7 drachmas; to the man who wins in the javelin throwing, three spears and a helmet, 8 drachmas; second prize three spears, $1\frac{2}{3}$ drachmas; to the man who wins

with the catapult, a helmet and a pole, 8 drachmas; to the second man, a pole, 2 drachmas; to the winner in the torch race, a shield, 20 drachmas. The gymnasiarch must also arrange a contest for the boys and give prizes: to the boy who wins the archery, a share in the sacrificial meat; to the boy who wins the javelin throwing, a share in the sacrificial meat. The out-going chief magistrates are to provide the arms and hand them over to the incoming magistrates. The financial officer is to give them the money. A share in the sacrificial meat also to be given to the rhapsode. The chief magistrates also to leave a catapult and 300 bolts until such a time as the council thinks that these are useful. No one is to sell the prizes that he receives: the generals shall require them to be displayed in the inspection. The secretary is to write up the names of the victors on a white board in order, and if the law proves to be good, write it up on a stone pillar and set it up in the sanctuary.'[14]

By the sacrifices and the games at this festival the city of Koressia publicly displays its own civic values. The meat from the sacrifices is used to reward public services, for it is given to citizens, non-citizen benefactors, and tax-payers. The games reaffirm the continuing commitment of the city to being a city of soldiers. The only boys who are given a share in the meat from the sacrifice are those who win the archery and javelin competitions. By giving these boys meat the city effectively promotes them to the citizen body before their time. The link between sacrifice and the military life is an essential one. Sacrifice relies on the production of the countryside; military service defends that production. Agriculture makes sacrifice possible, and sacrifice is a mark of civilized life. But because civilized life depends on agriculture, it must also be a life of warfare.

The scale of animal sacrifice in Classical

cities in fact put a considerable strain on the agricultural resources of the countryside. The Athenians had magistrates called 'Ox-buyers' whose job it was to procure beasts for sacrifice. In the year 334/3 the Athenians had an income of nearly 6000 drachmas simply from the re-sale of the ox-hides of victims of public sacrifice, and that at a time when hired labour could be had at $1\frac{1}{2}$ drachmas a day! Earlier in the century, during the years 377/6 to 375/4 the authorities at the sanctuary of Apollo on Delos spent 8419 drachmas on the purchase of 109 oxen for sacrifice and an uncertain but large further sum on their transport to the island and food on the way.

Even outside major religious centres the number of victims killed was large. Here is an extract from a calendar of sacrifices from late third-century Mykonos, giving the sacrifices for a single month: 'On the seventh of Hekatombaion sacrifice a bull and ten lambs to Apollo Hekatombios. Cut the chine of the bull and give the tongue and the shoulder to the priest. Of the lambs which the boys sacrifice, a tongue is given to the priest and to each boy. Of the lambs which the bridegrooms sacrifice, a tongue is given to the priest and to each bridegroom. On the same day an unblemished ox and ten lambs are sacrificed to Akheloios the river: three of these, the ox and two others, are slaughtered at the altar, the others at the river. The man who cultivates the land sacred to Akheloios is to pay his rent into the treasury of the god for this purpose. On the fifteenth the annual sacrifice to Arkhegetes. . . .'[15]

Some cities kept sacred herds of cattle and flocks of sheep to meet the need for sacrificial victims (see p. 49), but in others the provision of animals for sacrifice constituted an important part of the exchange between country and town. Where the sanctuaries, whether those of the town or those of the country, paid for the animals they needed with coinage, this was an important source of liquid cash for the countryside.

Cities which sacrificed had to be cities which engaged in agriculture. Where there was no agriculture there could be no sacrifice. Sacrifice thus signals man's control of the wild world, and marks the separation of man from beast. The way in which sacrifice and feasting were means of displaying control over the natural environment is well illustrated by the following story: 'When Xenophon was in exile from Athens and living in Skillous near Olympia where he had been settled by the Spartans, the Persian Megabyzos arrived on a visit to Olympia and gave him his money. Xenophon accepted the money and bought a plot of land for the goddess where the god indicated. It happened that there was a river Selinous flowing through the plot, and in Ephesos too a river Selinous flows beside the temple of Artemis, and there are fish and mussels in both. In the plot at Skillous there are also animals of all the sorts that men hunt. Xenophon made an altar and a temple from the money dedicated to the goddess, and from then on he always made a sacrifice to the goddess of a tithe of the seasonal produce from the land, and all the citizens and neighbouring men and women shared the feast. The goddess provided barley, bread, wine, fruit and nuts and a share of the beasts that were sacrificed from the holy pasture for the picnickers, and also hunted animals. For Xenophon's sons and those of the other citizens made a hunt for the feast along with some of the men who wanted to join in. Some of the animals were caught in that sacred place, and some from Pholoe, wild boar, roe deer and stags.'[16]

The feast which Xenophon gives combines enjoyment of sacrifice with enjoyment of the spoils of the hunt. It celebrates the enormous productivity of this rural retreat, but in doing so it also makes an open statement about man's control of his environment and his free ability to exploit it.

When man's relationship with and control over the animal world is upset, ordinary sacrifice becomes impossible. In his travels (related in the *Odyssey*) Odysseus meets a whole series of beings who are not quite human and do not stand clearly separated from the beasts. These creatures all stand in an odd relationship to both agriculture and sacrifice. The Cyclopes are shepherds who do not till the ground; they live off the produce which the earth spontaneously brings forth for them. They do not butcher and they do not cook. When the Cyclops eats members of Odysseus' crew he consumes them raw. Odysseus himself is unable to make a proper sacrifice in this land, for he has only cheese. Odysseus' own companions subsequently seal their own fate by killing the cattle of the sun. This is an unacceptable act partly because they are unable to sacrifice the cattle in the normal way. The cattle are really wild, and there are no cultivated barley grains with which to sprinkle them and only water and not wine with which to pour libations.

The close connection between sacrifice and the civilized life is further brought out, and given a moral dimension, in the complex of stories which concern Aristaios and Orpheus. Aristaios is the exemplary countryman. A master pastoralist, he watches over the herds of the Muses and is the first man to make cheese. A pioneer of cultivation, he is the first to get edible olives from the oleaster and the first to manage bees with hives. A hunter, he is credited with the invention of various trapping devices.

Aristaios' success in agriculture is intimately linked with sacrifice. When the people of Keos were suffering from plague brought on by unrelieved summer heat because of an unavenged murder, Aristaios had them build altars and make sacrifices. The winds immediately began to blow from the north, and the plague ceased. In this episode the wild climate is controlled by sacrifice just as the wild countryside is controlled by farming. In a second episode Aristaios had his bees die. He went to consult his nymph mother and, after a sacrificial feast, is told where he can learn what to do. He finds out that the death of his bees is a result of the fact that he caused the death of Orpheus' wife Eurydike, who had died of a snake bite when fleeing Aristaios' amorous pursuit. To regain his bees Aristaios has to sacrifice four bulls and four heifers and then leave their carcasses in the open, where, after nine days, they will generate bees. Aristaios' knowledge and success as an agriculturalist are dependent upon his offering sacrifices.

The story of the bees reveals the link between sacrifice and civilization in a still stronger way. Aristaios' success and failure as a bee-keeper relate not just to sacrifice but to his personal behaviour. When he pursues Eurydike Aristaios departs from the norms of civilized sexual relations within marriage. This is why his bees die. When he sacrifices the cattle he does not cut up the carcasses and share them with men; the civilized society needed to consume the sacrificial meat is provided by the bees. Bees were popularly thought to be a model of civilized society and were considered to have a marked aversion to all that smacked of sexual desire.

'Bees carry those of their number who die out of the hive. In other respects also the bee is the cleanest of animals. They often release their excreta when in flight, because of its nasty smell. They dislike both unpleasant odours and the smell of myrrh, and so they sting all those who use perfume.'[17]

'Why are bees keener to sting those who

have enjoyed illicit sex? Perhaps because the bee is the animal that is most observant of cleanliness and neatness, and because it has the keenest sense of smell. Since irregular intercourse is usually more unclean because of the unchastity and uncontrolled lust, bees detect it more quickly and conceive a greater hatred towards those involved. That is why in Theokritos the herdsman sends Aphrodite jokingly away to Anchises to be stung by bee stings because of the adulterous act saying "Off you go to Mt Ida, off you go to Anchises, where the oak and the galingale grow and the bees buzz in their hives".'[18]

Aristaios' improper conduct towards Eurydike put him outside civilized society and hence made it impossible for him successfully to keep bees. By sacrificing, Aristaios socializes himself again, and he regains his bees.

Eurydike's death sent her husband Orpheus into deep grief. In many ways Orpheus is the perfect complement to Aristaios. Aristaios is the farmer; he domesticates wild nature through agriculture and hunts what remains wild. Orpheus blurs the distinction between wild and domestic by the way in which he charms animals and trees and rocks to follow his music. Orpheus almost manages to blur the boundaries between life and death by gaining permission to retrieve Eurydike from Hades. This inversion of the pattern of civilized life is matched by Orpheus' problematic relationship to sacrifice. Orpheus was seen as the inventor of the vegetarian way of life, preaching that the sacrifice of animals is wrong and that blood should not be shed. When Eurydike was finally lost, the all-too-uxorious Orpheus cut himself off from female society and was torn to pieces by the resentful married women of Thrace. Orpheus will not sacrifice and his relationship with the civilized world is thus upset. The man who will not

sacrifice is himself sacrificed.

This group of stories about Aristaios and Orpheus explores the relationship between society, agriculture, wild nature and the gods. It shows how murder and adultery upset the natural order and destroy the proper conditions for agriculture, and it illustrates the restoration of these conditions through the sacrifice of cattle to the gods. It also shows how improper sacrifice, the vegetarian sacrifice of Orpheus, fails to make the distinction between wild and domestic that is essential to civilized life. Without that distinction normal social relations cannot be maintained: the civilized women become slaughterers and the priest becomes the victim. In the story of Aristaios agricultural society is temporarily disrupted but finally returns to its proper order. In the story of Orpheus the order of agricultural society is systematically inverted: Orpheus tries to live in a utopia where the normal rules of nature do not apply. In the end the breakdown becomes complete and Orpheus is the victim of his own transgression of civilized norms.

Sacrifice was not just the central religious rite; it was perceived as essential to society. Sacrifice itself depended upon the agricultural countryside, not only for the provision of its animal victims but for the model of productive consumption which it exploited. As long as Greeks sacrificed they put the farmer at the centre of civilized life and ensured that Greek culture was quintessentially agricultural. When they consumed sacrificial meat, even more than when they consumed other food, the citizens of the Greek city declared their dependence upon the countryside.

The countryside revised: dedications

Sacrificing an animal was not the only way to display piety. Greek sanctuaries were packed with objects of all sorts which individuals and groups had dedicated to the gods. Offering a sacrifice was always a communal activity, at least to some extent. Dedications could be made by an individual on his own. Sacrifice was a one-off act which left no permanent trace. Dedications remained on display to exhibit the individual's piety to his contemporaries and even, in some cases, to future generations.

Dedications took a large number of different forms. Just as various personal crises could lead a man or a group to make a sacrifice, so also dedications marked various con-

cerns. But unlike sacrifices dedications often reflected in their form the particular occupation or preoccupation of those who made them. A dedication from sixth-century Rhodes bears the inscription 'Onesos the bronzesmith dedicated me to Apollo – the wheel of a cart'[19] and takes the form of a miniature bronze cartwheel. Because their form is sensitive to the particular concerns of the dedicator, dedications reveal something of the changing worries men had and how

61 This small bronze cartwheel (7.5 cm in diameter) was dedicated to Apollo by a Rhodian bronzesmith in the late Archaic period. The smith presumably derived part of his livelihood from putting bronze tyres onto cartwheels.

the way in which men perceived their relationship to the gods changed.

The connection between the form of the dedication and the motive of the dedicator is by no means always clear. Archaic sanctuaries were frequently crowded with near life-size standing male and female figures, called *kouroi* and *korai*. The sanctuary of Apollo on Mt Ptoion in eastern Boiotia had at least 120 such statues. But despite the number of dedications which took this form it is impossible to determine what the dedicators thought they were doing. The statues cannot represent the dedicator, since men dedicate female figures; but equally they cannot represent the divinity to whom they are dedicated either, since goddesses receive male figures. These statues seem to have derived much of their special power from this anomalous status, and they provide a timely warning that dedications may be far from easy to interpret.

During the Geometric and early Archaic periods many sanctuaries received large numbers of small bronze animals as dedications. The selection of animals varies from sanctuary to sanctuary, but the number of animal statuettes is almost always very high, only exceeded in some places by pins and rings. At the Kabirion sanctuary near Thebes virtually the only sign of cult activity from the tenth to sixth centuries is the dedication of a large number of bronze oxen. At Olympia 99 per cent of the early bronze statuettes are of horses or large cattle. At Delphi horse statuettes are the most numerous, but cattle, deer, rams, and a number of birds are also found. Birds and horses dominate the bronze statuettes at the sanctuary of Artemis Orthia at Sparta and the Thessalian site of Pherai. At Philia, also in Thessaly, birds and deer are found but practically no horses.

We know that dedications were sometimes made in place of sacrifice or as a permanent memorial of sacrifice. A dedication from fourth- or third-century Cyrene was inscribed: 'Hermesandros set this up above the fountain as a memorial when he made a sacrifice to the goddess at the festival of Artemis, bringing 120 oxen. This is his glory and memorial and good fame.'[20] But the numerous animal statuettes cannot stand for sacrifices, for they include large numbers of animals which were never sacrificed – horses, deer, and birds. Also, these animals are not the animals of agriculture. The horse was never a beast of burden in ancient Greece, and birds and deer were wild animals. The dedicators cannot have been consecrating the animals with which they worked and on which they depended, any more than they were making substitute sacrifices. Part of the special interest of these dedications is that they show quite clearly that men were thinking in terms of the animal world, but they also show

62 This small bronze statuette of a horse (8 cm long), dating to c. 700 BC, is typical of the small animal figures which appear in large numbers in sanctuaries of the Geometric and early Archaic periods. This example comes from Pherai in Thessaly. (Compare Figure 5.)

that animal world was the whole animal world and not simply the world of agriculture.

In the late Archaic period animal statuettes die out almost completely. Bronze statuettes in general decline in number after 650 and are very rare after 500. At the Kabirion bronze cattle continue to 500. Cattle are still found after that but are now made of terracotta and accompanied by figures of men and of other animals. At Olympia there had always been a tradition of terracotta animal dedications, but these die out with the bronzes. At Artemis Orthia terracottas take over from bronzes in the middle of the seventh century and horses remain numerous. In Thessaly, on the other hand, the terracotta tradition which takes over from the bronzes is dominated by human figures.

Animals hardly figure in the dedications of the Classical period. Small dedications largely take the form of pots, and when these have painted decoration that decoration shows human or heroic scenes. Where terracottas are found they take the form of figures of the god or goddess involved or of human figures. Nor is it the case that animal dedications were made, but were of perishable material. Inventories from a number of different sanctuaries make it clear that various objects were dedicated which have since perished, but these tended to be items of clothing or pots made of precious metal.

Most Classical sanctuaries received a great variety of dedications. The only exceptions seem to be sanctuaries which were predominantly concerned with one particular aspect of life. Thus the sanctuary of Artemis at Brauron went on receiving the same limited selection of items of clothing throughout the Classical period because women made dedications here in connection with childbirth. This exception suggests that the variety of

dedications elsewhere was a product of the very different concerns that men had when they made their offerings.

If changes in types of dedication are seen as a reflection of the changing concerns of the dedicators, then it is clear that the decline of animal dedications implies a change in the way in which men thought about the animal world. In the Geometric and early Archaic period men seem to have regulated their relations with the divine in terms of the animal world; in the Classical period this was no longer the case. Whereas it is images of animals which dominate early dedications, as indeed they dominate early art, it is figures of men and the gods themselves which dominate the imagery of Classical dedications.

Something of the changing pattern of men's concerns in their relations with the gods can be seen in the history of the Kabirion sanctuary. Bronze and lead figurines of oxen are the first signs of cult activity on the site. In the late sixth century the first terracotta figurines appear, and with the change in material comes the introduction of human and other animal figures. At the same time two peculiar types of pot appear in the dedications: open bowls with fluted bodies and large handles called *kantharoi*, which are also found on some other sites, and bowls of a form unique to this sanctuary (Figure 64). The pots are decorated with scenes showing human figures, including what may be illustrations of myths in dramatic performance. The sanctuary seems to have used the natural auditorium provided by the hillside as its religious space from the beginning, but the first buildings on the site, which appear in the Classical period, seem to have been dining rooms. The sanctuary acquired a proper temple only in the Hellenistic period.

The sanctuary belonged to a very shadowy figure called Kabiros. Kabiros appears in the earliest inscriptions and the sanctuary seems to have been his from the beginning. But the changing nature of the dedications and of the buildings of the sanctuary suggest that the elements of the cult which were seen as important changed over time. Bone remains indicate that the normal sacrificial victims at the sanctuary were sheep and goats, and it seems unlikely that the cattle figurines are simply a reflection of the sacrificial practice. In the Archaic period Kabiros was clearly closely associated with large cattle, but from the fifth century onwards he develops other associations which end by swamping the bovine connection. The unusual predominance of large cattle in the early dedications suggests that cattle had a special and precise role, and were not simply symbolic of a general concern for agriculture. There is no way, however, that the cattle imagery could avoid being rooted in agriculture, or a cult with such a public face not engage in a dialogue with the life of the countryside. The changing appearance of the sanctuary and of its dedications implies that from the fifth century onwards the countryside became less pervasive as the medium for thinking about human relations with the gods.

63 This view across the Kabirion sanctuary shows the theatre, and the temple which was first constructed in the Hellenistic period. The natural hillside seems to have formed the auditorium for earlier rituals.

64 RIGHT This typical Kabirion cup shows a shaggy-haired centaur confronting two grotesque beardless male figures (possibly a parody of Peleus bringing his son Akhilleus to the centaur Kheiron to be educated).

The countryside made wild: Dionysos and Pan

Cult innovations in the Classical period were not limited to changes in what men dedicated to the gods. Cults of particular deities waxed and waned, old sanctuaries fell into disuse and new sanctuaries were built. Two cults which attained a new importance in the Classical period promoted a view of the countryside which contrasts quite markedly with the agricultural countryside of sacrifice and the religious calendar.

The cult of Dionysos can be traced well back into Greek antiquity, but the Greeks themselves always represented this god as an outsider. In several temples of Dionysos the cult statue was said to have been brought from outside. 'They say that the statue comes from Euboia. When the Greeks coming home from Troy were shipwrecked at Kaphereus, the Argives who managed to reach the land suffered badly from cold and hunger. They

prayed, and some god saved them in their misery. As soon as they moved on they came across a cave of Dionysos with his statue in the cave and wild goats huddling inside from the storm. The Argives slaughtered them, dined on their meat, and dressed in their skins. When the storm was over, they fitted up ships and travelled home, bringing with them this wooden idol from the cave. They still pay honours to it to this day.'[21] The Athenians themselves related how their cult and statue of Dionysos came from the town of Eleutherai ('Liberation') on the borders of Attica and Boiotia.

The temples and official rites of Dionysos were firmly based on the town. The Great Dionysia at Athens became almost as much a display of civic finery as the Panathenaia, involving a parade of the ephebes who were shown off to the city's allies. But Dionysos had another side.

The characteristic rites of Dionysos were

189

ABOVE AND ABOVE RIGHT
65 *Dionysiac revelling featuring music, drinking, playing with wild beasts, erotic dancing and ecstatic behaviour is shown here on the exterior of a drinking cup painted by the Brygos painter in the early fifth century.*

66 *Dionysos, garlanded and wearing the skin of a big cat, tears apart a goat. The tearing apart of wild animals was one of the most notorious activities associated with Dionysiac worship.*

private and essentially rural. These private rites did not involve normal sacrifices or dedications. They were marked by the abandonment of cultural constraints. Associated with the frenzy of drunkenness and of mental derangement, Dionysos was seen to promote the transgression of all boundaries. Worshippers ran in disorganized frantic hordes over the mountains, pulling up plants, killing animals with their bare hands, and tearing them up to eat in bleeding chunks. The countryside of the Dionysiac reveller is the countryside as a place outside the city, where nature is uncontrolled and the worshipper can escape from his social identity. The countryside of Dionysos lies at the limits of the world and has little that is human about it: 'It is difficult even for an active man to reach the peaks of Parnassos; the peaks are

above the clouds and the Thuides run raving up there for Dionysos and Apollo.'[22]

The fully liberated worshipper of Dionysos existed more in the telling than in the action. Drunken revelling in the streets of the town was probably the nearest most came to experiencing Dionysiac ecstasy. But what is important is the telling. The stories and images of raving worshippers of Dionysos conjured up a picture of a countryside which was outside civilization, a countryside which had nothing to do with agriculture, a countryside which was wild.

Pan really was a new arrival in Attica in the historical period. The history of his cult suggests that there had been a real change in the perception of the countryside during the Classical period. Pan came not from the fringes of the Greek world but from Arkadia.

In Arkadia Pan was worshipped as a master-of-the-animals figure who controlled wild beasts and protected domestic creatures. He was worshipped in temples as a normal deity: 'You can climb up the steps to a sanctuary of Pan. It has a colonnade and a small statue – though Pan can answer prayers and give wickedness what it deserves as effectively as the most powerful of gods. A never-extinguished fire burns in front of Pan, and they say that in olden days this god used to give oracles.'[23] The god with whom Pan was most closely associated in Arkadia was Demeter.

Pan first appears in Attica around 500. He entered public cult because he was said to have met the runner the Athenians sent to Sparta for help against the Persian invasion, and to have promised to fight on the Athenian side. The cult of Pan was quickly dispersed through Attica, but it centred not on temples but on cave sites, which received large numbers of dedications. Pan was associated with mental derangement, with both panic and obsession, and being possessed by Pan was a condition to be avoided rather than courted. Pan's cult essentially involved individuals rather than groups.

The caves of Pan occupied a geographical position unlike that of any other sanctuary. They were well off the beaten track and sometimes demanded considerable feats of rock-climbing for access. Himself a goatherd, Pan was, in Attica, far from being a god of goatherds, with whom his relations were somewhat equivocal. All the evidence suggests that Pan's worshippers were not those engaged in pastoral activities, but prosperous citizens, many of them not local men but men from the town. For these men Pan stands for a countryside which is not the countryside of the shepherd, but a countryside of the mind. The rugged mountains of the caves of Pan provided an image of wildness which was in complete contrast to the civilization of the town. Worshipping Pan was a way of escaping from society (see frontispiece).

Here there is a peculiarly pointed version of the paradox of the Greek city with which this book began. The religious calendar and the practice of sacrifice put the working countryside at the centre of religious cult, and construed human experience in terms of the facts and value of the farmer's life. Yet the changing nature of dedications suggests that the animal world became much less central to men's conception of their relationship with the gods, and the cults of Dionysos and Pan imply that, in as far as the countryside continued to be a model for human relations with the divine, it was the wild countryside and not the agricultural countryside which was important. Sacrifice went on declaring that the countryside was the fundamental source of an ordered, cultured life-style. Worship of Dionysos and Pan declared that the countryside was outside society, the place of marginal experiences and the place of the wild.

9

EPILOGUE: THE USES OF THE COUNTRYSIDE

No two Greek cities were identical. Cities varied in size, in situation, in settlement pattern, in resources, in political arrangement. Some cities were too small to be securely independent, like Thisbe and Siphai in Boiotia which were only free of the control of Thespiai when Thespiai itself had been oppressed by the still more powerful city of Thebes. Other cities had so large a territory that controlling it created particular problems; Spartan control of the whole of the southern Peloponnese demanded extraordinary social arrangements. Many cities, especially in the central Peloponnese and in central Greece, were land-locked; other cities became dependent upon their access to and use of the liquid roads of the sea. The whole organization of Athens relied on its territory being sown with villages, but in other cities the territory had no villages at all and sometimes little in the way of permanent residential settlement outside the town. The rich silver resources of the tiny island of Siphnos made it exceptionally prosperous during the Archaic period; the rather ordinary stone resources of the Corinthia became a major resource because Corinth enjoyed the highly advantageous position of having ports on two seas.

The arrangements in any single city varied enormously over time. Mineral resources were discovered and exploited; in time they were exhausted or became unworkable, as on Siphnos. Residential preferences changed. Rural buildings for temporary or permanent residence sprang up and were deserted with amazing rapidity. Whole settlements of considerable size were abandoned: the Aegean islands in particular are littered with well-built and carefully planned small towns of the Geometric period which came to nothing – sites like Lefkandi on Euboia and Zagora on Andros. Political regimes enjoyed no longer life. Many Greek cities were repeatedly split by strife between men of opposing political ideologies. At different times political power lay with a single man, a small group of wealthy men, heavily armed soldiers, or all adult males. In the Classical period cities frequently had their form of government influenced by outside forces, by a major imperial power such as Athens, or just by a bigger neighbour.

But there are limits to the diversity. The Greek city does have a unity. What is distinct about the Greek city is best revealed by the contrast between that city and the cities of the Roman, medieval, and early modern periods. The Greek city is not just a town, it cannot be divorced from its countryside. By the Roman period this was no longer true even in Greece itself. By the later Roman era the countryside ran itself almost independently of the town: village markets obviated the need for travel to the town to exchange goods; men thought of themselves as from a village rather than from a city and recorded villages as their places of origin; village and city politics had little or nothing to do with each other. The later Roman city foreshadows the enclosed medieval city of which Pirenne has written, 'Once outside the gates and the moat we are in another world, or more exactly, in the domain of another law'.

The Greek city was as far from the early modern city as it was from the medieval city dominated by crafts and guilds. In the early modern period a system of cities developed in which individual cities were functionally differentiated and each enjoyed a peculiar position in the larger economic system. Classical Greece, where exchange was consumer-dominated, knew nothing like this. The difference between the Classical and the early modern city can be illustrated by comparing the measures taken by the Athenians to ensure that shippers sailing from Athens brought corn back to Athens with the English Navigation Acts of the mid seventeenth century. The English Navigation Acts, passed to combat Dutch control of Atlantic commerce, limited the importation of most goods to English vessels or to ships of the country which produced the goods carried, and required English vessels to be built and manned domestically. The Athenians were only concerned with securing imports for consumption; the English Acts encourage production and export.

Urbanization was unknown in Greece. European urbanization took off, before the Industrial Revolution, when it became possible to invest in areas other than land, and when the peasant was forced into the market. The investment market was created by government debt, rapidly expanding trade, and new mortgage laws. The peasant was forced to continue to work, even when wages and incomes rose, by increased government exactions to support larger bureaucracies and standing armies. But even in Athens there was no government debt, property was mortgaged almost exclusively for non-productive purposes, such as raising a dowry for a daughter, and trade never acquired the regularity or the proportions to encourage regular or large investment. Money taxes were few and small, and they fell very largely on the very rich. There was no standing army, and the cost of the administration was trifling, not only by modern standards but also when compared with the cost of a gold and ivory cult statue. Slaves had little motive to increase efficiency, and free labour was almost certainly in limited supply, as peasants were content to survive and had little desire to improve their economic position if it meant working harder. None of the conditions necessary to encourage a significant proportion of the population to devote themselves to non-agricultural occupations were met in any city in Classical Greece.

Only in very peculiar circumstances did anything like an 'urban system' develop. In the fifth century, after driving the Persians from mainland Greece, a number of Greek cities got together under Athenian leadership to continue the struggle against the barbarians. This demanded prolonged campaigns with a large military force. These campaigns were expensive, and the Athenians came to be prepared to use force to extort tribute from other Greek cities in order to pay for them. Here, and only here in all Greek antiquity, a network of cities came close to being an economic network, albeit in a very partial sense. But although the Athenian empire did leave a mark on the territories of its allies (see pp. 132–133), the political links and the fiscal exactions created nothing in the way of an independent economic system with its own momentum which could outlast the decline of Athens as an imperial power.

The Greek city will not fit any model derived from subsequent urbanization, because it was not an urban unit. The essential mark of the Greek city is political independence, the possession of an administration and facilities for administration. Political independence is neither a necessary nor a sufficient condition for a town. Urban units are characterized by the size and density of their population, by the proportion of the population engaged in occupations other than farming, and by the range of non-agricultural professions. Even the cities of Greece were in many cases but tiny villages in population; Koressia on Keos had a total population of perhaps 700 to 800. The central settlements were often highly dispersed, loose groups of villages separated by tracts of farmland (see pp. 116 and 155 on the polyfocal settlements of Sparta and Tegea). All Greek cities were overwhelmingly agricultural, with a very restricted range of manufacturing. The most important non-agricultural production, in economic terms, frequently went on well outside the confines of the major settlement, as with the mining of silver at Athens and Thasos (Chapter 4).

The Classical city was embedded in the countryside. Agriculture made the Greek city possible and established its limits. The agricultural production of the countryside shaped the social structure. Patterns of residence and land-holding played a major part in establishing the political framework and the nature of political crises. The tone of life in the city was dependent on the city's ability to feed itself from its own territory. Some parts of the Greek world could rely on fairly predictable agricultural production. In other parts it was always touch and go whether the land would

produce enough to live on. The risk of harvest failure was always high, the range of plant and animal life which the countryside could support always tightly circumscribed. Cities frequently in need had to look outside for sustenance and had to rely in part on men not engaged in agriculture. Harvest failures hit the poor harder than the rich and threatened to split the citizen body. But it is a measure of the fact that the community was *not* divided between producers and consumers that food riots, which were frequent in Rome and a major form of political expression in early modern Europe, are all but unknown in Classical Greece.

Individual Greek cities and individual Greek farmers both aimed to be self-sufficient, but with very different consequences. The farmer reduced his risks by growing a variety of crops and by growing them in a number of different locations. The city, by contrast, endangered its position by trying to grow all its own food. The Greek peninsula as a whole probably produced enough food for its own subsistence demands in all but the most extraordinary harvest failures, but individual cities faced shortage, if not famine, with monotonous repetition. The more a small city pursued a policy of subsisting from its own resources, the more vulnerable it became to shortage.

Fluctuations in agricultural production were not a thing peculiar to Classical Greece. The whole history of Europe until the eighteenth century is scarred by cycles of crop failure, high prices, and resultant social and political tension. Eighteenth-century Europe finally broke the cycle, not by technological innovation but by changes in the social organization of production and by improving the means of distribution. In Classical Greece agricultural production was limited by social choice, and the distribution network remained under-developed because of the political commitment of the city to self-sufficiency. The social organization of the Greek city assumed that all were farmers; the politics of self-sufficiency forced the city to be countrified.

The special value which the Greek city placed on its own particular countryside put the peasant at the centre of political life, as citizen and as soldier. It made the borders of the city a particularly sensitive area. The borders rarely had any permanent residents or any important resources, agricultural or otherwise, but since the countryside was the city, for a city to allow the borders to be raided was to allow its integrity to be breached. The connection between the city as independent political unit and the city as countryside was intimate. Once the Greek city lost its political autonomy, the pattern of exploitation and occupation of the countryside began. The loss of city autonomy led directly to the development of urban units and the independent life of the countryside characteristic of the Roman period.

Even within the Classical period there are signs that the role of the citizen was changing, and with it his relation to the countryside. The identity of citizen and soldier began to be undermined. Wars remained predominantly border raids until well into the Hellenistic period, but new 'rules' of combat began to develop during the late fifth and the fourth century as wars became more political and cities looked to annex whole territories. This change moved the emphasis away from the citizen hoplite and battles in the fields, and towards walled towns and ultimately expendable territory. The new warfare demanded specialists, and this meant mercenary soldiers and professional generals. The citizen now became less of a jack-of-all-trades – farmer, politician, civil servant, soldier –

and the process of differentiation had begun which led eventually to the birth of the urban city and rustic countryside out of the inseparable unit of town and country which was the Classical Greek city.

Greek religious practices signal the way in which the city remained bound to the country but began to see that country as separate. The timing and the nature of the central acts of religious cult were structured around the production and exploitation of the countryside. But changing patterns of dedication show that it became less and less automatic to think with and through the animal world. New cults suggest that for some men the countryside was no longer perceived as the source of sustenance and comfort, but as a wild place where the bonds of society could be thrown off.

Most Greeks could not help thinking with the countryside. The young Spartiates being trained in the long Spartan schooling were formed into 'herds' under an 'ox-driver', were seen as 'foals' to be 'broken', and became, in the ritual at the sanctuary of Artemis Orthia, 'young foxes'. But although they thought *with* the countryside, they rarely thought about it. The countryside stamped its mark on the Greek city, but the city did little consciously to reform the countryside. Only with the peculiar shrines to Pan in Attica in the fourth century do we see man imposing their own views of the countryside on the landscape.

The beginnings of conscious thought about the countryside went with the beginnings of conscious thought about the town. The differentiation of the citizen body made clear what was special about the town just as it made clear what was special about the countryside. In the late fourth century the countryside makes virtually its first independent appearance in literature, in the pastoral poetry of Theokritos. Theokritos' countryside is not the working productive countryside of the citizen farmer, grinding his living out of the stony soil; it is the erotic countryside of young men looking after sheep, goats and cattle, a countryside not of war but of song. Theokritos both gives us this, the first countryside independent of the town, and also the first town which is distinctly urban, in the bustling scene of urban love and charms in Idyll 2.

The paradox of the Greek city is neither accidental nor benign. It was essential to the nature of the city that the countryside should be both vital and unmentioned. The Greek city was not a town and its territory, it *was* its citizens, as Classical authors not infrequently noted. The citizens lived in various forms of settlement, but all were dependent upon the production of the countryside, and most of them had a direct hand in that production. Citizens fought for the countryside and the life-style they enjoyed, and they thought with and through that same country. The particular landscapes of individual cities shaped citizens' lives in particular ways, but the common emphasis on the corporation of citizens gave Greek cities a shared ideology which had the countryside at the centre. The central position of the countryside in citizen ideology was precisely what prevented it being discussed. Only in the fourth century are there signs that the conventional ideology of the city was beginning to be questioned. It was questioned precisely in those two cities, Athens and Sparta, about which we know most but which, for very different reasons, were set apart from the majority of Classical cities. This book attempted to set Athens and Sparta in a wider perspective and to give them a broader context. Having started with a paradox the book ends with an irony. The achievements which are central to the Western Classical tradition and to our conventional picture of the Classical Greek city came from cities which were essentially marginal in the array of Greek cities.

Bibliography

Abbreviations

The following works are cited in abbreviated form in the notes.

Austin   M. Austin, *The Hellenistic world from Alexander to the Roman Conquest* (1981).

BCH   Bulletin de Correspondance Hellénique.

Fornara   C. Fornara, *Translated Documents of Greece and Rome, Vol. 1, Archaic Times to the end
                of the Peloponnesian War* (1977).

Fouilles de   *Fouilles de Delphes exécutées par ordre du gouvernement francais et publiées sous la direction
Delphes   de M. Théophile Homolle*, 4 vols (1904–   ). ii. Topographie et architecture; iii.
                Epigraphie; iv. Monuments figurées: Sculpture; v. Monuments figurées.
                [NB Publication still ongoing.]

Fraser and Bean P. Fraser, G. Bean, *The Rhodian Peraea and Islands* (1954).

Harding   P. Harding, *Translated Documents of Greece and Rome, Vol. 2, From the end of the
                Peloponnesian War to the Battle of Ipsus* (1985).

Insc. Dél.   Inscriptions de Délos

IG   Inscriptiones Graecae

IJ   R. Dareste, B. Haussoullier, T. Reinach, *Recueil des inscriptions juridique grecques* (1891).

Lazzarini   M. Lazzarini, *Le formule delle dediche votive nella Grecia arcaica* (Memorie
                dell'accademia dei Lincei, Ser. VIII 19.2) (1976).

ML   R. Meiggs, D. Lewis eds, *A Selection of Greek Historical Inscriptions to the end of the
                fifth century* BC(1969).

Pleket   H. Pleket, *Epigraphica* I (1964).

*SIG*³   W. Dittenberger ed., *Sylloge Inscriptionum Graecarum*, 4 vols (1915–1923).

Tod   M. Tod, *A Selection of Greek Historical Inscriptions, Vol. 2, from 403 to 323* BC (1948).

References to the *Proceedings of the Cambridge Philological Society* refer to the New Series, which is indicated by the letters ns.

Ancient Authors

The following is a guide to the translations and editions of the works of ancient authors quoted in the text.

Aineias the Tactician, *What to do about a siege*. Text, translation and commentary by L. Hunter, Aeneas, *On Siegecraft* (1927).

Aristophanes, *Peace*. Edition by M. Platnauer; Aristophanes' *Peace* (1964). Translated with commentary by A. Sommerstein, *The Comedies of Aristophanes, Vol. 5, Peace* (1985).

Aristotle, *Constitution of Athens*. Full-scale commentary by P. Rhodes, *A Commentary on the Aristotelian Athenaion Politeia* (1981). Translated with notes by P. Rhodes, *The Athenian Constitution* (Penguin Classics 1984).

Aristotle, *Enquiry into Animals (Historia Animalium)*. Translated with parallel Greek text in the Loeb Classical Library by A. Peck, Aristotle, *Enquiry into Animals*, 3 vols (1965–70).

Aristotle, *Meteorologica*. Translated with parallel Greek text in the Loeb Classical Library by H. Lee, Aristotle, *Meteorologica* (1952).

Aristotle, *Politics*. Translated with explanatory notes by E. Barker, Aristotle, *Politics* (1946).

Athenaios, *The Deipnosophistai*. Translated with parallel Greek text in the Loeb Classical Library by C. Gulick, Athenaeus, *The Deipnosophists*, 6 vols (1927–37).

Demosthenes, *Orations 37, 42, 47*. There is a new commentary on Demosthenes 37 in C. Carey, R. Reid, Demosthenes, *Selected Private Speeches* (1985). Otherwise these speeches are best read in the French translation with facing Greek text by L. Gernet, Démosthène, *Plaidoyers civils*, vols 1 and 2 (1954, 1957).

Diodoros, *World History*. Translated with facing Greek text in the Loeb Classical Library by C. Oldfather, C. Bradford Welles, R. Geer, F. Walton, Diodorus, *World History*, 12 vols (1933–67).

Hellenika Oxyrhynkhia. Commentary by I. Bruce, *An Historical Commentary on the 'Hellenika Oxyrhynchia'* (1967). Translated in J. Wickersham, G. Verbrugghe, *Greek Historical Documents. The fourth century* BC (1973).

Herodotos. There is no good modern commentary. There is a good translation by A. de Sélincourt (with introduction and notes by A. Burn), Herodotos, *The Histories* (Penguin Classics 1972).

Hesiod, *Works and Days*. Edition and commentary by M. West, Hesiod, *The Works and Days* (1976). Translated by D. Wender, *Hesiod and Theognis* (Penguin Classics 1973).

Hippocratic corpus, *Airs, Waters, Places*. Translated in G. E. R. Lloyd ed., *Hippocratic Writings* (1978).

Homer, *Iliad*. The best translation is that of R. Lattimore, *Iliad* (1951).

Isokrates, *Speech 4 (Panegyricus)*. There is an edition of this speech by J. Sandys, Isokrates, *Ad Demonicum and Panegyricus* (1872, reissued 1979).

Lysias, *Speech 22*. The speeches of Lysias are best consulted in the French translation with facing Greek text by L. Gernet, M. Bizos, Lysias 2 vols (1964, 1967).

Menander, *The Disagreeable Man*. There is an edition with commentary by E. Handley, *The Dyscolus of Menander* (1965).

Pausanias, *Guide to Greece*. The classical translation and commentary is J. G. Frazer, *Pausanias' Description of Greece*, 6 vols (1898). Readily available is the translation by P. Levi, Pausanias, *Guide to Greece* (Penguin Classics, 1971). The fullest and best illustrated archaeological commentary is in the edition with modern Greek translation by N. Papakhatzis, *Pausaniou Ellados Periegesis*, 5 vols (1974–81).

Photios, *Bibliotheca*. The only modern edition is the French translation with facing Greek text by R. Henri, Photius, *Bibliothèque*, 8 vols (1959–77).

Plato, *Laws*. Translated by T. Saunders, Plato, *The Laws* (Penguin Classics, 1970).

Plutarch, *Greek Questions*. Edition with translation and commentary by W. Halliday, Plutarch, *Greek Questions* (1928).

Plutarch, *Life of Lykourgos*. Translation and facing Greek text in Loeb Classical Library by B. Perrin, Plutarch's *Lives*, Vol. 1 (1914).

Plutarch, *Life of Perikles*. Translated by I. Scott-Kilvert, Plutarch, *The Rise and Fall of Athens* (Penguin Classics, 1960).

Plutarch, *On Sokrates' Divine Sign*. Translation with parallel Greek text in Loeb Classical Libary by P. Lacy and B. Einarson, Plutarch's *Moralia*, Vol. 7 (1959).

Plutarch, *Questions About Nature*. Translation with parallel Greek text in Loeb Classical Library by F. Sandbach, Plutarch's *Moralia*, Vol. 11 (1965).

Plutarch, *Table Talk*. Translation with parallel Greek text in Loeb Classical Library by E. Minar, Plutarch's *Moralia*, Vol. 9 (1961).

Polybios. There is a massive commentary by F. Walbank, *A Historical Commentary on Polybius*, 3 vols (1957–79). A selection of the whole work is translated by I. Scott-Kilvert, Polybius, *The Rise of the Roman Empire* (1979).

Porphyry, *On Abstinence*. Best consulted in the French translation with facing Greek text by J. Bouffartigue, M. Patillon, Porphyry, *De Abstinentia*, 2 vols (1977–79).

Strabo, *Geography*. Translated with facing Greek text in the Loeb Classical Library by H. Jones, Strabo's *Geography*, 8 vols (1917–32).

Theophrastos, *Characters*. Edition with commentary and translation by R. Jebb and J. Sandys, Theophrastus, *The Characters* (1909).

Theophrastos, *Enquiry into Plants (HP)* Translated with parallel Greek text in the Loeb Classical Library by A. Hort, Theophrastus, *Enquiry into Plants*, 2 vols (1916).

Theophrastos, *On the Causes of Plants (CP)*. Books 1 and 2 are translated with parallel Greek text in the Loeb Classical Library by B. Einarson, G. Link, Theophrastus, *De Causis Plantarum* (1976).

Theophrastos, *On Stones*. Edition with translation and commentary by D. Eichholz, Theophrastus, *De Lapidibus* (1965).

Thucydides, *Histories*. Translated by R. Warner with introduction and notes by M. Finley, Thucydides, *The Peloponnesian War* (Penguin Classics, 1972).

Xenophon, *Oikonomikos*. Translation with parallel Greek text in the Loeb Classical Library by E. Marchant, Xenophon, *Memorabilia and Oeconomicus* (1923).

Xenophon, *Hellenika*. Translated by R. Warner with introduction and notes by G. Cawkwell, Xenophon, *A History of my Times* (Penguin Classics, 1979).

Xenophon, *The March Up Country*. Translated by R. Warner with introduction and notes by G. Cawkwell; Xenophon, *The Persian Expedition* (Penguin Classics, 1972).

Xenophon, *Ways and Means*. There is a splendid commentary by P. Gauthier, *Un Commentaire historique des Poroi de Xenophon* (1976).

General Bibliography

For a general introduction to the history of Greece from the Archaic to the Hellenistic periods, the reader is recommended to consult the volumes of the Fontana History of the Ancient World: O. Murray, *Early Greece* (1980), J. Davies, *Democracy and Classical Greece* (1978), and F. Walbank, *The Hellenistic World* (1981).

In as far as the questions addressed in this book have been tackled at all before, they have been tackled by scholars dealing with the Archaic period; see in particular A. Snodgrass, *Archaic Greece: The Age of Experiment* (1980). For a programmatic statement see S. Humphreys, 'Archaeology and the social and economic history of Classical Greece' and 'Town and country in ancient Greece' in *Anthropology and the Greeks* (1976), 109–35. There are general remarks of considerable interest in M. Finley, *The Ancient Economy* (1973), 123–49, and G. de Ste Croix, *The Class Struggle in the Ancient Greek World* (1981), 9–19, 208–26.

Some ancient sources are usefully collected, with commentary, by M. Austin, P. Vidal-Naquet, *Economic and Social History of Ancient Greece* (1977).

The best discussion of the constant factors governing Greek history, which bulk large in chapters 1–5 here, is to be found in F. Braudel, *The Mediterranean and the Mediterranean World in the Age of Philip II*, Vol. 1 (1972).

1   The Paradox of the Greek City

The passages from ancient authors quoted in the text are:

1 Hippocratic corpus, *Airs, Waters, Places* 168–9.
2 Hesiod, *Works and Days* 639–40.
3 Hesiod, *Works and Days* 744–5.
4 Xenophon, *Oikonomikos* 5.1.
5 Plutarch, *Life of Perikles* 16.
6 Xenophon, *Hellenika* 5.2.7.
7 Xenophon, *Hellenika* 6.5.3.
8 Xenophon, *Hellenika* 7.5.14f.

Warfare: for bibliography and further discussion see Chapter 7. For the longest invasion of Attica in the Archidamian war see Thucydides 2.57.2.

Building: for bibliography and further discussion see Chapter 4. The inscriptions from Eleusis are *IG* ii² 1672 and 1673, on which see further R. Osborne, *Demos: the Discovery of Classical Attika* (1985), 105–7. The Delphic evidence may be found in *Fouilles de Delphes* iii. 5. 20 lines 15, 27, 47, 54 and 98 ff.

The site of Askra is discussed by A. Snodgrass, 'The site of Askra' in P. Roesch, G. Argoud eds, *La Béotie antique* (1985), 87–96.

On the Attic stelai the basic work is that of W. Pritchett, 'The Attic stelai. Part 1', *Hesperia* 22 (1953), 225–9, and 'The Attic stelai. Part 2', *Hesperia* 25 (1956), 178–317. See also D. Amyx, 'The Attic stelai. Part 3: Vases and other containers', *Hesperia* 27 (1958), 163–310, and D. Lewis, 'After the profanation of the Mysteries' in E. Badian ed., *Ancient Society and Institutions: Studies presented to Victor Ehrenberg* (1966), 177–91. The latest texts of the inscriptions are published in *IG* i³ 421–30. The long list of cloaks is 421.212–49; Axiokhos' pictures are found at 427.59–62; large quantities of grain appear especially at 421.108–40.

For the property of Axiokhos see 422.201–2 424.10–11, 427.63–85, 430.33; of Euphiletos see 426.78, 430.14–19; of Panaitios 422.204–7, 426.53–64.

On Mantineia the basic monograph is G. Fougères, *Mantinée et l'Arcadie orientale* (1898). There is a useful survey of the archaeology of the area in S. and H. Hodkinson, 'Mantineia and the Mantinike. Settlement and society in a Greek polis', *Annual of the British School at Athens* 76 (1981), 239–96.

2 Farming the Country

The passages from ancient authors quoted in the text are:

1 Aristotle, *Meteorologica* 1.13.
2 Theophrastos, *Enquiry into Plants* 8.7.6.
3 Aristotle, *Meteorologica* 2.4.
4 *SIG*³ 963 1–36.
5 *IJ* XXIII C.
6 *BCH* 89 (1965), 665 ff. Col. 3 lines 2–7.
7 *SIG*³ 986.
8 *IG* v 2. 3.1–21.

A convenient, if technical, introduction to the geology of Greece for the English reader can be found in D. Ager, *The Geology of Europe* (1980), 500–14. The fullest description of the Greek landscape is to be found in A. Philippson, *Die griechischen Landschaften*, 4 vols (1952–6).

For an introduction to the climate of Greece see D. Furlan, 'The climate of southeast Europe' in C. Wallén ed., *Climates of Central and Southern Europe, World Survey of Climatology, Vol. 6* (1977). For the debate about the causes of soil erosion and whether erosion in various parts of Greece and the Mediterranean occurred at the same time see C. Vita-Finzi, *The Mediterranean Valleys* (1969), and J. Wagstaff, 'Buried assumptions: some problems in the interpretation of the "Younger Fill" raised by recent data from Greece', *Journal of Archaeological Science* 8 (1981), 247 ff.

The shipment of grain from Cyrene is recorded in Harding 116, Tod 196. Tod has a helpful commentary.

Questions related to the uses of timber in the Greek world are dealt with in R. Meiggs, *Trees and Timber in the Ancient Mediterranean World* (1982). For timber and relations between Athens and Macedon see *IG* i³ 89 and 117. *IG* i³ 89 receives commentary in ML 91 and translation in Fornara 161.

The estate of Phainippos is described in [Demosthenes] 42.2 and 5–7, and discussed in G. de Ste Croix, 'The estate of Phainippus' in E. Badian ed., *Ancient Society and Institutions: Studies presented to Victor Ehrenberg* (1966), 109–14. Hesiod recommends wood-cutting in September in *Works and Days* 419 ff. The lands of Philokrates are discussed by R. Osborne, *Demos: the Discovery of Classical Attika* (1985) 52f.

For fragmented land-holdings in modern Greece see H. Forbes, '"We have a little of everything": the ecological basis of some agricultural practices in Methana, Trizinia' in M. Dimen and E. Friedl eds, *Regional Variation in Modern Greece and Cyprus. Annals of the New York Academy of Science* 268 (1976), 236–50. The discussion by J. Wagstaff and S. Augustson, 'Traditional land use', in A. C. Renfrew and J. Wagstaff eds, *An Island Polity* (1982), 106–33 covers strategies, methods and productivity, but the figures in the tables for the latter are not reliable.

For Hesiod on making a plough see *Works and Days* 427 ff. Theophrastos' observation that digging is good for all soils comes at *CP* 3.10.1. For working heavy soils in summer, light in winter see *CP*

3.20. For Theophrastos on leaching and deep digging see *CP* 3.20. 7f. Xenophon mentions green manure at *Oikonomikos* 16.12. For pulses as a fallow crop see *IG* ii² 2493 (compare ii² 1241). For leaving land fallow for two years see Theophrastos *HP* 9.11.9, *CP* 4.6.1. Problems of standing water appear in *CP* 3.6.3, 3.12.1, and the reaction of wood to wet conditions in *HP* 1.8.1, 4.11, 5.1.12, 5.9.2, *CP* 3.11.

The traditional pessimistic view of ancient productivity is classically represented by A. Jardé, *Les Céréales dans l'antiquité grecque : la production* (1925). The fluctuation in cereal yield in Thessaly is discussed by P. Halstead, 'From determinism to uncertainty : social storage and the rise of the Minoan palaces' in A. Sheridan and G. Bailey eds, *Economic Archaeology. Towards an Intergration of Ecological and Social Approaches* (1981), 187–213, and by P. Garnsey, T. Gallant and D. Rathbone, 'Thessaly and the grain supply of Rome during the second century BC', *Journal of Roman Studies* 74 (1984), 30–44. For an optimistic view of the possibilities of ancient cereal production see G. Sandars, 'Reassessing ancient populations', in *Annual of the British School at Athens* 79 (1984), 251–62, who explores the data from Melos since the seventeenth century. Melos has exceptional soils and Sandars' figures cannot be transferred directly to other parts of Greece. For the amount of grain consumed per head of population in Classical Greece see H. Forbes, L. Foxall, 'Sitometreia : the role of grain as a staple food in Classical antiquity', *Chiron* 12 (1982), 41–92.

The Eleusis inscription recording shares of wheat and barley dedicated to Demeter and Kore is *IG* ii² 1672. The discussion of the Rheneia estates here is based on the work of John Kent, 'The temple estates of Delos, Rheneia and Mykonos', *Hesperia* 17 (1948), 243–338. Some doubt is cast on Kent's assumptions by M-T. Le Dinahet-Couilloud, 'Identification des domaines d'Apollon à Rhénée' in *Les Cyclades. Matériaux pour une étude de géographie historique* (1983), 135–9. The Thespian land lease is most conveniently consulted in M. Holleaux, *Études d'epigraphie I* (1938), 99–120.

On pastoralism see H. Koster, J. Koster, 'Competition or symbiosis? Pastoral adaptive strategies in the southern Argolid, Greece' in M. Dimen, E. Friedl eds, *Regionai Variation . . .* (cited above), 275–85. On ancient transhumance see S. Georgoudi, 'Quelques problèmes de la transhumance dans la Grèce ancienne', *Revue des études grecques* 87 (1974), 155–85. The classic account of a transhumant pastoral society in modern Greece is J. Campbell, *Honour, Family and Patronage* (1964).For specific grants of the right to pasture animals at Tegea see *IG* v 2. 10, 11 and 17. For Aristotle on the large cattle of Epiros see *Enquiry into Animals* 3.21.

The goat pasture of the island of Herakleia is discussed by L. Robert, 'Les chèvres d'Herakleia', *Hellenika* 7 (1949), 161–70, commenting on *IG* xii.7 509. The boundary between Delphi and the Ambryssians and Phlygonians is published and commented on in *Fouilles de Delphes* iii. 2. 140–7.

3 A Settled Country?

The passages cited from ancient authors quoted in the text are:

1 Demosthenes 47.52f.
2 Strabo, Geography 8.1.1.
3 Strabo, *Geography* 8.3.2.
4 Thucydides 2.14.2.
5 Aristotle, *Politics* 1252b 29–30.
6 *IG* xii.8 683.
7 *Insc. Dél.* 503.33f.
8 *IG* xii.5 872 50–55.

9 *IG* xii.5 872 78–82.
10 *IG* xii.5 872 19.

There is, and as yet can be, no history of settlement in Greece as a whole. Sketches of the settlement history of particular areas appear in the publications of archaeological surveys mentioned below. For a perceptive study of the settlement history of one area of the Peloponnese in recent times see J. Wagstaff, *The Development of Rural Settlement: A Study of the Helos Plain in Southern Greece* (1982). For the human issues involved in settlement choice the best general guide is provided by J. Davis, *People of the Mediterranean* (1977).

The archaeological evidence: a good impression of the strengths and weaknesses of extensive survey can be gained from reading J. G. Frazer's tremendous commentary on Pausanias with its detailed descriptions of the remains mentioned by Pausanias as they could be traced at the end of the nineteenth century: J. G. Frazer, *Pausanias' Description of Greece* (6 Vols, 1898) (Vol. 1 is a translation of Pausanias, Vol. 6 has indices and maps).

An impression of the range of recent survey activity in Greece can be gained from D. Rupp and D. Keller eds, *Archaeological Survey in the Mediterranean Area* (1983). The issues raised are well discussed by John Cherry, 'Frogs round the pond: perspectives on current archaeological survey projects in the Mediterranean region' in that volume pp. 375–416. For settlement on Melos see A. C. Renfrew, J. Wagstaff eds, *An Island Polity. The Archaeology of Exploitation on Melos* (1982), especially 10–23, 136–55, 246–90, with additional comments on the density of early Archaic sites by R. Catling in *Classical Review* 34 (1984), 98–103. For Keos see J. Cherry, J. Davis and E. Mantzourani eds, *An Archaeological Survey of Northern Keos in the Cyclades* (1987).

The results of the Boiotia, Argolid and Megalopolis surveys await final publication. On Boiotia see J. Bintliff, A. Snodgrass, 'The Cambridge/Bradford Boeotian expedition: the first four years', *Journal of Field Archaeology* 12 (1985), 123–61. For a less complete survey of a wider area of territory see W. Mac-Donald and G. Rapp, *The Minnesota Messenia Expedition: Reconstructing a Bronze Age Regional Environment* (1972), the chronological scope of which is wider than the title indicates.

On Askra see bibliography for Chapter 1. On the villages of Attica see R. Osborne, *Demos: the Discovery of Classical Attika* (1985). On single towers see J. Young, 'Studies in south Attica: century estates at Sounion', *Hesperia* 25 (1956), 122–46, J. Pečirka, 'Homestead farms in Classical and Hellenistic Hellas' in M. Finley ed., *Problèmes de la terre en Grèce ancienne* (1973), 113–47, and A. Lawrence, *Greek Aims in Fortification* (1979). For further discussion of the towers of Thasos see R. Osborne, 'Island towers: the case of Thasos', *Annual of the British School at Athens* 81 (1986).

Discussion of the relationship between settlement and moral values in Italy will be found in S. Silverman, 'Agricultural organization, social structure and values in Italy', *American Anthropology* 76 (1968), 1–20.

For extended discussion of the Thespiai and Karthaia lease documents see R. Osborne, 'The land leases of Hellenistic Thespiai: a reconsideration', in P. Roesch and G. Argoud eds, *La Béotie antique* (1985), 317–23, and R. Osborne, 'Land use and settlement in Classical and Hellenistic Keos: the epigraphic evidence', in J. Cherry, J. Davis, E. Mantzourani eds, *An Archaeological Survey of Northern Keos in the Cyclades* (1987). For Rheneia see above Chapter 2. The Hyampolis document is published as *IG* ix.1 87. The Larisan document is discussed by F. Salviat and C. Vatin, 'Le cadastre de Larissa', *BCH* 98 (1974), 247–62, and C. Habicht in V. Milojcic *et al.* ed., *Demetrias 1* (1976), 157–73. See also more generally, T. Boyd and M. Jameson, 'Urban and rural land division in ancient Greece', *Hesperia* 50 (1981), 327–42.

4 The Country Disrupted

The passages from ancient authors quoted in the text are:

1 *IG* ii² 1582 63–69.
2 *IG* ii² 1180.
3 *Fouilles de Delphes* iii. 5. 19 lines 41 ff.

For Aristotle's distinction between things mined and things quarried see *Meteorologica* 378a.

Mining: for a general introduction to the ancient exploitation of metal resources see J. Healy, *Mining and Metallurgy in the Greek and Roman World* (1978). Older, but still important even for Classical Greece, is O. Davies, *Roman Mines in Europe* (1935).

On iron see A. Snodgrass, 'Iron and early metallurgy in the Mediterranean' in T. Wertime and J. Muhly eds, *The Coming of the Age of Iron* (1980).

Silver: the Laurium mines have long been studied by scholars with historical and technological interests. The best recent study, with good illustrations, is C. Conophagos, *Le Laurium antique* (1980). In English see R. Hopper, 'The Attic silver mines in the fourth century', *Annual of the British School at Athens* 48 (1953), 200–54, J. Ellis Jones, 'Laurion: Agrileza, 1977–83: excavations at a silver mine site', *Archaeological Reports* 31 (1984–5), 106–23, and R. Osborne, *Demos: the Discovery of Classical Attika* (1985), 111–26 and 29–36. The speech devoted to mining matters is Demosthenes 37; for Xenophon on the mines see *Ways and Means* 4. For Herodotos on the mines at Dysoron see Herodotos 5.17. For Diodoros on the Philippi mines see *World History* 16.8.6. On the mines of Thasos see A. Müller, 'Le mine de l'acropole de Thasos', *Thasiaca, BCH Supplément* 5 (1979), 315–44, and J. de Courtils, T. Koželj, A. Müller, 'Des mines d'or à Thasos', *BCH* 106 (1982), 409–17.

Quarries and stone: for Theophrastos on precious stones see *On Stones* 5.32. A fairly comprehensive survey of existing scholarship on Greek quarries is given by A. Dworakowska, *Quarries in Ancient Greece* (1975). Issues to do with building are well covered by A. Burford, *The Greek Temple Builders of Epidaurus* (1969) and by A. Burford, 'The economics of Greek temple building', *Proceedings of the Cambridge Philological Society* ns 11 (1965), 21–34.

On transport of stone see A. Burford, 'Heavy transport in Classical antiquity', *Economic History Review* 13 (1960), 1–18 and A. Snodgrass, 'Heavy freight in Archaic Greece' in P. Garnsey, K. Hopkins and C. R. Whittaker eds, *Trade in the Ancient Economy* (1983), 16–26. The latter addresses the question of the transport of *kouroi*. For the cost of transport at Delphi see *Fouilles de Delphes* iii. 5. 26–7. On the building of the temple of Zeus at Olympia see B. Ashmole, *Architect and Sculptor in Classical Greece* (1972), Chapter 1.

The quarries of Attica are discussed at greater length by R. Osborne, *Demos* (cited above) 93–110. See also R. Wycherly, *The Stones of Athens* (1978). For the quarries of Thasos see J-P. Sodini, A. Lambraki, T. Koželj, 'Les carrières de marbre d'Alikí à l'époque paléochrétienne', *Alikí 1* (1980), 79–137.

On the possibility of dating quarrying traces by the techniques employed see M. Durkin, C. Lister, 'The rods of Digenis: an ancient marble quarry in eastern Crete', *Annual of the British School at Athens* 78 (1983), 69–96. For the identification of marbles by traditional methods see G. Lepsius, *Griechische Marmorstudien* (1980). The article which first clearly showed the difficulties of marble identification was A. C. Renfrew, J. S. Peacey, 'Aegean marble. A petrological study', *Annual of the British School at Athens* 63 (1968), 45–66. See more recently K. German, G. Holzmann, F. Winkler, 'Determination of marble provenance: limits of isotopic analysis', *Archaeometry* 22 (1980), 99–105.

5 Exchange and Society

The passages from ancient authors quoted in the text are:

1 Theophrastos, *Characters* 4.11.
2 Theophrastos, *Characters* 10.13.
3 Hesiod, *Works and Days* 388–402.
4 Hesiod, *Works and Days* 348.
5 Aineias the Tactician, *What to do about a siege* 7.
6 Austin 116, *SIG*³ 976.
7 Aristotle, *Constitution of Athens* 51.3–4.
8 Lysias 22.
9 Fornara 63, ML 30.
10 Austin 115, *SIG*³ 493.
11 Xenophon, *Hellenika* 5.4.56–7.
12 Demosthenes 50.6.
13 Austin 50.
14 Austin 97, *SIG*³ 495.
15 Austin 111 §3, *IG* ii² 1013.
16 Pleket 2.
17 Xenophon, *Ways and Means* 4.9.
18 Theophrastos, *Characters* 5.6.

The place of trade in the ancient economy has attracted much academic attention in the past century. The best introduction to the debates is provided by K. Hopkins, 'Introduction', in P. Garnsey, K. Hopkins and C. R. Whittaker eds, *Trade in the Ancient Economy* (1983). All discussions of exchange have to be set against the background of the means of transport and communication. These are well discussed by J. Landels, *Engineering in the Ancient World* (1978), Chapter 6, 'Ships and sea transport', and Chapter 7, 'Land transport'.

Peasant loans and Hesiod are discussed by P. Millett, 'Hesiod and his world', *Proceedings of the Cambridge Philological Society* ns 30 (1984), 84–115. On debt bondage and the Solonian agrarian crisis see M. Finley, 'Debt bondage and the problem of slavery' in B. Shaw and R. Saller eds, *Economy and Society in Ancient Greece* (1981), 150–66. On loans and debt in Classical Athens see M. Finley, 'Land debt and the man of property in Classical Athens', *ibid.* 62–76.

Study of trade in staple crops has been much advanced by recent work. This is best represented by P. Garnsey, 'Grain for Athens' in P. Cartledge and F. Harvey eds, *Crux. Essays presented to G. E. M. de Ste Croix* (1985), 62–75, and by the contributions to P. Garnsey and C. R. Whittaker eds, *Trade and Famine in Classical Antiquity* (1983) by Bravo, Jameson, and Rathbone. Demosthenes' claims about Athenian cereal imports are made in Demosthenes 20.31–3. The episode of Rhodian interception of Spartan grain ships is related by Diodoros, *World History* 14.79. For Athens' continued need to get home grain harvested see Austin 44. The classic treatment of the politics of benefaction is P. Veyne, *Le Pain et le cirque* (1976).

Thasos. For the various wine laws see J. Pouilloux, *Recherches sur l'histoire et les cultes de Thasos* I (1954), 37–45, 130–2. For the amphora kilns and the amphora stamps see Y. Garlan, 'Les timbres amphoriques thasiens', *Annales, économies, sociétés, civilisations* 37 (1982), 837–46.

The best general treatment of pottery production and pottery trade is provided by D. Peacock, *Pottery in the Roman world* (1982), especially 12–74. The standard text-book on Greek pottery is R. Cook, *Greek Painted Pottery* (1960).

6 The Politics of Settlement

The passages from ancient authors quoted in the text are:

1 Thucydides 1.2.2–5.
2 Aristotle, *Politics* 1319a 19–38.
3 Plutarch, *On Sokrates' Divine Sign* 580 D-F.
4 *Hesperia* 20 (1951) 223.
5 Austin 83 (Herakleides Kretikos (?) 1.1).
6 Thucydides 1.10.2.
7 Pausanias 10.4.1.
8 Pausanias 8.13.5.
9 Polybios 4.73–4.
10 Isokrates 4.42.

The best short introduction to ancient politics is provided by M. Finley, *Politics in the Ancient World* (1983). Relations between space and politics are well explored, but in a way not at all like that pursued here, by J-P. Vernant, 'Space and political organization in ancient Greece', *Myth and Thought among the Greeks* (1983), 212–34.

The excavation of the area of the street of the Hermoglyphs in Athens is published by R. Young, 'An industrial district of ancient Athens', *Hesperia* 20 (1951), 135–288. The best introduction to the public buildings of Athens is provided by J. Travlos, *A Pictorial Dictionary of Ancient Athens* (1971).

For Olynthos see D. Robinson ed., *Excavations at Olynthos* (14 vols, 1929–52); vols 8 and 12 are particularly important for the matters discussed here.

The most recent archaeological and historical monograph on Corinth is J. Salmon, *Wealthy Corinth* (1984). For the Punic amphora building see C. Williams, 'Corinth 1978. Forum SW', *Hesperia* 48 (1979), 106–24, C. Williams 'Corinth excavations 1979', *Hesperia* 49 (1980), 107–34.

For the remains at Arkadian Orkhomenos see F. Hiller von Gärtringen and H. Lattermann, *Arkadische Forschungen* (1911), 18–31, and G. Blum and A. Plassart, 'Orchomène d'Arcadie', *BCH* 38 (1914), 71–88. The proxeny inscriptions from Orkhomenos are published by G. Blum and A. Plassart, 'Inscriptions d'Orchomène d'Arcadie', *BCH* 38 (1914), 447–78. A very similar picture is found at Lousoi, see W. Reichel and A. Wilhelm, 'Das Heiligtum der Artemis zu Lusoi', *Jahreshefte der österreichischen archäologischen Instituts in Wien* 4 (1901), 1–89.

On Sparta see generally P. Cartledge, *Sparta and Lakonia* (1979), P. Oliva, *Sparta and her Social Problems* (1971), and S. Hodkinson, 'Social order and the conflict of values in Classical Sparta', *Chiron* 13 (1983), 239–81. For the importance of the helot threat in determining Sparta's foreign policy see G. de Ste Croix, *The Origins of the Peloponnesian War* (1972).

The Thasian evidence is assembled and commented on by J. Pouilloux, *Recherches sur l'histoire et les cultes de Thasos* 1 (1954). The best description of Thasos town is to be found in G. Daux and others, *Guide de Thasos* (1968). For the signpost inscription from Alikí see F. Salviat and J. Servais, 'Stèle indicatrice thasienne trouvée au sanctuaire d'Alikí', *BCH* 88 (1964), 267–87.

Elis: for the union of Elis in the early fifth century see Diodoros, *World History* 11.54, Strabo, *Geography*

8.3.2 and Herodotos 4.148. For the inscriptions suggesting loose connections between centre and villages see W. Dittenberger and K. Purgold, *Inschriften von Olympia* (1896) nos 16 and 10. For the survey of the area of the Peneios valley near Agrapidokhori prior to flooding for a reservoir see *Arkhaiologikon Deltion* 20 B (1965) 215–18, 23 B (1968) 174–94, 24 B (1969) 155–61, and 25 B (1970) 197.

On the political organization of Attica see J. Traill, *The Political Organization of Attica* (1975), and R. Osborne, *Demos: the Discovery of Classical Attika* (1985). For the nature of the Council see P. Rhodes, *The Athenian Boule* (1972). On Kleisthenes' reforms see D. Lewis, 'Cleisthenes and Attica', *Historia* 12 (1963), 22–40, and P. Lévêque and P. Vidal-Naquet, *Clisthène l'Athénien* (1964).

For the possible effects of Athenian imperialism on settlement patterns in the Aegean island see A. C. Renfrew, J. Wagstaff eds, *An Island Polity* (1982), 246–90.

On the history of Boiotia in general see R. Buck, *A History of Boiotia* (1979); on the first Boiotian confederacy see P. Salmon, *Étude sur la confédération béotienne (447/6–386)* (1978): on the second confederacy see J. Buckler, *The Theban Hegemony 371–62* (1980); on the third confederacy see P. Roesch, *Thespies et la confédération béotienne* (1965). For the evidence of Aristotle see Aristotle fragment 611.76 (Rose). For Polybios' testimony see Polybios 20.6 (Austin 84). The inscription mentioning the Thespians 'and those with them' is published by P. Siewert, 'Eine Bronze-urkunde mit elischen Urteile über Böoter, Thessalier, Athen and Thespiai', in A. Mallwitz ed., *Bericht über die Ausgrabungen in Olympia* X (1981), 228–48.

7 The Field of War

The passages from ancient authors quoted in the text are:

1 Xenophon, *Hellenika* 3.2.21–7.
2 Plutarch, *Greek Questions* 17.
3 Thucydides 1.5–6.
4 *Hellenika Oxyrhynkhia* 13.3–4.
5 Aristotle, *Politics* 1330a 20–23.
6 Polybios 18.31.
7 Polybios 13.3.
8 Herodotos 6.42.
9 Pausanias 10.14.4.
10 Austin 91, *SIG*[3] 527. 1–104, 137–163.
11 Polybios 24.3.
12 Thucydides 5.42.1.
13 Plutarch, *Life of Lykourgos* 28.
14 Thucydides 3.15.
15 Xenophon, *Helenika* 3.2.29–31.
16 Thucydides 3.94. 1–2.
17 Thucydides 1.15.
18 Herodotos 1.17–18.
19 Thucydides 4.103–6.
20 *SIG*[3] 471.

The best general introduction to Greek warfare is provided by Y. Garlan, *War in the Ancient World* (1975). Generally speaking, the modern scholarship on warfare is divided between works of English-speaking scholars interested primarily in the material conditions of warfare, methods of fighting, armour, and logistics of campaigns, and works of French scholars more interested in war and society and in the ideological aspects of military training and practices.

For the way in which wars were fought see F. Adcock, *The Greek and Macedonian Art of War* (1957), J. Anderson, *Military Theory and Practice in the Age of Xenophon* (1970), and A. Holladay 'Hoplites and heresies', *Journal of Hellenic Studies* 102 (1982), 84–103. On Greek armour see A. Snodgrass, *Arms and Armour of the Greeks* (1967). On the logistics of campaigning and similar issues there is the compendious work of W. Pritchett, *The Greek State at War* (4 vols 1974–85).

For the origin of hoplite warfare see P. Cartledge, 'Hoplites and heroes: Sparta's contribution to the technique of ancient warfare' and J. Salmon, 'Political hoplites' in *Journal of Hellenic Studies* 97 (1977), 11–27 and 84–101. On the ideology of the hoplite see P. Vidal-Naquet, 'La tradition de l'hoplite athénien' in J-P. Vernant ed., *Problèmes de la guerre en Grèce ancienne* (1968), 161–81. On ritual aspects of warfare see A. Brelich, *Guerre agoni e culti nella Grecia arcaica* (1961). The treaty between Argos and Sparta in 420 is recorded in Thucydides 5.41.

On military training and ephebes see P. Vidal-Naquet, 'The black hunter and the origin of the Athenian ephebeia' in R. Gordon ed., *Myth, Religion and Society. Structuralist essays by M. Detienne, L. Gernet, J-P. Vernant and P. Vidal-Naquet* (1981), 147–62. For the situation in Sparta see M. Finley, 'Sparta and Spartan society' in R. Saller and B. Shaw eds, *Economy and Society in Ancient Greece* (1981), 24–40, and P. Cartledge, 'The politics of Spartan pederasty', *Proceedings of the Cambridge Philological Society*, ns 27 (1981), 17–36. The Damonon inscription is *IG* v.2 213. For Aristotle on the standing army see *Politics* 1268a 20–5. The inscription from Gortyn is *SIG*³ 525 (Austin 105).

The question of the relationship of war to the countryside has mostly been dealt with in terms of the (un)suitability of Greek terrain for hoplite warfare. The classic treatments are G. Grundy, *Thucydides and the History of his Age* (1911), Chapter 9, and A. Gomme, *A Historical Commentary on Thucydides*, Vol. I (1945), 10–24. The typical campaign of Tolmides against Sikyon is known from Pausanias 1.27.6. For the limits of crop ravaging see V. Hanson, *Warfare and Agriculture in Ancient Greece* (1980).

There are a number of fine works on fortifications. For the relations between changing strategies, changing fortifications and the countryside the best treatment is Y. Garlan, *Recherches de poliorcétique grecque* (1974). More concerned with the material remains are F. Winter, *Greek Fortifications* (1971), A. Lawrence, *Greek Aims in Fortification* (1979), and, with the best photographs, J-P. Adam, *L'Architecture militaire grecque* (1982). For the Spartan forts see, on Belmina, W. Loring, 'Some ancient routes in the Peloponnese', *Journal of Hellenic Studies* 15 (1895), 25–89 at 36–41, and on Teuthrone, *Arkhaiologiki Ephemeris*, Chron. 10–22 (1981). For the fortifications of fourth-century Attica see J. Ober, *Fortress Attica* (1985). On the Dema wall, see J. E. Jones, L. Sackett, C. Eliot, 'To Dema: a survey of the Aigaleos-Parnes wall', *Annual of the British School at Athens* 52 (1957), 152–89. For the Aniforitis wall in eastern Boiotia see Bakhuizen, *Salganeus and the Fortifications on its Mountains* (1970).

The inscription relating to the border between Corinth and Epidauros is discussed by J. Wiseman, *The Land of the Corinthians* (1978), 136–38. For the Khremonidean war forts in Attica see J. McCredie, *Fortified Military Camps in Attica* (1966).

8 The Country of the Gods

The passages from ancient authors quoted in the text are:

1 Pausanias 8.44.
2 Athenaios, *The Deipnosophistai* 138f–39b.
3 Pausanias 8.23.6.
4 Photios, *Biblioteca* 322.13 ff (Bekker).
5 Homer, *Iliad* 4.45–9.
6 Aristophanes, *Peace* 937–1059 (excerpts).
7 *SIG*³ 1030.
8 *SIG*³ 1031.
9 *SIG*³ 1033.
10 *SIG*³ 1032.
11 Plutarch, *Table Talk* 729f.
12 Hesiod, *Works and Days* 42–52.
13 Porphyry, *On Abstinence* 2.29–30.
14 *SIG*³ 958.
15 *SIG*³ 1024.29–40.
16 Xenophon, *The March Up Country* 5.3.7–10.
17 Aristotle, *Enquiry into Animals* 626a.
18 Plutarch, *Questions About Nature* 36.
19 Lazzarini 779.
20 *Annuario della scuola archeologica di Atene* 39–40 (1961–2), 312–3.
21 Pausanias 2.23.1.
22 Pausanias 10.32.5.
23 Pausanias 8.37.11.

The best introduction to Greek religion is J. Gould, 'On making sense of Greek religion' in P. Easterling, J. Muir eds, *Greek Religion and Society* (1985) 1–33. The most recent text-book is W. Burkert, *Greek Religion* (1985).

There is no good treatment of religious space in English, but an excellent one in French: F. de Polignac, *La naissance de la cité grecque. Cultes, espace et société viii*ᵉ*–vii*ᵉ *siècles avant J-C* (1984). On the suburban sanctuaries of Athens see M. Jameson, 'Apollo Lykeios in Athens', *Arkhaiognosia* 1 (1980), 213–35. The group of Boiotian cults with similar sites and features is discussed by A. Schachter, 'A Boiotian cult-type', *Buttetin of the Institute of Classical Studies* 14 (1967), 1–16. The Thesmophorion on Thasos is discussed by C. Rolley, 'Le Sanctuaire des dieux patrooi et le Thesmophorion de Thasos', *BCH* 89 (1965), 441–83. On Artemis Brauronia see R. Osborne, *Demos: The Discovery of Classical Attica* (1985). On Artemis at Kaphyai see H. King, 'Bound to bleed. Artemis and Greek women' in A. Cameron and A. Kuhrt eds, *Images of Women in Antiquity* (1983), 102–27. On the herms of Attica see R. Osborne, 'The erection and mutilation of the hermai', *Proceedings of the Cambridge Philological Society,* ns 31 (1985), 47–73.

On Athenian festivals the basic textbook is L. Deubner, *Attische Feste* (1932). In English see H. Parke, *Festivals of the Athenians* (1977). For the dates of the festivals see J. Mikalson, *The Sacred and Civil Calendar of the Athenian Year* (1975). On the festivals of Pyanepsion see P. Vidal-Naquet, 'The black hunter and the origin of the Athenian ephebeia' in R. Gordon ed., *Myth, Religion, and Society* (1981), 183–214. On the Arrephoria see W. Burkert, 'Kekropidensage und Arrephoria', *Hermes* 94 (1966), 1–25. On the Skira see A. Brumfield, *The Attic Festivals of Demeter and their relation to the Agricultural Year* (1981). On the Genesia see F. Jacoby, 'Genesia. A forgotten festival of the dead', *Classical Quarterly* 38 (1944), 65–75.

The discussion of sacrifice here is heavily indebted to recent work by French scholars. See in particular, J-P. Vernant, 'Sacrificial and alimentary codes in Hesiod's myth of Prometheus' in R. Gordon ed., *Myth, Religion and Society* (1981), 57–79; P. Vidal-Naquet, 'Land and sacrifice in the Odyssey: a study of religious and mythical meanings', *ibid.* 80–94; M. Detienne, J-P. Vernant eds, *La Cuisine du sacrifice en pays grec* (1979); G. Berthiaume, *Les rôles du mageiros* (1982); and J-L. Durand, A. Schnapp, 'Boucherie sacrificielle et chasse initiatique' in *La cité des images* (1984), 44–66. Much evidence on sacrifice is collected and interpreted in a very different way by W. Burkert, *Homo Necans* (Eng. trans. 1983).

The information on Athenian sale of ox-hides comes from *SIG*^{3} 1029.29 (*IG* ii^2 1496.92). The Delian accounts are *SIG*^{3} 153.31–40 (*IG* ii^2 1635.31–40).

For Aristaios and Orpheus see M. Detienne, 'The myth of the "honeyed Orpheus"' in R. Gordon ed., *Myth, Religion and Society* (1981), 95–109. For further remarks about the problematic position of the hunter in myth see M. Detienne, 'The perfumed panther' in M. Detienne, *Dionysos Slain* (1979), 20–52, and J. Fontenrose, *Orion: The Myth of the Hunter and the Huntress* (1981).

On dedications see F. van Straten, 'Gifts for the gods' in H. Versnel ed., *Faith, Hope and Worship* (1981), 65–151, and W. Rouse, *Greek Votive Offerings* (1902). For bronze animal figurines see W. Lamb, *Greek and Roman Bronzes* (1929), 30–111. For the Kabirion bronzes see B. Schmaltz, *Das Kabirenheiligtum bei Theban, Vol. 6, Die Statuetten aus Bronze und Blei* (1980). For the Kabirion terracottas see B. Schmaltz, *Die Kabirenheiligtum bei Theben, Vol. 5, Terrakotten* (1974). On the general history of the Kabirion see A. Schachter, *Cults of Boiotia*, Vol. 2 (1986).

On Dionysos the best introduction to the modern literature is P. McGinty, *Interpretation and Dionysos. Method in the Study of a God* (1978). On Pan see P. Borgeaud, *Recherches sur le dieu Pan* (1979).

9 Epilogue: The Uses of the Countryside
On the Greek city during the Hellenistic and Roman period see A. Jones, *The Greek City from Alexander to Justinian* (1939). My remarks about the early modern city here are heavily in debt to J. de Vries, *The Economy of Europe in an Age of Crisis* (1976) and J. de Vries, *European Urbanisation 1500–1800* (1984). On food riots in early modern Europe see C. Tilly, 'Food supply and public order in modern Europe' in C. Tilly ed., *The Formation of National States in Western Europe* (1975).

Index